Humanities World Report 2015

Also by Dominic Scott

RECOLLECTION AND EXPERIENCE

PLATO'S MENO

MAIEUSIS: Studies in Ancient Philosophy in Honour of Myles Burnyeat (ed.)

Also by Arne Jarrick

ONLY HUMAN
Studies in the History of Conceptions of Man

THE NEED TO BE NEEDED
An Essay on Humankind, Culture, and World History

Humanities World Report 2015

Poul Holm

Arne Jarrick

and

Dominic Scott

Except where otherwise noted, this work is licensed under a Creative Commons Attribution 3.0 Unported License. To view a copy of this license, visit http://creativecommons.org/licenses/by/3.0/

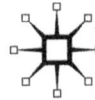

© Poul Holm, Arne Jarrick and Dominic Scott 2015

The authors have asserted their rights to be identified as the authors of this work in accordance with the Copyright, Designs and Patents Act 1988.

Open access:

 Except where otherwise noted, this work is licensed under a Creative Commons Attribution 3.0 Unported License. To view a copy of this license, visit http://creativecommons.org/licenses/by/3.0/

First published 2015 by
PALGRAVE MACMILLAN

Palgrave Macmillan in the UK is an imprint of Macmillan Publishers Limited, registered in England, company number 785998, of Houndsmills, Basingstoke, Hampshire,RG21 6XS

Palgrave Macmillan in the US is a division of St Martin's Press LLC, 175 Fifth Avenue, New York, NY 10010.

Palgrave is the global academic imprint of the above companies and has companies and representatives throughout the world.

Palgrave® and Macmillan® are registered trademarks in the United States, the United Kingdom, Europe and other countries

DOI: 10.1057/9781137500281
E-PDF ISBN 978–1–137–50028–1
E-PUB ISBN 978–1–137–50029–8

ISBN 978–1–137–50026–7 hardback
ISBN 978–1–137–50027–4 paperback

A catalogue record for this book is available from the British Library.

A catalog record for this book is available from the Library of Congress.

Transferred to Digital Printing in 2014

Contents

List of Tables viii

Acknowledgements ix

1 **Introduction** 1
   The purpose and scope of this report 1
   Some qualifications 2
   Our sources 4
   Outline of the report 7
   Prospects for the future 10

2 **The Value of the Humanities** 12
   Introduction 12
   Intrinsic value 16
   Social value 18
   Heritage, culture, memory 22
   The economic value of the humanities 25
   Contribution to other disciplines 27
   Innovation 30
   Critical thinking 32
   Personal and spiritual development 34
   Aesthetic appreciation 35
   A distributional survey of the interview responses 36
   Strategies for justification 38
   Conclusions 40

3 **The Nature of the Humanities** 42
   Part I 42
   Thematic orientations 43
   Part II 51
   Reactions to the term 'findings' 54
   Knowledge 57
   Breakthroughs 58
   Perception of the humanities 61
   Conclusion 63

4 The Digital Humanities — 64
- The world of professional digital humanists — 64
- Research trends — 68
- Resistance to digital humanities — 72
- Interview responses — 74
- Conclusion — 82

5 Translating the Humanities — 84
- Translational research practices — 84
- Translational medicine — 86
- Evidence from interviews — 88
- Evidence from national reports — 103
- Conclusion — 108

6 The Culture of Humanities Research — 111
- Introduction — 111
- Internationalisation — 113
- Interdisciplinary research — 122
- The value of interdisciplinary research — 125
- Institutional tensions — 128
- Conclusion — 133

7 Funding and Infrastructure — 136
- Core funding for research — 136
- Non-governmental funding in developing countries — 140
- Competitive funding streams in developed countries — 141
- Research institutes — 146
- Infrastructure — 148
- Conclusion — 157

8 Humanities and Public Policy — 160
- The United States — 160
- China — 163
- South Africa and Australia — 164
- India, Japan and Latin America — 166
- The European Union — 167
- Conclusion: the politics of the humanities — 175

9 Conclusion — 179
- Overview — 179
- Recommendations — 186

Appendix: The Interview Questionnaire — 193

Notes	199
References	207
Index	209

List of Tables

3.1	Respondents who mentioned socially relevant themes	48
3.2	Respondents pointing to the value of cross-fertilisation	50
3.3	Reactions to the term 'findings'	55
3.4	Answers to the question 'Do the humanities advance knowledge?'	57
3.5	Answers to the question 'Do the humanities produce breakthroughs?'	59
4.1	Digital humanities centres and individuals by region, July 2013	66
5.1	Translational practices among respondents	89
5.2	Respondent views on universities and translational practices	90
8.1	European humanities-relevant national research priorities	168

Acknowledgements

We would like to thank our funders: the Swedish Research Council, the Swedish Riksbankens Jubileumsfond and the Netherlands Organisation for Scientific Research (NWO Humanities). Without their support, this project would not have been possible.

We are also grateful to SHM Productions Ltd for their constant support in running the logistics of the project and conducting desk research, in particular Maurice Biriotti and Chris Paouros, as well as Maroussia Bednarkiewicz, Eliott Champault, Zuzana Figerova, Gabrielle Guillaume, Damian Low, Sofya Pattenden, Kate Peden, Steve Potts and Jon Turner.

We are indebted to several other individuals and organisations for their input and support: Alexander Etkind and the Department of Slavonic Studies, University of Cambridge; Jonathan Harle and the Association of Commonwealth Universities; Dele Layiwola, University of Ibadan, Nigeria; Michael Levenson and Keicy Tolbert, Institute for the Humanities and Global Cultures, University of Virginia; Chun-chieh Huang and Kirill Ole Thompson, Institute for Advanced Studies in the Humanities and Social Sciences, National Taiwan University; the Swedish Collegium for Advanced Study; the Olsson Center for Applied Ethics, Darden School of Business, University of Virginia; Gwen Nally, University of Virginia; and Charles Travis, Trinity College Dublin.

In June 2014, the Volkswagen Foundation and the Riksbankens Jubileumsfond organised the Herrenhausen Symposium on the Global Humanities. We are grateful to the organisers, particularly Wilhelm Krull and Göran Blomqvist, for inviting us to discuss some of our findings at this event.

In the run-up to publication, we have benefited greatly from the professionalism and expertise of Paula Kennedy and Pete Cary at Palgrave Macmillan.

Finally, we would like to thank all our interview respondents, who have been the backbone of this project.

OPEN

1
Introduction

The purpose and scope of this report

This is a first attempt to assess the worldwide state of the humanities. We present this report fully conscious that it will be found wanting in important aspects. Yet we believe that an attempt, however faltering, must be made to map on a global scale what humanists think about what they do and how the field is changing. There has been no shortage of commentary on the humanities over the last few years. The topic has been discussed intensively in national reports, essays, books, newspaper articles, not to mention social media. Most of the commentary on the subject to date tends to come from the perspective of a particular country or region. Our aim is to look at some familiar – and some less familiar – questions from a global perspective by listening to voices from all continents.

The report will be of use firstly to the research community and secondly to academic leaders and research policy stakeholders. We aim to set a baseline against which future developments in the world of the humanities may be evaluated. Our main topics are:

- Attempts by researchers and others to articulate the value of the humanities worldwide
- The ways in which humanists describe the nature of what they do and the degree to which it is seen as distinct from the natural and social sciences
- The channels through which humanists attempt to communicate their research beyond the Academia
- Features of the culture of humanities research: attitudes towards interdisciplinary research; responses to globalisation; reactions to the ever-increasing role of digitisation

- Changes in funding patterns and problems of research infrastructure
- Relations between the humanities and the societies that fund them

This report is not a battle cry for the humanities in the 21st century since we think that there is a need for cool analysis and reflection. We end by making some recommendations about ways forward and challenges to be met. These conclusions are based on our analysis of the state of the art presented in Chapters 2–8. We are, of course, deeply committed to the humanities, but we have tried not to let our findings be occluded by wishful thinking.

Some qualifications

In this introduction we set out in more detail the questions that have framed our work and describe each chapter's agenda. We also detail the sources on which we have relied and describe the process by which we conducted our research over a period of 30 months. But first we need to make three qualifications.

First, this report focuses upon humanities research rather than education. In this respect it differs from much of the commentary on the humanities, whether in national reports or books, which often considers (or laments) the fate of teaching in the humanities. Our main reason for limiting the project in this way is practical since including undergraduate education as one of our central themes would have meant a considerable expansion in the scope of the project. Of course, we do not deny that education and research are connected. Where small group teaching is concerned, seminars with undergraduates allow for an exchange of ideas that can stimulate new research. Even when such a luxury is not on offer, giving a class to a large group of students can lead a researcher to familiarise themselves with an area that may then become a research interest. Finally, there is the basic fact that changes in undergraduate numbers affect the numbers of researchers, since the same people typically teach as well as research (regardless of whether the former activity feeds the latter). So, for all these reasons, there is no denying the link between the two. Nonetheless, it is still feasible for a humanities report to focus on research, introducing undergraduate education only as a subordinate theme. Making teaching one of the principal themes would certainly have added breadth to our work; but it is not as if our conclusions and findings are somehow undermined because we have limited our focus.

Second, there is the old question of how to define the humanities. What is the rationale for grouping together a particular set of academic disciplines as 'the humanities'? This is a notoriously difficult question. An obvious answer – that the humanities study the human – is clearly too superficial, because the medical sciences and psychology also study 'the human', as do the social sciences. Despite all the attempts that have been made to answer this question, there is no consensus; some even suspect that the grouping is merely a contingent fact about the recent history of academia.

We take no stand on whether 'the humanities' are a *bona fide* group of academic disciplines, whether they constitute a 'natural kind' and what it is that might unify them into a single group. Instead, our approach is entirely pragmatic. We start from the fact that, as things are in most universities around the world, a particular set of disciplines happens to be grouped together under the umbrella term, 'the humanities': history, archaeology, anthropology, philosophy, religious studies, literature, linguistics, musicology, art history, classical studies, media studies and cultural studies. It is true that the grouping differs from one region to the next. The separation between the social sciences and the humanities is more sharply drawn in Europe and the US than, say, in Latin America or Russia. Thus, sociology might well be included among the humanities in some regions, but not in others. But we have, on the whole, limited ourselves to the list of disciplines just mentioned.

Finally, we should say something at the outset about who we are as authors of this report. We call this book a report because it attempts to give an account of the state of the humanities, together with some recommendations about the future. Such is the remit of many documents that call themselves reports. However, many such reports are commissioned and funded by national (or regional) bodies and publish their findings and recommendations on behalf of a national agency or some similar body. As such, they need to be representative of the entity for which they speak. For instance, in 1999 UNESCO sponsored and produced the *World Social Science Report*. This project involved the formation of a committee and the selection of several authors from around the world, in such a way as to satisfy the need to be a truly representative body appropriate to UNESCO. The same organisation produced follow-up reports in 2010 and 2013. We applaud the efforts of the editorial board and the authors. However, we are doing something different. We are not claiming to represent any organisation, region or country. We are three academic researchers who sought and obtained funding from different organisations in Europe. Using these funds, we ran our own research project and have written up the results accordingly. Doubtless the product reflects our backgrounds and perspectives. But we hope that it will be judged on its own merits like any other piece of academic research. In short, this is a report about the world, but not (as it were) *by* the world (i.e. commissioned by some kind of world organisation).

Our sources

Our work started in earnest in August 2011. Prior to that, we had written a proposal that outlined the purposes of the project and set out what we intended to cover in each chapter. To begin, we embarked upon a survey of existing national reports into the humanities (though sometimes these covered the humanities and social sciences). For instance, reports existed about the US, Canada, the UK, Germany, France, the Scandinavian countries, India, sub-Saharan Africa and Australia. In addition, the EU had commissioned an ongoing project of reports into the humanities and social sciences not just in EU countries, but also in other European nations, Brazil, Israel, Japan and Turkey (these are known as the METRIS reports). Our first task was to collate all these reports, mine them for information and data, and compare the results across regions. We then turned our attention to books and articles by prominent advocates of the humanities, as well as commentaries in the press and elsewhere.

Perhaps what makes our work distinctive is that we have conducted a series of interviews with leading humanities scholars around the world: 89 interviews, covering 41 countries in 5 continents. These have proved an invaluable source of information and insight, and most of the chapters use the results extensively. Although we interviewed some scholars at the beginning of their careers, the great majority were senior academics: many were heads of departments or humanities deans; a few had taken a leading role in national associations or funding bodies. All showed a detailed knowledge of the state of the humanities in their country or region. Some were also scholars who had worked in more than one country, such as a European now working in Asia, or an Asian working in North America.

The guiding methodological principle was to ensure a diversity of opinions, achieved by interviewing scholars from a wide variety of disciplines and from many different nations around the globe. Throughout, we opted for qualitative rather than quantitative analysis. The scholarly community of the humanities in Europe probably consists of more than 100,000 academics and in the world there may be upwards of a million humanists.

We did not have a database and manpower at our disposal to do a representative sample and questionnaire. Instead, we opted for discursive analysis and carried out in-depth, 45–60 minute interviews based on a fixed set of questions or, in some cases, received written responses to our questions. We tested our preliminary interpretations of interviews by bringing informants to regional workshops. The goal was to map the range of opinions and approaches to a strict set of questions. This methodology ensures a depth of understanding of the difference of opinions that are likely to exist in a given community. The methodology works on the principle that within a bounded rationale there is a limited set of positions available and it is therefore possible to map opinions by using a relatively small sample. But the method does not yield results that are quantitatively representative; we cannot say which statements or opinions are representative of the humanities, but we can say which line of reasoning resonates within a certain region. In a sense, the respondents were chosen at random; sometimes they were contacts we already had, or were contacts of contacts. Sometimes, we identified them as a result of attending a particular humanities conference. But we arrived at the final list of respondents by many different routes. On the whole, the respondents did not know each other, and so we are confident that we have avoided the risk of 'group think'. Certainly, there is a great deal of variety among the answers.

We compiled a list of questions initially, and then tested it out on a small group of humanists. Having made some revisions, we conducted around 40 interviews in several countries. As a result of this process, we saw that the questions could be changed, so we created a slightly different questionnaire for the remaining half of the process. However, the two questionnaires are so similar that there have been few problems in collating the results of the interviews as a whole. Both sets of questions are reproduced in the Appendix.

The questions covered all the main points of our original proposal (and more besides). The interviews were conducted in different ways: sometimes a respondent would simply fill in the questionnaire and send it back over e-mail; in other cases we conducted an interview, recorded it and then wrote up the transcript; in some cases, the interviewer asked the questions, took notes, wrote up the interview and then sent back a draft to the respondent, who was then free to comment and change as appropriate.

The interviewees covered the following disciplines:

- Archaeology 3
- Cultural studies 5
- Classics 4

- History 20
- Linguistics 5
- Literature 17
- Media studies 3
- Philosophy 15
- Religion 2
- Other (mostly a humanities/social sciences blend) 15

The breakdown by region was:

- Africa (Af): 13 (Ghana, Kenya, Malawi, Mozambique, Nigeria, South Africa, Tanzania, and Zambia)
- Asia (As): 16 (China, India, Japan, Mongolia, Taiwan and Thailand)
- Australia (Au): 4
- Europe (E): 16 (Denmark, Estonia, France, Germany, Ireland, the Netherlands, Norway, Romania, Spain, Sweden, Switzerland and the UK)
- Latin America (LA): 9 (Argentina, Brazil, Mexico, Peru and Uruguay)
- MENA region (ME): 6 (Algeria, Egypt, Jordan, Lebanon, Tunisia and Turkey)
- North America (NA): 16 (Canada and the US)
- Russia (R): 9.

Respondents were 28 female, 61 male.

To preserve respondent anonymity we use a code, such as Af1/ME2, when quoting them.

To validate our preliminary interpretation of the interviews, we subsequently held workshops focused on particular regions. In May 2013 we held one in Taipei involving scholars from Taiwan, Japan, Thailand and Asianists from the US. In June 2013 we held a workshop at the University of Cambridge, to which we invited a group of Russian humanists. In October 2013 we held a workshop at the University of Virginia, to which we invited scholars from Latin America (Mexico, Argentina, Uruguay, Peru), the workshop also included scholars from the US who were from or were working on Latin American countries. Finally, we co-funded a conference on the humanities in Nanjing, China, in May 2013 involving participants from China, India, Europe and the US. These events gave us the opportunity to go beyond the information we had already received via the interviews. Typically, the workshop participants had done an interview before attending.

Outline of the report

In the chapters that follow, we pursue what we consider to be some of the most important topics for a humanities report.

In *Chapter 2*, we start with perhaps the best-known issue: the value of the humanities. How do people, especially advocates of the humanities, articulate the value of humanities research in different countries around the world? Are there any patterns that come to light when one compares the answers to this question in different countries? We start with a list of the values most typically attributed to the humanities, such as social cohesion, cultural heritage and critical thinking. We then give an outline account of each, and show which values are most commonly highlighted around the world. Although much of our discussion is descriptive, sketching 'the state of the art', we also offer some more critical comments, and warnings, about the risks of espousing certain values.

In *Chapter 3*, we turn to the nature of the humanities and break the chapter into two parts. First, we ask what sorts of themes or approaches are most prevalent in humanities research today and what ones may be emerging. For instance, are phenomena such as digitisation or internationalisation having any effect on the sorts of themes researchers are choosing to work upon? In the second part we broach the question of how humanities scholars conceive of their disciplines. Do they see them as fundamentally different from the sciences (natural or social)? In particular, do they attempt to make advances in knowledge, to attain findings and make breakthroughs? Or do they consider their role to be more one of raising questions than answering them, or of telling narratives and trying out new perspectives?

Chapter 4 is devoted to another area where recent developments may or may not be meshing well with humanists' attitudes and culture. This is the area of digital humanities (DH). In the first half of the chapter we try to give a snapshot of the sheer scale of activities around the world and the different kinds of digital projects pursued. Based on information available online, we provide a survey of DH centres around the world and give a classification of the kinds of projects they fund and promote. There is no doubting the scale of activity. But what about mainstream humanists? Are they convinced that these new technologies and projects are paying real intellectual dividends? Do they even understand what is going on? In order to answer such questions, we asked our interviewees for their views on the digital humanities.

Chapter 5 considers the ways in which humanists communicate or conduct their research beyond the borders of the Academia. Interestingly, there is not even an agreed term for this. As a starting point we take, by way of comparison, the way in which medical science tackles this issue, as in the process by which research gets from 'bench to bedside' – not to say that the humanities should ape the medical sciences, but because they provide an interesting point of reference. They also provide us with a term to use, 'translation' ('translational medicine' is the expression used for the process of bringing research into clinical use). In this chapter we gather together information about the attempts of humanists to move beyond academic boundaries. There are several quite different modes in practice: reaching out to high schools; consultancy; museum work and public exhibitions; media work (newspaper, radio or TV); and working with policy makers. We have gathered information on such activities from a few national reports (particularly in the US), but most of our data comes from our own interviews, where we asked respondents directly about their attitude to, and their experience of, translation. As well as surveying the different kinds of translation, we raise the question of how far institutional conditions actually facilitate or obstruct it.

Chapter 6 considers some issues about the culture of the humanities and the extent to which it is keeping pace with certain technological or institutional developments. We look at two phenomena from this perspective: interdisciplinarity and internationalisation. Many humanists have long felt attracted to the idea of crossing disciplinary boundaries in their research and there is evidence that funding bodies encourage or even require this. Although the interest in interdisciplinary research is not new, it is important to ask whether the pressure to engage in it actually meshes both with researchers' own inclinations and with basic professional incentives. Is interdisciplinary research actually of benefit to researchers as they attempt to rise up the career ladder or is it rather a risk to move out of mono-disciplinary expertise, especially in terms of publication prospects? In short, are professional conditions really aligned with institutional aspirations towards interdisciplinary research? In the second half of the chapter we consider what might be called a parallel question about internationalisation. It is a cliché to talk of globalisation and the breaking down of national boundaries. It is a fact of life everywhere and affects the humanities profoundly. Communications have been transformed over the last few years by e-mail and the Internet (our own project would have been impossible without all this). International networks and publishing outlets have mushroomed. So, the question arises as to how humanists themselves are reacting to this. Is globalisation leading to homogenisation of research, especially through the use of English as a common language?

Chapter 7 is about funding and infrastructure, also issues that we raised in the questionnaire. We were interested first in whether respondents had noticed significant changes in funding in recent years. Obviously, in some countries funding is a great deal better than in others. But what about actual changes for better or worse? This question is particularly salient in the wake of the financial crisis and the subsequent (if slow) recovery. Does economic progress in some developing countries spark investment in the humanities? Are there clear regional differences in the perception of challenges and opportunities? In the second half of the chapter we consider what infrastructure needs our respondents have. It is quite typical for humanists to say that they are cheap and need little funding, but is this actually the case? If offered the chance for more resources, where do our interviewees think they should be spent?

Finally, in *Chapter 8* we turn to the relation between humanities and politics. In many ways, this has been an undercurrent in previous chapters since many think the value of the humanities is precisely its contribution to society (such as social cohesion and social decision-making). Translation (or outreach) is very much about the ways in which academia makes its work known and used by society at large. Issues of funding sooner or later involve references to the taxpayer. But in this last chapter we bring the relation between humanities and society to the forefront. Specifically, we are interested in the expectations that humanists have of their society and, in turn, what their society expects of them, especially as evidenced by the attitudes of governmental bodies towards the humanities. In this chapter we make particular use of national reports (especially from the US, South Africa and the EU). Given the time at which we are writing, we have ended up with a particular focus on two regions: the US, especially the arguments between Congress and the National Endowment for the Humanities (NEH); and the EU where, at the time of writing, the Commission is in the process of deciding how to distribute research funds over the next seven years. On the one hand there is the very real prospect of significant funding coming to the social sciences and the humanities; on the other, there is the likelihood that this will come with strings attached – such that only projects focused on quite specific and 'utilitarian' themes will have any chance of being funded.

At the end of the report, we provide a conclusion, to draw out the main themes of our research, and then a list of recommendations.

Although it has taken us considerable time and effort to compile this report, we hope it will not take long to read. Throughout, we have taken a 'straight talking' approach, the organisation of the material is straightforward and the topics have been arranged in a relatively intuitive list. There is no necessity to read the chapters and subsections in order. Instead, the report can be used as a reference compilation or handbook, it invites the reader to dip in and out of sections without reading full chapters.

Prospects for the future

In our research we have had innumerable conversations and encounters, not just in the course of conducting the interviews or giving presentations at workshops and conferences, but also around the fringes of conferences, or as part of soliciting interviews and inviting feedback. Among all the comments we have had, two stand out as the most common. On a positive note, a large number of people commented on the importance of what we are doing, they described a world humanities report as timely and necessary, sometimes even as urgently needed. But there was another kind of reaction when our project was described as 'very ambitious'. After all, we were attempting to survey the state of the humanities worldwide and assess the challenges for the future. That itself is a challenge of almost bewildering proportions.

We agree. Our project is as ambitious as it is worthwhile. But we make no apology, it had to be done, or it is at least one step in a longer-term process that has to be started. Many of the issues we address are already well-known (the value of the humanities, similarities to or differences from the sciences, interdisciplinarity, the digital humanities, funding and the relation between the humanities and society). But to come at them from a global perspective, comparing reports, commentaries and interviews from many countries brings an entirely new perspective to these well-worn issues. Furthermore, the very process of conducting the research – creating the contacts, building the goodwill, setting up a template for future research – might help build a worldwide platform for the humanities.

So we see our effort, substantial as it has been, as a first step. Doubtless there are all sorts of ways in which future (or follow-up) reports can improve upon what we have done: more interviews, with different questions, covering a larger number of countries; the systematic collection of statistical data. We also explored the possibility of an electronic survey to elicit responses to our issues from a thousand humanists around the world, and have created a pilot questionnaire. This would in itself create a set of important and valuable statistics. In the end we decided not to do this because of a shortage of time and manpower. But it is important for someone to take the first step towards a truly global look at the humanities. If it is distinctive of the humanities to study our humanity, it should study our collective and global humanity. That is the spirit in which we have conducted our work and we trust that it will be read and judged in that way.

Except where otherwise noted, this work is licensed under a Creative Commons Attribution 3.0 Unported License. To view a copy of this license, visit http://creativecommons.org/licenses/by/3.0/

OPEN

2
The Value of the Humanities

Introduction

What is the value of the humanities? This is a question that guides us throughout this report as we seek conceptual clarity and credibility for practices in digital humanities, knowledge exchange, globalisation, interdisciplinarity, infrastructure and public policy. In this chapter, however, we address the question head-on as we report on how humanities researchers themselves articulate the value of their work. This chapter reveals that humanists across the globe more often than not identify a social value to humanities research.

By way of our interviews and literature review, we have identified a bounded set of answers to the question of the value of humanities research. They are as follows:

Intrinsic value: humanities research has a value in and of itself. Even if it leads to other benefits (as listed below), it should also be pursued for its own sake.
Social value: the humanities benefit society in a number of ways. They help create tolerance and understanding between citizens, thereby leading to social cohesion. They aid decision-making, especially on the complex ethical issues that confront society as a whole. In addition, they can benefit society by challenging established positions (see also 'critical thinking' below).
Cultural heritage: the humanities enable citizens to understand, preserve and sometimes challenge their national heritage and culture.
Economic value: there are direct economic benefits from humanities research, for example in publishing, media, tourism and, of course,

the training humanities scholars provide to their students, who go into the job market across a wide range of professions.

Contribution to other disciplines: humanities research feeds into other fields, most obviously the social sciences, but also into medicine, computer science and engineering/design.

Innovation: the humanities deal with questions of motivation, organisation and action, which are essential components of creativity and entrepreneurship, and so the humanities promote a culture of innovation.

Critical thinking: it is of the essence of the humanities to develop critical thinking. This is epitomised by the Socratic tradition in philosophy, but by no means confined to that discipline.

Personal and spiritual development: humanities research can enhance one's personal and spiritual wellbeing through the study of different texts and traditions – religious, philosophical or spiritual.

Aesthetic appreciation: literary research, art history and musicology promote aesthetic discrimination, enhancing the appreciation and enjoyment of artistic works.

We argue that this list represents a plausible taxonomy of the most prominent attempts to articulate the value of the humanities around the world. It is, of course, possible to classify the value of the humanities at different levels of generality. At the very general end of the spectrum one hears claims such as 'the humanities make us human'. At the other extreme one might take examples from a particular discipline that have led to some benefit or other, e.g. philosophical research in bioethics. But we think that dividing the terrain at an intermediate level of specificity (as above) will bring clarity to a topic often marked by excessive abstraction and hyperbole.

Our purpose is not to advocate any of the values in particular; it is to describe and analyse them and to offer some critical reflections. We also wish to show how support for these values is weighted differently around the world.

The list is based on research from a number of different sources:

- A literature review of national reports, opinion pieces in the media, books (scholarly and popular) and articles in journals and edited books
- Interviews with 89 humanities researchers worldwide
- Workshops with scholars from several countries, especially from East Asia, Russia and Latin America.

In the interviews, all respondents were asked the following questions:

> Why fund research in the humanities? If you had to give a succinct answer to this question, what would it be? How would you articulate the value of humanities research to an impatient and potentially hostile audience?

We phrased the question in this way to avoid taxing the patience of our interviewees with a completely open-ended question about the value of the humanities. In effect, we were asking as much about the rhetoric of justification as the justification itself. Nonetheless, the responses to this question have been a very useful guide towards understanding people's own opinions on the value of the humanities.

In the first 45 interviews, we confined ourselves to this question. However, as we gathered more information on the issue, we decided to add an extra component to this section of the questionnaire. Since we had by this point a reasonably clear classification of the different values that humanities research might be thought to have, we decided to present them in a list to respondents and ask for their reactions. This is how we phrased the additional request:

> Here are some ways of expressing the value of humanities research:
>
> (a) *Intrinsic value*
> (b) *Informing social policy*
> (c) *Understanding cultural heritage*
> (d) *Promoting economic value*
> (e) *Contributing to other academic disciplines (e.g. in the natural or social sciences)*
> (f) *Feeding through to undergraduate education*
> (g) *Promoting critical thinking and innovation*
>
> Which of these in your own view is (or are) the most important? Which of these is considered most important in your country/region?

This allowed us to distinguish what the respondents themselves thought about the value of the humanities from the dominant discourse in their country. In the analysis below, we have highlighted the extra information that came out of the revised question.

Reports, books and articles allow their authors to articulate a particular value in detail. But there is a risk that such pieces tell us more about the individual authors than about frequently held attitudes in the regions from which they come. By complementing these sources with our interview results, we hope to provide a somewhat broader perspective, although the risk of idiosyncrasy remains. In addition, the HWR workshops have allowed us to talk around the interview results and the literature review to deepen our understanding of the different types of value and the distinctions and tensions between them.

All the items on the list feature somewhere in the interviews and, although the list is not a completely exhaustive account of everything said in those interviews, we have tried not to omit any significant categories of value. We hope that this list does indeed represent the approaches that are dominant in different regions of the world.

The values overlap in different ways. For instance, many would see social value and cultural heritage as continuous with each other. Or, as we have already indicated, one of the social benefits of the humanities is critical thinking and innovation is often closely associated with economic and social value. But our task is first and foremost to report on the different values commonly attributed to humanities research. It is certainly useful, for the sake of clarity, to start with some distinct categories, even if they eventually become blurred in the broader discussions that we hope to stimulate. Another point to bear in mind is that these values can come into conflict with each other in specific instances: pursuing intellectual curiosity because of intrinsic value may conflict with economic value (though this need not necessarily be the case); critical thinking and innovation may not always be conducive to social cohesion. But our task is not to reconcile these tensions, but to articulate the different values espoused around the world.

One question we had to confront was whether to include undergraduate education as a distinct benefit of humanities research. After some reflection, and discussion in the workshops, we have decided against this for the following reason. As well as the distinction between the different kinds of value that humanities research may have, one can distinguish different ways in which humanities researchers might deliver such benefits: by appearing on TV; by writing popular books; by working with museums and galleries to create content for the general public (audio or written); by sitting on government committees to formulate policy or on ethics committees (e.g. in hospitals). These categories are precisely those to be discussed in Chapter 5 under the heading of 'translation'. But one of the most important ways of delivering these benefits is through undergraduate education. That is, the outcomes of humanities research typically filter down to undergraduate courses, which in turn may make their students better qualified for the workplace (economic value), better citizens (social value), better at critical thinking or appreciating works of art and so on. However, it would be a mistake to list education as a distinct value alongside the nine listed above since it is a distinct mode of delivery.

In Sections 1–9, we describe and analyse each of the values listed above more closely, adding in some critical remarks where appropriate. As already indicated, the sources for this work derive from the literature review, the interviews and the workshops. Sections 10–11 will focus directly on the interview results in more detail, first to illustrate how support for these values is distributed in different regions of the world, and second to highlight respondents' views on the very idea of 'justifying' the humanities.

Intrinsic value

Analysis

Any academic discipline can be defended on the grounds of intrinsic interest. That pursuing knowledge and understanding is valuable for its own sake and does not actually require some further goal in order to be of value (of course, researchers who are driven by intrinsic value may have additional and more personal motivations, which may explain their particular choices of field and topic). In the case of the humanities, the intrinsic value argument is that, as human beings, we ought to have an interest in our history, culture, ideas, languages and so on. As part of our interviews, we found this approach widespread in almost all regions. It can also be found in discussions of the humanities, one of its major proponents in the US being Stanley Fish,[1] but it is certainly not a new idea. Again in the US, it has featured prominently in discussions of the liberal arts, when their advocates claim that undergraduates (no less than their professors) should study these subjects just for their own sake. The nineteenth century Harvard professor Charles William Eliot, who was one of the most important figures in the development of the liberal arts in the US, talked of 'the enthusiastic study of certain subjects for the love of them without any ulterior object'.[2]

One of our interview respondents made the point quite succinctly:

> NA8: To me the justification for humanities research is quite basic, quite fundamental. It extends human knowledge and human appreciation of language and literature and the arts. It is a good in and of itself.

Three others, from quite different regions, made related points even more briefly (though with a hedonistic twist in one case):

> As16: The humanities are just interesting!
> ME2: The nicest thing about history is that it might be of no use. That's a definition of luxury.
> R8: 'Why fund the research in the humanities?' Just because it's fun. And that's it.

Intrinsic value and justification

Intrinsic value may seem highly problematic as a way of defending the humanities, however much support it has among scholars themselves.[3] It could invite charges of self-indulgence, especially from people outside academia and in times of economic hardship. So, if one is concerned with defending the humanities, the temptation might be to abandon appeals to intrinsic value and resort immediately to arguments that appeal to the social or economic benefits of the humanities (even if this goes against what we actually believe as scholars).

But perhaps this is too simplistic. The idea that the humanities have intrinsic value is by no means confined to academics. There are funding contexts in which the intrinsic value approach does have force, notably when dealing with philanthropic donors.[4] Even in the public arena the intrinsic value approach should not be dismissed. At least in some countries, evidence from publishers and TV and radio outlets suggests that the broader public has a strong interest in subjects such as history, literature and archaeology.[5] A successful defence will attempt to change the perception of the humanities from being a mere burden on the taxpayer to a set of disciplines whose subject matter already engages the interest of large swathes of the public.[6] Interestingly, although the intrinsic value approach applies as much to the natural sciences as to the humanities, it may actually be easier to apply in the case of the humanities, as the subject matter is somewhat closer to people's concerns. This point came out of a few responses, as in the following from Europe:

> E6:...there is a broad interest in the society at large in the subjects that are studied within the humanities, such as history, religion, literature, art, theatre, language, etc. Even if these are interests that most people pursue in their pastime and/or as concerned citizens, they are important in their own right, and we therefore need people who study these subjects professionally and in that capacity are able to transmit knowledge to the rest of society.

A hybrid approach

It is also worth mentioning a hybrid approach to the value of the humanities, which combines instrumental and intrinsic elements (though it is ultimately instrumental in character). In discussing the economic and other benefits of the sciences, there is a well-known line of argument that one cannot always know in advance what research will yield benefits, whether technological, commercial or medical. So, the argument runs, the best course is to allow intellectual curiosity to run its course, to allow scientists to work as if they value research for its own sake, and then let the economic and other benefits fall out serendipitously. The same argument can be made for the humanities, especially in respect of certain items on the list such as social and economic values, innovation and the benefit the humanities may bring to other disciplines. If one is confined to what seems economically or socially useful, one may miss out on the most fruitful avenues of research. So, as in the sciences, it is best to embark on one's research with a non-instrumentalist mindset and to proceed as if one is pursuing it for its intrinsic value. However, this is still an instrumentalist approach, the ultimate value here is not intrinsic value but, psychologically, it embraces the intrinsic approach.

Social value

The social value of the humanities could be broken down into various kinds, perhaps the two most frequent being cohesion and decision-making.

Social cohesion

The humanities have been thought to promote social cohesion. One way is through undergraduate education, a point widely discussed in the commentary on US liberal arts, where the role of the humanities in enhancing our ability to communicate is central: by making people better able to articulate their viewpoints, they ease communication within society. Also, by equipping them to understand different viewpoints, they make citizens more tolerant of each other (a point that applies across national boundaries, of course, and so the humanities can be seen to be useful in an increasingly globalised world).

The link between the humanities and social cohesion can be clearly made for specific disciplines. History gives a sense of the past, especially of other people's pasts, which is vital for democratic citizens living together in an increasingly globalised world. Literature opens up our imaginative potential, as do the arts more generally, thus making us more sensitive to the attitudes and emotions of our fellow citizens. Religious studies help us understand different religious and spiritual traditions. Philosophy requires its practitioners to understand other viewpoints, even when they disagree with them.[7] Although there are plenty of references to social value in the North American literature, it is by no means confined to that region. In South Africa, for example, it is part of the public discourse about the humanities.[8]

Here are some examples making this point, one from a Japanese respondent, two from the US and one from Latin America:

> As1: [w]e need the understanding of the humanities, which restores human cooperation and partnership, more than economics or technology.
>
> NA2: The humanities are what keep us human ... : [i.e.] the abilities associated with reading, writing, thinking clearly and communicating with other people. If you can't relate with other human beings, what is any of this for? ... People are losing touch with each other and it is, paradoxically, getting worse with social media. And the humanities are the secret to maintaining an appreciation for what makes human beings special.
>
> NA12: A world without the humanities is one without value, meaning and a sense of shared community with each other.
>
> LA10: [the] humanities are essential to overcome certain trends that are highly contrary to minimal social stability, e.g. xenophobia, racism, aggressive behaviour, addiction and fanaticism.

Social decision-making

Another aspect of the social value of the humanities concerns decision-making in politics, international relations, medicine, welfare; and with the use of new technologies societies have increasingly complex decisions to make. The humanities are, it is argued, indispensable here.

The level at which decisions need to be made varies. It could be a matter of individual citizens being equipped to contribute to public debate, to vote, or make decisions in their place of work. Humanities research can exert an influence, albeit sometimes indirectly, not only through undergraduate education, but also by dissemination through public media. But humanities researchers might also be enlisted to inform public policy directly. Whether or not this actually happens, and to what extent, is a question for later chapters. Here, we are merely pointing out that humanists tend to think that, in principle, their disciplines could make such a contribution.

One could illustrate the point in more specific terms by looking either at individual disciplines, or at areas of policy (e.g. health, environment or security). Where individual disciplines are concerned, one of the clearest ways in which philosophy can contribute to policy is through bioethics, on such issues as stem cell research and informed consent. There are also plenty of examples of the value of linguistics research, as in the understanding (and preservation) of minority languages, and sociolinguistic issues about differences of dialect and their relation to social status.[9]

If one wants to look at policy areas, a recent example concerns security in the US. In May 2011 the National Humanities Alliance and the Association of American Universities co-sponsored a meeting on Capitol Hill in Washington entitled *Addressing National Security & Other Global Challenges Through Cultural Understanding*.[10] Also, the EU Commission's *Horizon 2020 Programme* includes a call for research projects on 'Secure Societies'. Another good example is environmental policy, which can draw upon many different disciplines – history, archaeology, anthropology, philosophy, literature and theology.

Several of our interview respondents from different regions noted the importance of the humanities for social decision-making:

> Af8: [The humanities'] results will help us to understand the context of social and economic phenomena and enable us to attempt to influence policy makers in their decisions.
> ME1: The SSH help us to solve social problems. First we must understand human beings, only then can we help people control social phenomena like violence and poverty.
> As11: Where there is controversy in social issues, this may arise (or does arise) because people have a specific worldview or life view. Philosophy is able to isolate their assumptions and see what traditions or thought systems these assumptions are embedded in.

Some respondents made the point in the context of technological innovation. Here are some examples from North Africa, the US, Japan and China:

> ME4: We need the humanities to think about the challenges of the new informational age.

NA6: The standard humanities defence: we're the field that studies history and language and then integrates that with ethical concern and inquiry. [My University] now has [an] initiative that studies tech and society, for example. You need a human perspective around scientific innovations and their applications.

As4: Natural sciences create technologies and social sciences propose various policies, but it is only humanities who can tell us how they can be used wisely.

As16: Philosophy helps us foresee the impact of new technologies (or gives us the tools to do so).

Challenging social norms

Humanities research can often be the source of challenges to widely accepted social values and traditions. In this way it may actually be in tension with social cohesion. This role overlaps with critical thinking, being a specific instance of it, so we shall have more to say below. But for the moment, here is one of our interviewees testifying to the critical value of the humanities in a social context:

As2: I would just say that it is only in the humanities and social sciences that we still produce a 'critical discourse'. Science, technology and even economics have stopped performing that function. The curricula in these areas have no element of criticism *per se*, making it difficult for them to contribute to the formation of critical citizenship. It has proved more than once in the course of the last century that pure science and economics have failed to produce an understanding of the symbolic life that makes us social and therefore human.

This point was also stressed at our Latin American workshop.

Institution building

Finally, it is worth recording three interview responses (from India, Lebanon and Russia) that linked the humanities to the creation and nurturing of strong institutions:

ME3: The humanities are essential for building strong institutions.

As6: You need some insight into the relation between the subject and the world in order to make institutions stronger.

R1: The humanities help people to be aware of how they think and why they do certain things. It is like cement that holds together social practices and institutions. The humanities enable social institutions to evolve and become better. That is why having the humanities in society is the same thing as enabling society to continue to exist.

Heritage, culture, memory

Preserving cultural memory and identity

Preserving and promoting cultural heritage has long been viewed as a function of the humanities, as is obvious not only in the case of history and language, but also literature, the arts, philosophy and religion. The value of the humanities here could lie not only in preserving cultural identity, but also in rediscovering it. As seen in China with the revival of interest in Confucius as a reaction to the Cultural Revolution of the 1970s, which attempted to root out Confucianist traditions. Other examples can be found in the wake of major political transformations where there is an emphasis on nation building and national histories, as discussed in our Russia workshop, when the humanities acted as an important tool to define nations in the post-Soviet republics. The same emphasis on nation building also applies within Russia, and the government actively promotes an interest in Russian history to this end.[11]

As an extension of this approach, some also refer to the way nations might promote their heritage abroad, perhaps as a way of developing 'soft power'. A current example also concerns China, and the initiative to establish Confucius Institutes around the world, not just to promote the learning of Chinese, but also a wider appreciation of Chinese culture. Again, such initiatives provide an obvious role for humanities research.

Aside from the use of history, literature, philosophy and religion, the preservation of a linguistic culture is yet another category to be noted. This is an acute issue where minority languages are concerned, though this is not the only context. With the growing dominance of English, governments of non-Anglophone countries have felt the need for a language policy, and here the expertise of humanities researchers is obviously relevant.

Here are some interview responses, mainly from Europe, that highlight cultural heritage:

> Af1: The humanities are our heritage. We must sustain it. We must preserve it.

R2: Humanities are crucial for upbringing of a new generation as they provide those who participate in the process (parents, children, teachers, educational structures, etc) with the notion of culture, tradition and cultural transmission.

R3: One of the few absolute treasures of Russia is its literature, replacing her history, philosophy, and religion. Until the end of the 20th century (before the era of postmodernism) literature was the distinguishing feature of the national culture. ... I am convinced that Russian culture can be understood adequately with help of its literature.

E8: We're the keepers of memory and have to pass this on to our students.

E10: Humanities give a sense of belonging. Without humanities, identities (ethnic, national, cultural, etc.) could not exist.

Nationalism and essentialism

The idea of preserving or rediscovering a heritage raises a number of problems. It can lead to extremely superficial research (e.g. the promotion of 'cosmetic Confucianism'), and nationalist agendas may lead to downright falsification of the past. More fundamentally, these approaches may be faulted for assuming the existence of a fixed national culture waiting to be preserved. Typically, objections to 'cultural essentialism' will come from within academia, so it is easy to see humanities scholars coming into conflict with the state over the issue. Clear examples can be found when a state wishes to set the national history curriculum for schools and tries to enlist the support of humanities researchers. This is becoming an acute problem in Russia, as discussed in the HWR workshop, but also mentioned by one respondent:

R6: Russian higher education is suffering from the ministry's excessive control over its content. The ministry or its affiliated agencies check course syllabuses and programs, establishing, e.g., syllabus writing guidelines. This has a double effect, stifling faculty's creativity (since they have to submit the documents in a single standard form) and creating an opportunity for ideological control in the humanities. The latter is clearly observed in such initiatives as a single normative history textbook for secondary schools or government control over History Society and other fledgling professional associations. The case of a researcher from Murmansk (and numerous scientists) prosecuted for allegedly divulging classified information to foreign collaborators came as a warning for many in the field of history of Russia.

This phenomenon can also be found elsewhere, in much milder forms, perhaps. In the UK, for instance, prominent academics and others spoke out against what they saw as a naïvely nationalist curriculum being proposed by the then Education Secretary.[12]

Confronting and coping with the past

All this points to another function for the humanities in relation to cultural heritage, that of challenging conceptions about national identity. Indeed, by rejecting myths about the past, good humanities research might actually fend off bad national ideology. But this is just part of a broader function for humanities research – particularly in history – of confronting difficult aspects of a nation's past, which at the most extreme might concern acts of genocide. In turn, confronting the past in this way can lead to the process of *coping* with the past and reconciliation. Again, this is a context in which humanities research is essential.

Here are three interview responses that raise some of these issues, from Turkey, Russia and Mozambique:

> ME2: We have an ongoing and deep conflict with national history as perceived by the state, the government, and the public opinion in general.... In general, the political establishment has a very negative view of the humanities, which is shared by the great majority of the population: unless they espouse nationalist historiography, scholars are seen as snobbish intellectuals or even traitors, kowtowing to Western demands. But there's no outright censorship.
>
> R4: The state has a more significant ideological influence on research of the history of Russia. A major concern for the Russian scientific community has caused a politically motivated prosecution of Arkhangelsk historian Mikhail Suprun, who the court found guilty of 'illegal gathering of information about the private life'. He studied the biographies of German prisoners of war and ethnic Germans, Soviet citizens interned in the post-war years in the Arkhangelsk region.
>
> Af8: I'm working with questions related to memory that are a deconstruction of the official history...

Understanding and negotiating other cultures

In addition to understanding, promoting or challenging one's own culture, humanities research can enable one to understand other cultures. Understanding one's trading partners is increasingly important in an era of globalisation. The same applies in the area of security (as in US attempts to understand the Muslim world).[13] What is important to note is that governments understand the need to research deeply into the histories of countries that are of economic or political concern to them. Perhaps an extreme example is the way new programmes are being established in China for the study of Greek and Roman classics, as a step towards greater understanding of the West.

Overlaps

Cultural heritage and social value clearly overlap in important ways. Understanding and promoting national heritage may provide social benefits, in particular by creating more social cohesion,[14] though confronting it may of course reduce cohesion. Perhaps the cultural value of the humanities might be seen as a species of social value, but it seems legitimate to keep them apart, as made clear by our Russia workshop. Much of what we have discussed above would be more appropriately called political than social, for instance creating cohesion by promoting national history is very different from doing so by developing skills of communication and empathy.

The economic value of the humanities

Analysis

Humanities research may have economic value in issues of welfare, poverty, distribution of income, employment and business activity. For instance, businesses need to understand the cultures in which they operate, and this involves the use of historical, cultural and media research. Also, the use of language is essential to business, so both literature and linguistics are important. More specifically, the humanities contribute crucially to particular kinds of industry. They are responsible for productive output in the creative industries, like theatre, film and TV, all of which may be informed and enhanced by humanities research. The tourist industry depends in part on museums and other heritage institutions. In addition, there is direct economic value in popular books on history and literature, not to mention TV documentaries.

Employment of graduates is an important issue in discussions about education in the humanities and liberal arts. The claim is that humanities disciplines prepare students for the world of work, whatever that may turn out to be. For instance, they teach students how to scan large bodies of text and information to detect patterns; how to use language to persuade; how to evaluate and construct arguments. There are, of course, difficulties in measuring the economic impact of the humanities and these are discussed in Chapter 5.

A few of our interviewees took up the economic argument:

> E6: I would try to persuade the audience that people with degrees from the humanities have acquired (unique?) transferable skills that may be very useful in a much wider context than in professions where such degrees are directly relevant. In the humanities we study and interpret human behaviour as manifested by singular events – historical battles, works of art, all kinds of texts, etc. – and try to integrate them into larger patterns in order to understand them as well as possible. This is very different from what one does in the sciences, where the aim is to establish generalisations that, without exception, hold over a range of phenomena. Such singular events are what our lives are made up of, and the ability to interpret and understand them is therefore important at almost every workplace, of course in combination with more specialised knowledge.
>
> As5: If you fund humanities studies, you develop analytical skills and a definite philosophy in life which help you in any profession eventually.
>
> ME1: The more we invest in understanding human beings through SSH research, the more productive they will become.

A conspicuous appeal to the economic value of the humanities has been made by the UK Arts and Humanities Research Council, which has embraced the argument wholeheartedly.[15] Strong arguments in favour of the economic value of the humanities to the creative and cultural sectors have also been made by Scandinavian and EU reports.[16] However, the economic argument has provoked a backlash among other humanities scholars. A number of prominent figures in the UK have founded the Council for the Defence of British Universities (CDBU) partly to promote an understanding of the broader value of universities (not just in the humanities).[17] A recent national report on humanities and social sciences in South Africa makes a trenchant critique of those who appeal to economic value, certainly in any narrow sense.[18] In the US, commentators such as Stanley Fish and Martha Nussbaum are also well-known critics of the economic approach.[19]

Contribution to other disciplines

Several humanities disciplines contribute significantly to the social and natural sciences. Regardless of whatever claims are made about the value of humanities research in general, this indirect utility has been promoted by some to demonstrate the value of the humanities.

Humanities and the natural and social sciences

A simple list of humanities contributions to interdisciplinary collaboration may demonstrate this point:

- Archaeology, more than any other humanities discipline, benefits from the natural sciences (and their associated technology). But, increasingly in the field of environmental and climate science, the influence may be working the other way around. Archaeological research is becoming a more important source of evidence in these fields.[20]
- History is closely intertwined with the social sciences, all of which include a historical dimension or subdivision, whether political, legal, social or economic. Indeed, the fact that history so obviously contributes to the social sciences says something about the arbitrariness of the distinction between humanities and social sciences. Also, history is becoming increasingly important in the understanding of environmental change. This is part of a wider trend, the 'historical turn', where more and more academic disciplines are embracing an interest in historical perspectives. Historical research over long time-periods can bring a new perspective to the social sciences. For example, it has been shown that over time the world has witnessed a substantial decline in violent interpersonal conflicts. For instance, in Europe over the last three or four centuries there has been a substantial drop in homicide rates.[21] Furthermore, it seems clear that there is a close and sustained correlation between manslaughter and alcohol consumption.
- Linguistics clearly influences the fields of psychology and sociology through social linguistics and psycholinguistics. It is also relevant to computer science.

- In philosophy, striking examples are the use of logic in computing and, from the 'hard end' of philosophy, the influence of decision theory in economics. The different branches of philosophy of science – physics, mathematics, and biology – can also, in principle, contribute to the relevant areas. Philosophers in the 'continental' tradition, e.g. Foucault, have been highly influential in the social sciences; political philosophers (from both the continental and Anglo-American traditions) have also influenced sociology and economics. The dividing line between political philosophy and political science is obviously porous.
- Research in the arts (literature, visual arts and music) also impacts upon the natural and social sciences. Recent developments in musicology provide some good case studies because of the link with psychology and brain science.[22] Work done by art departments is contributing to computer science as visualisation is becoming the way of understanding complex data; graphics is also becoming an interpretative tool (cf. 'the iconosphere'). Yet another example would be the contribution of literary studies to sociology, for instance in the area of youth culture.

Humanities and the professional schools

One could also claim that the three areas of international relations, law and management are beneficiaries of humanities research. These areas are interdisciplinary by nature and there is an increasing recognition that both humanities and social sciences have a vital contribution to make.

The fact that the humanities do feed into other disciplines was mentioned by our respondents:

> As16: [Philosophy is] also useful for other disciplines, offering helpful weapons to analyse the basic assumptions of their theories that might otherwise pass unnoticed within their own approaches.
> Af3: Humanities research is the basis on which all other knowledge is developed, communicated and translated into practical human development.... If you do not understand human beings, how can you understand any knowledge that these human beings seek to generate, communicate and apply?
> Af7: Research in the natural and other social sciences may need the intervention of humanities research to be meaningful and turned

into user-friendly products. Thus, humanities research contributes to the work of other academic disciplines.

However, this value was only occasionally mentioned, and then only in very general terms. Two exceptions come from US respondents, who answered the question about emerging research themes as follows:

> NA11: There is a lot of new interesting stuff at the border between music and sound. Reconceptualising music as 'sound', thinking about music in a broader way than has been thought before. Also, in connection with visual studies, new media (there's a New Media Center here), visual studies, sound and music and culture, which would also include literature, history and anthropology. A lot is going on in those focus points. Some of it overlaps with people doing computer and cognitive science. So, along with that, I'm sure you've heard of the emerging relationship between cognitive science and the humanities. We're starting to do that here, and that means talking to people ranging from hard neuroscience, to history of science, literature, art history or history.
>
> NA7: Neuroscience, for example, is at the cutting edge of contemporary understanding of the diseases that plague societies with increasingly ageing populations. The genomic and proteomic levels of analysis of that become so abstract that they require philosophers of mind to participate in it. And they're actually looking for people in philosophy – not really in psychology, because that's too clinical, it's not abstract enough – but they are looking for highly theoretical humanist scholarship to participate in what they're engaging in. It's a meeting point of science and art, where the difference between the two becomes extremely blurred. I think whether this becomes a larger trend is dependent upon whether people in the humanities want to participate in it.

The last extract raises an important question. Even if the humanities have a proven track record of contributing to other disciplines, and even if there is the potential for much more to be done, is all this sufficiently recognised? Do disciplinary and other institutional divides inhibit important contributions from being made? These divides take different forms: non-humanities disciplines may be reluctant to admit the influence of the humanities and may set up barriers to dialogue; humanities scholars may help to increase a sense of cultural divide between themselves and non-humanities scholars; university structures may impede effective communication; and publishers may be reluctant to venture into the terrain. These issues will be taken up in Chapter 6 in our discussion of interdisciplinary research.

Innovation

Several sources in a wide range of countries make a strong link between innovation and the humanities: national reports,[23] blogs,[24] media articles[25] and a number of our interviews. In the UK, the AHRC (Arts and Humanities Research Council) worked with NESTA (National Endowment for Science, Technology and the Arts) to produce a report entitled *Arts and Humanities Research and Innovation*. From the first page the authors discuss 'the distinctive contributions of arts and humanities knowledge':

> The arts and humanities cover a very wide range of research disciplines, including archaeology, English literature, history, music and philosophy. They contribute to a constantly growing body of knowledge on human experience, agency, identity and expression, as constructed through language, literature, artefacts and performance. This knowledge nourishes the UK's cultural existence, and inspires creative behaviour, as well as innovative goods and services. The arts and humanities have a particularly strong affiliation with the creative industries. There is growing evidence that this research helps to fuel those industries...

The link between the humanities and innovation shot to the headlines with a famous interview by Steve Jobs of Apple. Talking in the context of product innovation, Jobs said: 'the reason that Apple is able to create products like iPad is because we always try to be at the intersection of technology and liberal arts, to be able to get the best of both.' We also found the link to innovation had taken root in Russia. Participants at the HWR workshop referred to the interest in Richard Florida's concept of the Creative Class, especially in the context of urban planning, where the arts and humanities are playing an important role.

Of course, one can question whether innovation is a distinctive feature of the humanities as opposed to other disciplines, but it is no less significant in the humanities than elsewhere. At any rate, those who advocate innovation as a value typically see the humanities as promoting innovation in a way that complements the sciences and cannot be replaced by them. This is the point made by Jobs. And in a companion AHRC report to the one just quoted, we found the following claim:[26]

> Arts and humanities knowledge tends to be more particularistic, more tacit and less easy to communicate formally. This has implications for how this knowledge is created and shared with others. Yet, because they are less amenable to codification, the arts and humanities are better placed to disrupt and challenge standardised practices and conventional wisdoms.... The arts and humanities add to the overall diversification of knowledge creation. They offer distinctive approaches to the understanding of human experience and activity. If innovation is to thrive, it must exploit the knowledge from the entire spectrum of an integrated research base.

We have already mentioned the fact that the different values of the humanities can overlap. It is particularly important to stress this in the context of innovation. For instance, when commentators talk of the humanities promoting innovation, they might well be using this as a way of talking up their economic value as in, the humanities help promote economic value by providing innovative ideas and models to business. In social policy, the humanities may lead policy makers to consider proposals that would otherwise not have occurred to them, to break out of old habits of thinking.[27] In the case of cultural heritage, we have already mentioned the way in which the humanities can serve to question and revise preconceived views (or even myths) about national memory. This is yet another form of innovation. In current European Union policy thinking a strong case is often made for the necessity of nurturing social innovation alongside technological innovation and, as we shall see in Chapter 8, this is a point that is often picked up by humanities advocates, who argue that social innovation may be nurtured by research into human motivations, behaviour and entrepreneurship.

On the other hand, many humanist scholars mistrust appeals to innovation as a 'buzzword'. They may claim that innovation is not an end in itself; that not all innovation is good (e.g. in the arena of cultural heritage, governments can misuse the humanities in order to invent nationalist identities).

Looking at our interview responses, it is interesting that few people mentioned innovation unprompted. Perhaps the most articulate expression of the role of innovation was this one, explaining the role of humanities as a vital part of a knowledge ecosystem:

> NA6: Our society, especially in the recession era and era of privatisation, is fixated on market value. They think that the straight path to market growth is to put all your money in the STEM (science, technology, engineering, and mathematics) fields. What's not considered in that view is where ideas and innovations actually come from, and what the best system is for producing that. I'm a believer in the 'rich ecology' thesis. You don't get great discoveries and inventions by locking a thousand engineers in a room. You need the entire pyramid of engineers and artists and humanists with everyone sharing each others' points of view and ideas. You need a jungle.

Critical thinking

> This move, the intrinsic questioning purpose of the Humanities, was summonsed both as a means of overthrowing dominant understandings but also of advancing the Enlightenment belief that questioning [sc. and] knowledge are one and the same thing. This tradition of critique appears in almost every discipline in the Humanities—its purpose is (as the philosopher Walter Benjamin proclaimed) 'to brush against the grain' of established understandings.
>
> At its heart lies the genius of critical thought: the technique of asking deep-seated questions with the aim of gaining profound insights into the multiple challenges that face the human condition. (South Africa, *Consensus Study*, p. 29)

The claim that the humanities promote critical thinking is commonly made. It is particularly prominent in discussions of the value of a humanities education. In our context of humanities *research*, the point would be that research in humanities epitomises the use of critical thinking, and researchers pass on such virtues to their students.[28] But the same type of argument can be used beyond the teaching context; books, articles and media presentations might all be thought to promote critical thinking among the wider public.

The value of critical thinking found some robust advocates among our interviewees, for instance:

> NA5: Skills and sensitivities involved in learning how to think critically about the world around you are the skills and sensitivities

that succeed across the board, whether you work in medical imaging or are poet laureate. Critical thinking is part of being human. Right now, we have a lost generation of people who really will believe anything, and that's a real educational failure. We can turn it around, but it's going to take some work.

It is not difficult to be critical of the critical thinking argument. Why, it has to be asked, is this an argument for the humanities rather than any other academic subject? Surely any discipline depends on critical thinking? Progress is made when one researcher takes on the conclusions of another and subjects them to close and critical scrutiny. It seems odd to claim this as the preserve of the humanities.[29]

Some may still contend that, although all disciplines thrive on critical thinking, the humanities epitomise it. This touches upon the nature of the humanities, the topic of the next chapter. Consider the following extract from one of our interviews on the question about the nature of humanities research:

> As3: [Please give up to three examples of things that, due to humanities research, we know today that we did not know before, either in your own field or in the humanities in general.] I do think that this runs counter to our sense of the humanities as a dynamic discipline, and we should refuse to answer such queries because it puts the humanities in competition with, and defensive about, the knowledge that is generated by the sciences. Of course, we know much that we did not know before because of humanities research, but the most important lesson we have from the humanities is that we can still keep thinking about what we know, and see if we can unknow it, unravel it in some way, or build upon it. Do you think it is appropriate to describe the results of humanities research as 'findings'? Not if the findings are to be taken as the final word of wisdom. All findings in the humanities are provisional and subject to questioning and clarification and change and modification and dialogue and conversation.

This response seems to indicate that the end goal of research is the process of critical thinking itself. If so, it would be appropriate to single out the humanities in this way. But this comes at a price, namely that of conceding that, while the sciences do advance by way of finding answers to specific questions, the humanities do not.

Finally, a point of clarification, critical thinking is not the same as innovation. Both seem to have something in common since they might start from a widely accepted mode of thinking, which they then seek to change. But critical thinking is about analysis; innovation typically involves the imagination. Indeed, the creativity required by good innovation may even be stymied by too much analysis or critical thinking. This was a point made quite forcefully in our Russia workshop, as both critical thinking and innovation turned out to be important values for the participants. We realise, however, that not everyone will agree; some still hold that the two values go hand in hand. One of our respondents made exactly this point:

> LA2: The main thrust of the humanities is to foster critical thinking. We need to return to the Socratic maxim, 'the unexamined life is not worth living'. If we produce citizens unable to have their own ideas, they won't be innovative and creative. I was recently talking to a Chinese scholar who made exactly this point about Chinese society; however much scientific research they do, they still need to develop creativity and innovation. In fact, this point was made in China decades ago in the 1950s.

Personal and spiritual development

Many humanities disciplines study religious and spiritual traditions through their histories and their texts. One way of doing this is self-consciously 'clinical' and detached, for instance when scholars seek to understand such material 'from the outside'. But at our East Asia workshop, participants stressed the importance, especially in that region, of studying texts and traditions in a more 'devotional' way. That is, they might study them as a means to their own spiritual fulfilment (or, more broadly, their own personal development) and that of their students and readers. Both Buddhism and Confuciansim are commonly studied in this way by scholars in the Far East.

The idea is not alien elsewhere. Values-based universities in Africa and the US, especially those associated with a religious tradition, will typically approach many humanities disciplines in the same way. Nor is the idea necessarily religious. The study of the humanities and liberal arts explicitly for personal growth and development has been revived and advanced in the US quite recently by Anthony Kronman, interestingly enough, a Yale law professor.[30] A number of our respondents saw the value of the humanities in this way, notably in Russia and Asia:

R3: The value of the humanities is in fact that they provide tools with which a person becomes aware and realises [himself or herself] in the world.

R6: This [sc. the 'alternative academia' of biography and non-fiction authors, bloggers, museum curators, etc.] is all part of the growing demand for human self-realisation and betterment. It cannot proceed without knowledge of the past and criticism of the present.

NA13: Humanities research is about values, the meaning of existence, and of our life. Nobody can ignore this, even though most people might rarely think about this in their daily life. It is like the air, for example, or breathing, which we almost never think about in our daily life, unless there is a problem such as air pollution, or asthma, and then one suddenly realises that breathing is the fundamental activity of any being's state of being alive. Like the nutrition that one consumes every day, education of humanities offers individuals the necessary nutrition for existence. Deficiency of a specific nutrition in our body is not always visible and noticeable unless one gets sick, but if [you] wait until the illness occurs, cure might not be possible. I believe humanities research and humanities education function [in a] similar way.

As7: In the rapid development of high meaning in Asia, the first thing is of paramount importance. East Asia is all about traditions, Confucianism and all kinds of profound teachings. These things, I feel our 21st Century people are starved of and are dying for. I am a Buddhist myself...

As8: It helps people to leave a spiritual and enriched life, helps them have a rested mind and an active imagination.

Aesthetic appreciation

In music, literature and the arts generally, humanities research provides new insights to promote and deepen the appreciation of artistic beauty. Aside from the obvious ways in which humanities scholars may perform this function through undergraduate education, examples could include art historians writing material for exhibitions, and musicologists or drama scholars writing programme notes. All of these might also broadcast on radio or TV and write popular books. Literary scholars can communicate insights from their research through similar media, as well as book reviews.

That the humanities have such a role may seem obvious, but it turns out to be a disputed area. Academic research in literary criticism, art history and music has certainly had an aesthetic function in the past. Nowadays, there is no shortage of critics *outside* academia, writing and talking in the media, who aim to guide the general public in its appreciation of different kinds of artwork. But is this something modern-day academics do in the humanities? In the case of literature, it may actually be controversial to attribute such a role to researchers, perhaps because of trends such as postmodernism or, more generally, the 'democratisation' of public life, and hence the demise of academic expertise in matters of aesthetic appreciation.[31]

It was notable that very few of our respondents mentioned aesthetic appreciation as a value of the humanities. Here are two exceptions, both from North America:

> NA11: I would remind [an impatient and potentially hostile audience] first, that the way they live their lives and the pleasure they get from the world, some high percentage of that comes from their education in the humanities. Learning how to distinguish between good [and bad] forms of communication..., between canned and serious things, between superficial things and profound things. And this doesn't just go for aesthetic experience, but just being an intelligent consumer of media, politics, business and sciences. Again, I know this sounds old-fashioned but it helps people think broadly and deeply with discrimination. If they don't care about that, then there's not really much to say. You can't convince them.
>
> NA14: I'd prioritise aesthetic appreciation, i.e. the way research can make possible new and sophisticated forms of aesthetic pleasure. This is bound up with the way it shows how aesthetic pleasure has changed over time.

But note that in the first of these quotes aesthetic value is mentioned only briefly and is considered 'old-fashioned'.

A distributional survey of the interview responses

So far, we have been using the interview results alongside other sources to help characterise the different values of humanities research. In this section we examine the interviews on their own. First, we shall see how, according to these interviews, support for the different values is distributed around the world. In the final section (Strategies for justification), we look at the ways in which our respondents reflected on the idea of justifying the humanities.

Responses to the original question on reasons to fund the humanities varied widely. One point of difference was the level of generality. Some were broad-brush, others gave specific examples to illustrate the value of humanities research. But it is fair to say that in each region almost all the values we have discussed were mentioned at least once. As regards overall patterns, we can mention two: (i) one positive, a significant proportion of our respondents mentioned the social value; (ii) the other negative, very few, in answer to this question at least, mentioned economic value.

(i) Overall we found that most respondents made some sort of reference to society or the social, or at least a reference to our collective life as human beings, or to collective decision-making (e.g. about technological innovation). Europeans seemed less inclined than others to mention societal value, while more than two thirds of respondents from other regions mentioned social value. On the other hand, Europeans tended to mention cultural heritage more often than others.
(ii) Only a handful of respondents mentioned the economic value of the humanities. The small number of these references is striking, given the way the original question was set. It challenged respondents to think of themselves defending the humanities to a hostile audience. This ought to have invited them to make use of whatever arguments might resonate with their critics. Yet very few took up the opportunity to mention economic value. Perhaps this reflects something we mentioned earlier, that the economic argument is viewed with suspicion in academic circles. Those who did mention it referred to it in somewhat deflationary terms.

It is particularly interesting to reflect on this result in the US context. There, public pronouncements about the value of the humanities, whether from within academia or without, often focus on the employability of humanities graduates. Critics complain that humanities disciplines are irrelevant to the workplace and try to promote STEM subjects instead. Academics, worried that parents of students and potential students will be persuaded by this, try to fight a rearguard action. So it is interesting that, with two exceptions, our group of interviewees steered away from the topic, despite the terms of the question.

As indicated above, after conducting 45 interviews, we added a component to the questionnaire, which gauged respondents' reactions to the values we have been discussing in this chapter. We asked them which values they considered most important, and which their society did. We had 44 responses from Africa, Australia, Latin America, the MENA region, Russia and Asia.

The responses to the added question showed a disparity between the interviewees' own attitudes and those they felt prevailed in their own country. Although intrinsic value is popular among the respondents themselves, far fewer thought that it would gain any purchase in society at large. It is also noteworthy that, while the interviewees tended to believe in the social value of the humanities for policy making, they are less sanguine about whether their societies would agree. The same applies to the responses regarding critical thinking and innovation. On the other hand, there is a relative alignment between attitudes on cultural heritage. Yet again, we see that economic value is not something many humanities scholars espouse, though more think that it is something society expects of them. There is clearly more work to be done in future studies on the preferences of humanists.

Strategies for justification

Finally, we turn to a meta-issue arising from the interviews. Because of the way the original question was framed, some respondents took it as a cue to discuss the very idea of justifying the humanities. Occasionally, respondents counselled against arguing with a hostile audience at all; or they warned about the dangers of responding to critics operating within narrow, short-term paradigms.

If these responses were right, perhaps the entire thrust of this chapter might be considered misconceived. Haven't we been talking all along about justification, simply assuming that it is something worth doing? But this would be a mistake, because there is an important distinction between *justifying* and *articulating* the value of the humanities. By articulating, we mean explaining and differentiating the different values or benefits humanities research is thought to have. This is, in fact, all we have been doing for most of this chapter. Justifying the humanities is subtly different as it involves defending the humanities in the face of a challenge. Unlike articulation, justification is self-consciously rhetorical. There are potentially hostile audiences to consider, for instance: politicians nervous of their budgets; people who consider STEM subjects worth funding but struggle to see the point of the humanities.

Now one could argue, like the respondents above, that one simply should not engage in this kind of defensive manoeuvre at all. But that does not mean that one should not engage in the distinct project of articulation. It is important, and interesting for other reasons, to be aware of the different ways in which the humanities contribute to our lives, individually and collectively. Besides, we do not agree that all attempts at justification are misplaced. We need to give some account of ourselves to those who fund us and it would be wholly impractical to disengage altogether (even if a few critics are beyond the pale). It is also useful for us to challenge ourselves about our own motivations and values, irrespective of what others may think. So, let us turn to another group of respondents who agreed that we should engage with impatient and hostile audiences, but held that there are better and worse ways of doing so. The idea of tapping into a pre-existent or at least implicit interest was one favoured approach. For instance, one European respondent described how a historian might ask people about their family, such as their grandparents' childhood. This starts a conversation about what it was like in that period. Once such interest has been generated, some kind of dialogue becomes possible, and the historian can then introduce what they know about the past. In the US seven respondents also offered some constructive thoughts about how to open up people's minds to the issue. One thought that the key was to find a topic, probably local in nature, in which an interlocutor would already be interested, for instance a poet from their own state. The strategy would then be to show how academic research could affect the way we think of this author and, by extension, the region from which they came. Others went further and stated that the humanities already play a significant role in people's lives. Both these responses suggest that interest in the humanities may lie just beneath the surface, even in an impatient interlocutor; they merely need 'reminding'. Other respondents went a step further and insisted that people outside academia are already interested in the humanities. 'The fact is that we engage in humanistic thinking whether we know we do or not – when we talk about drones or stem cell research.' Another thought that politicians' critiques of the humanities fail to recognise the crucial importance that the humanities (e.g. literature) play in so many people's lives.

If these optimists are right, we need to be able to exploit public interest in the humanities, be it only latent. This requires effective communication. But, according to two US respondents, humanities scholars may sometimes be their own worst enemy:

> NA7: I think the humanities are partially to blame. We've spent a decade talking to ourselves in an esoteric language that nobody else understands or thinks is relevant. I'm not saying that the humanities need to sacrifice complexity in order to communicate, but nevertheless the humanities need to become more self-reflective themselves. What is the culturally critical function of the intellectual interrogations that they are engaged in? The humanities must find a way to limit [their] esotericism, without compromising the complexity of [their] interrogations.
>
> NA10: There's a lot of appreciation for the humanities. We founded a programme called the free minds programme, a one-year humanities course for adults, most of whom are low-income, ethnic minorities, and never went to college. They value the humanities. They value being able to think through issues and to have exposure to that kind of cultural capital. I think it's a matter of speaking beyond the academy, of speaking in a non-jargony language, of speaking about issues that people really care about and about the meaning of human life. Much humanities scholarship has moved away from the issues that really motivate people. So I think it's important to stay centred in those issues that people are facing every day.

These comments act as a salutary reminder when it comes to advocacy. If there is a problem of hostility and impatience in public attitudes, part of the solution may lie in our own hands.

Conclusions

This has been a wide-ranging survey, though in many ways we have barely been able to scratch the surface. But, by pulling some strands together, we can make the following points:

1. Almost all the values we listed at the beginning find supporters right across the world. The social value of the humanities is particularly popular. If scholars wish to find a single value to unite rather than divide them, they should persist in articulating it. It makes the humanities not only noble, but also useful.

2. Several respondents mentioned the intrinsic value of the humanities. We identified a hybrid form of this approach, where the curiosity-based pursuit of knowledge can actually lead to significant instrumental benefits. This hybrid justification could be an essential part of the rhetoric, pointing to the long-term societal value of being indifferent to such value in the short-term.
3. The role of the humanities regarding cultural heritage is also very important, but it needs to be handled with care. As has long been the case, political pressures can lead to abuse of academic standards in this domain.
4. The economic value of the humanities receives only lukewarm support. In the main, our respondents tended to avoid it. So justificatory appeals to economics are likely to divide humanities advocates from one another. Nonetheless, if the evidence can be found to support the argument, there is no reason why it should not be articulated. Its opponents need to explain why, if it is rooted in fact, it should not be deployed as one argument among others.
5. Humanities scholars should always be on the alert not to become their own worst enemy. The merits of clear and accessible communication (without losing nuance and sophistication) should always be borne in mind.

Except where otherwise noted, this work is licensed under a Creative Commons Attribution 3.0 Unported License. To view a copy of this license, visit http://creativecommons.org/licenses/by/3.0/

OPEN

3
The Nature of the Humanities

This chapter falls into two parts and is based upon the interview responses. The first part asks whether there are any patterns detectable in the research themes or topics chosen for humanities research. We found that socially relevant themes were prominent (though less so among the European interviewees) and that interviewees often identified cross-fertilisation as the way forward, especially interdisciplinarity, collaboration and comparative research. The second part considers a set of epistemological questions: how do researchers conceive of their work? Do they see themselves as seeking to advance the frontiers of knowledge, making discoveries and sometimes even breakthroughs? Or do they consider that such attitudes are more suitable to the sciences? We found that most researchers believed that the humanities do produce knowledge but were pessimistic as to how society perceives and values the humanities.

Part I

In Section 3 of the questionnaire we asked:

> What themes have been dominating your own field?
> What themes do you expect to dominate your field?
> Where do you see the potential breakthroughs in your field?

We looked for patterns, either regionally or worldwide: were any particular themes pervasive, or did the responses indicate that humanities research is fragmented?

We should comment briefly on the way the respondents approached this section of the questionnaire. A very few did not answer the questions at all, and sometimes a respondent made no comment to one of the questions. The responses also varied greatly in length. Sometimes they used a single word and at the other extreme wrote a long paragraph with follow-up references. There were also variations in the level of abstraction. Some answered the question in very general terms; others gave very specific examples from their own field. Many gave both types of answer. Also, some respondents took the question to be about their own research or that of their institute, rather than about their field generally.

Some respondents challenged the terms of the questions, particularly in the case of the third question. A few asked whether talk of breakthroughs was actually appropriate in the humanities. This raises an epistemological issue, which we discuss in Part II. Occasionally, respondents queried whether there are dominant themes in research, past or present, but this response was quite rare.

Thematic orientations

Overview

We initially divided the responses into three categories. At the specific or micro-level, we were given examples of research themes such as:

Russian towns
Ottoman Empire as seen from the periphery
Early modern England
Palestinian refugees
Applied Buddhism
Athenian democracy
James Joyce and Wallace.

At the more general or macro-level, we had examples such as:

Race, class and gender
Modernism and modernities
Visual culture
Identity
Ethnicity and nationalities
Media
Memory (especially in relation to war)
Postcoloniality
History of crime.

At a still more abstract level, were some theoretical and methodological tendencies:

> The shift from economic historical perspectives to ideological transformation
> The cultural turn in history in contrast to the materialist turn in sociology
> Critical humanities
> Postmodernism, in contrast to the rapprochement between humanities and sciences
> The digital humanities
> Comparative history
> Post-critical sociology
> Interdisciplinarity.

The macro-level: socially relevant themes

We were unlikely to find many patterns by looking at the micro-level, given the relatively small size of our sample, but even when we looked at the macro-level, few themes reached double digits. The exceptions included gender, which appeared in 13 responses, and identity, which appeared in 12. By abstracting a little further we met with a little more success and when using 'culture' as a keyword we found over 20 responses that made some sort of reference to the word.

On their own, these results do not entitle us to draw any interesting conclusions. But things change if we consider these results in the light of some of the findings from the previous chapter: here we saw that over 50% of researchers stressed the social value of humanities research, and also that many researchers put a strong emphasis on heritage. For the purpose of looking at thematic patterns, let us now bunch these two together and look across the macro themes to ask: to what extent are humanities researchers connected to the societal concerns that surround them? How frequently did our respondents mention socially relevant research themes? A brief look at the topics listed under the heading of macro-themes suggests a social orientation in the research topics, which is borne out by a closer look.

To give a sense of how we understand the description 'socially relevant', here are the examples of themes and topics that we take it to include, listed by region.

Africa

Out of a total of 13 responses; 11 mentioned socially relevant themes. Not only is this a high number, but the socially relevant themes were prominent compared to others. Examples included:

- Politics: nationalism; armed struggle; peace processes; regional studies; mineral resources and their social impacts; democracy
- Language: language variation and identity; language policy (with multilingual populations)
- Development: religion and development; theatre for development; development versus conservation; gender and development; politics and development
- Culture: popular culture; performance studies; media
- Religion: the social role of religion; the role of the church in the process of democratisation; religion and development.

Other societal themes were: history and memory: globalisation: gender: identity: and public archaeology.

Asia

Of the 16 respondents, 13 of them mentioned socially relevant themes, such as:

- The environment: the protection of environment; animal welfare; agricultural ethics
- Culture: cultural exchange; cultural aspects of ethnic groups and traditional approaches to understanding; intra-Asia culture of actions
- Politics: political instability; the relationship between the people and government elites; politics and literature; globalisation and the role of the state; justice and conflicts
- Religion: religion and peace; politics, religion and literature; religion and globalisation; the study of Islam, especially the issue of secularism.

In addition, respondents mentioned: bioethics; gender; questions of ethnicity; and postcoloniality.

Australia

All four respondents mentioned socially relevant themes.

- Environmental humanities; food culture; sustainable food production

- Memory, especially in relation to war and conflict, e.g. in relation to Gallipoli
- Popular culture, especially radical culture.

Other themes mentioned include media; sexual ethics; and sport.

Europe and Russia

Of the 16 non-Russian European respondents, 10 mentioned socially relevant themes, as did eight out of the nine Russians. Examples being:

- Culture: history of popular culture and political culture; political and cultural anthropology, social history; cultural diversity (in comparison with biological diversity)
- Globalisation: transnational and international history; cultural interconnections; comparative studies, i.e. comparing the Ottoman with the Chinese, Russian and Mogul empires.
- Policy: philosophy of technology, bioethics, ethics in the public domain, social integration; humanities subjects that relate to economics, health sciences, social cohesion and interculturality
- Ideological transformation: in governance, mentalities and in the management of complexity and diversity
- Language: communication studies with social relevance, e.g. with respect to multiculturalism and immigration; bilingualism; the study of adults who learn a minority language
- Gender (property, sexuality): interplay between race, class, and gender, especially with regard to the situation of minorities.

In addition, the following themes were mentioned: political, social, and economic elites; history of crime and criminal justice; state building; space, place and displacement; Cold War studies; the relation between society and the media; environmental studies.

Latin America

Of the nine respondents from Latin America, seven mentioned socially relevant themes, including:

- Culture: cultural issues and identity; collective memory
- Public engagement: the status and role of humanities in relation to culture and society, e.g. philosophy and archaeology; developing the public face of the humanities

- Politics: political economy, specifically, the effects of newcomers to the International System, and how it might change the architecture of international regimes and institutions, and change the distribution of power; autonomy of the political and its bearing upon the authority of law, agency of political communities (e.g. particular or universal political communities)
- Justice: the authority and normativity of law; global justice; human rights; democracy; justice and war
- Religion: secularisation, laïcity, church–state relations
- Plurality: freedoms (civic and religious) and diversity; new challenges in a plural world; unity in a nation with a diverse population and a diversity of cultural expressions.

In addition respondents mentioned social movements in 20th century Latin America; and security.

The MENA region

All six respondents mentioned socially relevant themes. They included:

- Language: the relation between language variation and identity; language policy concerning multilingual populations
- Politics: political instability; the relationship between the people and government elites; globalisation and the role of the state; employment; refugees
- Religion: the study of Islam, especially on the issue of secularism.

Gender, identity, socialisation, family and ethnicity were also mentioned as research topics.

North America

Of the 16 respondents, 12 mentioned socially relevant themes. The main clusters were:

- Globalisation: the realm of the transnational; 'looking at globalisation in a very localised kind of way – the local impacts of global process and the forms of resistance to uniformity'; projects with a globalised/hemispheric context; the re-emergence of China and India; religion and globalisation
- Health: bioethics; working with the clinical sphere to develop therapeutic approaches that embrace values, understanding and knowledge traditionally embedded within the humanities

- The public and private: looking at ongoing privatisation; at the diminishing role of public funding; at suspicion of governmental programmes; issues of privacy, surveillance and social media
- Environmental studies: protection of the environment; climate change; animal rights; food studies

In addition, the following themes were mentioned: cultural awareness; security and terror; human rights; violence/non-violence; gender studies.

To summarise, Table 3.1 lists the number and percentage of respondents by region who mentioned socially relevant themes.

These figures are striking (though it is also interesting that Europe is at the lower end of the scale.). They also fit well with some of the findings from Chapter 2, where we analysed respondents' views about the value of the humanities, often as expressed in public and even defensive contexts. Here we have been looking at what researchers say about their fields from the inside, out of the public gaze, but their views seem to be in tune with the more rhetorical statements about the justification of the humanities. Prevalent themes within academia resonate strongly with what is going on outside it. This helps to challenge the accusation, all too often heard, that the focus of humanities research is asocial and esoteric.

The methodological level: cross-fertilisation

Turning from the macro themes, let us now focus on the third category of responses to our question, which mentioned theoretical and

Table 3.1 Respondents who mentioned socially relevant themes

	Social themes mentioned	Number of respondents	Proportion as a %
Af	11	13	85
As	13	16	81
Aus	4	4	100
E	10	16	63
LA	7	9	78
MENA	6	6	100
NA	12	16	75
Ru	8	9	89
TOTAL	71	89	80

methodological trends. A significant number of respondents saw interdisciplinarity as a key trend in current research and, even more in future research, possibly resulting in breakthroughs. Respondents differed as far as the nature of interdisciplinary work was involved: sometimes they were thinking of research that reaches out to other humanities disciplines; sometimes to the social sciences; sometimes to STEM subjects. A total of 29 respondents made some reference to interdisciplinary research in this section of the questionnaire.

This figure is certainly interesting, but things become far more so if we allow ourselves to see interdisciplinarity as an instance of a wider tendency towards cross-fertilisation. Typically, an interdisciplinary researcher is someone who has been trained within the confines of a specific discipline, with its own professional and methodological norms, and then reaches out to another discipline, with all the risks, uncertainties and opportunities that this involves. But there are other forms of cross-fertilisation. A substantial number of respondents mentioned some form of intercultural or transnational comparison in their answers. Comparative work of this type is not necessarily interdisciplinary (as is usually understood). So comparative and interdisciplinary research should be treated as distinct concepts. As examples of comparative research, we found references to historians who compare two sets of phenomena in different parts of the world and at different periods, such as comparing the Roman and Ottoman empires. Sometimes this might overlap with the project of writing 'global history', where the different segments of history are pieced together into a single framework. Similarly, historians of political thought might compare two periods in different regions and at different times – one respondent cited the example of comparing the ideas of the French Revolution with contemporary Japanese political thought. Within the discipline of philosophy, respondents mentioned opportunities for comparative work between Eastern and Western philosophies; and within Western philosophy itself, the notorious divide between analytic and continental traditions offers opportunities for bridge-building and comparison, which two respondents thought a possible source of breakthroughs. Also, under this heading, we might include the idea of bringing philosophies of much older periods to bear on contemporary philosophical problems: medieval philosophy for modern philosophy of mind; ancient Greek and Chinese philosophy for contemporary ethics. All these are examples of comparative research given in interview responses.

Like interdisciplinary research, international or intercultural work can quickly shade into collaborative research, as it is perhaps best conducted by building research teams across different countries (as noted by one of our Latin American respondents who works on secularisation and laïcity in different regions). Though distinct from one another, intercultural, transnational, interdisciplinary and collaborative research all fall under the heading of research cross-fertilisation. So we think we are justified in grouping them together, and in using this grouping to find a pattern in the answers about research themes.

In a similar vein, we found three other types of response that, taken on their own, would not seem statistically significant but become important once seen as part of this broader pattern. (1) Occasionally, respondents talked of research that works with local communities as an important category. Two archaeologists (from Brazil and Tanzania) and a historian (from Mozambique) fell into this category. Other respondents might have referred to such outreach later on in the questionnaire, under the heading of translation, but the point here is that these respondents linked such activities to dominant research trends. (2) Another case concerns researchers working with practitioners: two respondents from film studies (one from India, the other from Nigeria) underlined the importance of bringing together academic research and practice. (3) In the case of art history another example is working with museums, and through them the public, as opposed to pursuing research simply within academia. Note that all these cases are about conducting research, not (merely) communicating its results.

Putting all these categories together, we present the numbers in Table 3.2.[1]

Table 3.2 Respondents pointing to the value of cross-fertilisation

	Interdisciplinary	Comparative	Public engagement	Practitioner engagement	Number of interviews
Af	4	2	3	1	13
As	4	4	1	1	16
Aus	2	0	0	0	4
E/Ru	11	3	0	1	25
LA	2	3	1	0	9
ME	2	2	0	0	6
NA	8	5	0	0	16
TOTAL	34	18	5	3	89

TOTAL: 60 out of 89, or 67%, of our interviewees mentioned some form of cross-fertilisation.

There are two further observations to make. (1) There was no significant disciplinary spread in these results – i.e. references to the different categories were spread evenly around the different fields. So we have not presented a table separating the results by discipline. (2) On the whole, respondents saw the trend towards cross-fertilisation in future themes or breakthroughs.

So, at a very high level of abstraction, we have seen how the majority of our respondents referred to some form of cross-fertilisation when it came to identifying research themes and trends.[2] It did not have to be this way. It would have been quite plausible for a respondent to claim that the dominant themes are those where researchers plough the monodisciplinary furrow, confined within a traditional academic context and a specific time and period. Perhaps the best research results from mining ever more deeply in the seams already mapped out. Here is one response along these lines (Af10):

> *[What themes have been dominating your own field?]* My theoretical orientation in linguistics tilts towards the functional–typological option. In my restricted specialisation of syntax, issues regarding grammaticalisation, language documentation, grammar writing, usage-based analyses are some of the themes. *[What themes do you expect to dominate your field?]* I expect these to continue for the next few years.

There is no reason, a priori, why the majority of our respondents should not have gone down this route. But they did not.

Interdisciplinarity, transnational research (internationalisation) and outreach to the public are among the main subjects of subsequent chapters. In them we shall ask questions about institutional conditions, such as whether they are being imposed on researchers against their will and how well they are being enabled or resourced. At this stage, we are merely pointing out that, on the basis of our interview results, researchers themselves already think that these are important sources of research themes – past, present and future – and in some cases that they will facilitate the most important breakthroughs.

Part II

We now turn to the question of whether humanities scholars see themselves as attempting to make discoveries and to advance knowledge, as is regularly supposed in the sciences, or whether their objective is different, e.g. merely exploring new perspectives and ways of looking at familiar ideas and texts. The question is important in its own right, but a secondary reason for focusing on this issue concerns the public perception of the humanities. If the humanities conceive of themselves as fundamentally different from the sciences in this respect, policy makers and society at large may have a problem understanding just what researchers in the humanities do, and hence why they are worth supporting.

The interview questions

When we first started the interviews, the section entitled 'The nature of the humanities' consisted of the following questions:

> What are the major similarities and dissimilarities between the humanities and the sciences in the ways they conduct and present research?
>
> Could you give some examples (up to three) of important findings gained in the humanities?
>
> Aside from your own views, how do you think the humanities are perceived in this respect?
>
> What impact does the perception of the humanities in comparison to the sciences have on funding?

We conducted 38 interviews using these questions, mainly from Asia, Europe and the US. Some interviewees did not respond to one or other question in the cluster. When this happened, it was usually impossible to know whether the respondent was being absent-minded, tired, impatient, or whether they were being deliberately evasive. Nonetheless, most respondents did answer all the questions, so we had a good number to work with.

Our use of the word findings in the second question produced some interesting reactions. Given that this is a word less often associated with the humanities than with the natural and social sciences, the question might seem provocative. In the event, some interviewees simply went along with the question and gave examples. From this, one is entitled to assume that they had no problem with the use of the term findings in the humanities, or at least that we have no evidence to say that they objected to it. Other respondents queried the term and others explicitly objected to it. This then gave us further evidence for how they conceived of the difference between the humanities and the sciences.

Looking at those who queried or rejected the term, we asked ourselves why. One possibility was that a respondent objected to the term because they thought the humanities do not make discoveries or attain new knowledge. An alternative was that a respondent does think the humanities make discoveries and attain new knowledge, no less than the sciences do, but that they do not like to use the term findings to describe it. In this case, the issue may be more semantic than epistemological. In the responses we received to this question, we could usually tell what attitude interviewees took to the use of the term findings. Where they did have reservations, it was normally clear whether this was merely a semantic worry or whether it betrayed a deeper epistemological position about knowledge and the humanities. But to avoid the risk of any future uncertainty, roughly halfway through the interview process we decided to change the question slightly and separate out the two issues of whether the respondents conceived of the humanities as progressing in terms of knowledge and whether they objected to the use of the term findings.

So, across the next 51 interviews, we revised this section of the questionnaire to:

> What, in broad terms, are the major similarities and dissimilarities between the humanities and the sciences in the ways they conduct and present research?
>
> Please give up to three examples of things that, due to humanities research, we know today that we did not know before, either in your own field or in the humanities in general.
>
> Do you think it is appropriate to describe the results of humanities research as findings?
>
> What impact does the public perception of the humanities in this respect have on funding?

In other words, we were now asking directly what people thought of the use of the term findings, and distinguishing this question from the broader issue of whether they conceive of the humanities as knowledge directed.

Looking at all the responses to this section of the questionnaire (in both versions), we found an enormous amount of material to analyse. But, for the purposes of this chapter, we focus on the respondents' epistemological assumptions and attitudes, as evidenced mainly by their answers to the questions about findings and knowledge. (There are other issues about the relation between humanities and the sciences that are not so obviously epistemological, such as the role of collaboration and the use of quantitative methods, but we shall not discuss these here.) In the last section we turn to issues about public perception of the humanities, looking at the respondents' views and then drawing some conclusions of our own.

Reactions to the term 'findings'

In this section, we survey all the interview responses to gauge their reaction to the notion of findings in the humanities. When considering the first batch of interviews (38) we make inferences purely from they way they responded to the question: 'could you give some examples (up to three) of important findings gained in the humanities?' If the respondent simply gives some examples, we take that to imply that they accept the notion of findings in the humanities; if they stop to question the term, it is usually possible to say whether they are strongly negative, mildly negative or mixed, in the sense that they think the term is appropriate in some contexts of humanities research but not in others. With the second batch of interviews (based on the new question), the task of gauging respondents' reactions to findings is simpler, since we asked outright what they thought of the term.

With all the interviews, we have attempted to divide their reactions into the following categories:

- clearly/strongly *negative*
- mixed, but *mildly negative*
- *mixed* (ambivalent), but not taking a normative position either way
- mixed, but *mildly positive*
- clearly/strongly *positive*

The following are examples of each category:

> *Negative*: 'I don't think it's the function of the humanities to establish findings. We don't use those terms. We talk more about insights, perspectives and points of view. We don't talk in that quite definitive way about findings and measurable outcomes.' (NA10)
>
> *Mildly negative*: 'The difference [between the sciences and the humanities] lies in the fact that establishing findings cannot be obligatory for the humanities. That would change its essentially creative and fluid character. One cannot deny that a great deal of self-indulgent

work happens in the humanities, but the answer to that cannot be a scientistic demand for findings.' (As2)[3]
Mixed: 'Well, there are findings and there are other issues to do with reports and inferences.' (Af4)
Mildly positive: 'I do not have problems with the word "findings". It depends how you describe the word in your research.' (As13)
Positive: 'Yes! The humanities produce objective findings that are arrived at through a systematic process of study of specific phenomena.' (Af3)

Using this classification we can divide up the answers, as in Table 3.3, separated by region.[4]

If we group the *positives* and the *mildly positives* together, and similarly with the *negatives*, we can see that 35 respondents were positive about findings, and 26 were negative (around 40% and 29% of our sample respectively).

We now turn to the reasons given for the *negative* responses.

- Some rejected the findings terminology on the grounds that it excludes functions distinctive to humanities research, that it is about values, or interpretation or appreciation. For instance:

    NA8: No findings, not in general. In classics, there are some examples of a different model. In philology – study of texts – we do have findings. They are generally wrapped up in careful editing of texts in which you find the best reading for ancient work. Sometimes these readings involve making new discoveries and emending texts

Table 3.3 Reactions to the term 'findings'

	Negative	Mildly negative	Mixed	Mildly positive	Positive	n/c
Af	3	3	1	0	4	2
As	3	2	2	6	1	2
Aus	1		1		2	
E/Ru	0	4	3	7	5	6
LA		2	1	2	1	3
ME	2	0	0	0	2	2
NA	5	1	2	3	2	3
TOTAL	14	12	10	18	17	18

n/c = no comment.

in sometimes quite a dramatic way because you have established a better way of looking at an original work. That is what I would call scientific research. It is not just interpretative or appreciative. It is fundamental scientific work.

But these responses are not evidence that these interviewees deny their research is truth seeking since one can have true or false judgements about values, interpretation and appreciation.

- Three respondents reacted against the word findings because they thought humanities research lacks finality. For instance:

    As3: Not if the findings are to be taken as the final word of wisdom. All findings in the humanities are provisional and subject to questioning and clarification and change and modification and dialogue and conversation.

Of course, since researchers in the natural and social sciences would also admit that their findings are subject to revision, this point should not be used to drive a wedge between the humanities and the sciences.

- Perhaps two respondents took a stronger 'anti-objectivist'[5] stance, saying that the humanities (only?) look for new perspectives. For instance:

    ME4: Do the humanities have findings? In the exact sciences they have discoveries; in our fields we can discover a new way of thinking about a subject matter. There have been discoveries but, on the whole in the humanities, we discover new ways of thinking about existing ideas or texts; we find ways of reading something differently. But one does so scientifically; one needs to know what's been said before and understand it in an organised way. One needs arguments; one needs to form hypotheses and to demonstrate them.

When we looked at respondents who were *mildly negative* about the term findings, we found no clear pattern in the reasons given. Only three could be construed as making a gesture towards some form of anti-objectivism:

    As4: Instead of findings, I should rather call them as 'subjective perception/understanding'.

As for the remaining responses in this category, there were no patterns detectable in their reasons. One European reiterated the point found in some US *negative* responses that the humanities involve (critical) interpretation, which cannot be described in terms of findings. But in the other *mildly negative* responses, all gave different reasons, which do not crop up elsewhere.

Knowledge

Do the humanities advance knowledge?

As indicated above, after conducting 38 interviews we changed the section on the nature of the humanities, replacing the request for three examples of findings with the following:

> Please give up to three examples of things that, due to humanities research, we know today that we did not know before, either in your own field or in the humanities in general.

We were interested to see what would happen once respondents were asked to give examples in, what we considered, a less provocative way. Following on from the previous discussion, you might expect that respondents would not have a problem talking simply in terms of advances in knowledge. As we saw, very few objected to the term findings because it implied that the humanities, like the sciences, seek knowledge.

This expectation was justified. Of the 40 responses we had to this new question, 35 were happy to answer on the assumption that the humanities advance knowledge and 11 made no comment. But we cannot infer anything from this, we cannot say that they were evading the question (and therefore tacitly suspicious of knowledge claims in the humanities), they may simply have been distracted or fatigued. By way of a more detailed breakdown, Table 3.4 lists by region those who went along with the request for examples of knowledge.

Table 3.4 Answers to the question 'Do the humanities advance knowledge?'

	Accepted	Rejected	Mixed
Af	8	0	0
As	7	1	1
Aus	2	0	0
E/Ru	8	0	1
LA	6	0	1
ME	1	0	0
NA	3	1	0
TOTAL	35	2	3

Two respondents who rejected the terms of the question said:

> As3: I do think that this runs counter to our sense of the humanities as a dynamic discipline, and we should refuse to answer such queries because it puts the humanities in competition with, and defensive about, the knowledge that is generated by the sciences. Of course, we know much that we did not know before because of humanities research, but the most important lesson we have from the humanities is that we can still keep thinking about what we know, and see if we can unknow it, unravel it in some way, or build upon it.
>
> NA13: I feel that the question itself is biased. This is based on science or social science model of 'discovery.' Humanities research enables us to understand how value systems in our society are generated.

The important point is that they were the only ones who reacted negatively to the new question. If our sample of interviewees is representative, it would seem that, in general, humanities scholars do not oppose the idea that their fields are truth seeking and do not reject the idea that they work towards, and indeed achieve, knowledge.

Breakthroughs

We now turn to a related issue about the nature of the humanities, that of whether our respondents think there are breakthroughs in humanities research. As discussed in Part I of this chapter, we asked our respondents to comment on breakthroughs in another section of the questionnaire, under the heading of 'major research themes', when, after questions about recent and emerging research themes, we asked them:

> Where do you see the potential breakthroughs in your field?

In Part I we drew on these answers to see where respondents thought there might be breakthroughs. But now our interest is more epistemological. Just as with our question about findings later on in the questionnaire, the question about breakthroughs might seem provocative. It simply assumes that there are breakthroughs in the humanities. So, as with findings, we left it up to the respondents either to accept the terms of the question and give examples, or to challenge them and thereby reveal their own assumptions about the nature of the humanities. It is from this perspective that we now wish to look at the responses.

The answers broke down into the following respondents who:

- accepted the notion of breakthroughs, and gave examples
- accepted the notion of breakthroughs, but thought that there would not be any in their field (= mixed)
- disputed the application of breakthroughs to the humanities in principle
- made no comment: some did not answer the question, which may have been because the interviewer did not press it. There is no case where the respondent's failure to answer can confidently be read as a refusal to engage with the notion of breakthroughs.

Table 3.5 lists the results by region and worldwide (out of a total of 89).

It is noticeable that those who accepted the notion of breakthroughs in the humanities far outnumbered the sceptics. But since there are some sceptics it may be useful to indicate in outline what they said.

Two respondents made the very similar point that, although we should not talk in terms of breakthroughs, we should talk of discoveries:

> NA8: I don't think breakthrough is a term that fits very well in the humanities, particularly in the classics, given the nature of the material. But we do see new discoveries being made all the time. For example, there have been some very exciting discoveries made in the field of ancient reading. These discoveries illustrate how oral techniques and reading techniques merged for a while, before reading became a thing done with just the eyes. So that would be one example.
>
> NA6: I'll start with the breakthrough issue.... To take the narrative frame of breakthroughs, inventions, and innovations that fits the sciences very well and reframe the discourse under the word

Table 3.5 Answers to the question 'Do the humanities produce breakthroughs?'

	Accepted	Disputed	Mixed	n/c
Af	7	2	0	4
As	9	0	1	6
Aus	2			2
E	6	4	0	6
LA	5	0	0	4
ME	1	1	3	1
NA	6	5	1	4
Ru	6		1	2
TOTAL	42	12	6	29

discovery rather than breakthrough. The thesis is that the humanities are as important as any of the other disciplines in that they expand the horizons of human discoveries. If you think about the grand challenges – energy and water shortage and food – both have a natural and human cause and effect. We need not only the STEM sciences but also the humanities, the cultural sciences.

In other words, they did not want their rejection of breakthrough terminology to be linked to anti-objectivism. Another respondent replaced breakthrough terminology with reinterpretation:

> E13: In the humanities we're not so much concerned with discovering new stuff, the content is already there. The task is to find new methods of engaging with it. People take their questions from the world around them and use them to reinterpret works from the past. For a good example, look at the Globe Shakespeare project, which brings people from all over the world to perform and present their own perspectives on his plays.

These were in fact the only respondents who rejected talk of breakthroughs outright. If we turn to the other sceptics, we see that they were all milder. Some (two from history, two from literature) sounded sceptical about breakthroughs, but became more optimistic as they went on:

> E15: To me the idea of a breakthrough seems to make more sense in the sciences than in the humanities. But in my field, perhaps something like a breakthrough will come through intercultural comparison, e.g. with China, which has its own classical culture.

Finally, there were some who seemed to allow for the possibility of breakthroughs in principle, but didn't think their field was going to yield them (in the near future):

> ME3: I don't foresee any breakthroughs in philosophy. That's not to say there aren't breakthroughs in the subject, but that you can't predict them. An example of a breakthrough is Rawls, but it takes time for people to absorb such work. If there are breakthroughs they will come as a result of the international environment of philosophical research.

There seems to be no pattern to the discipline of the sceptics. True, the staunchest two were from linguistics, but other than that it is difficult to associate scepticism about breakthroughs with any particular discipline.

Perception of the humanities

We now return to the section of the questionnaire about the nature of the humanities. In the final part of this section, we asked respondents for their views about the public perception of the humanities. Specifically, we wanted to know what effects they thought the public perception of the humanities had on funding. In the first version of the questionnaire we asked:

> And what impact does the perception of the humanities in comparison to the sciences have on funding?

In the second we altered the question to:

> What impact does the public perception of the humanities in this respect have on funding?

(By 'this respect' we were referring to the issue tackled in the other questions in this section, about examples of knowledge gains and the question of whether the humanities produce findings.)

Almost all those who responded to this question were negative; only three answers showed any optimism. As to the reasons for such pessimism, about half the pessimists thought the diagnosis quite straightforward, since the sciences are perceived as being more useful than the humanities they get more funding. The utility at issue varied slightly. Many respondents talked about technology, referring to engineering benefits or to medicine. Others were more general. Among the African respondents (and only among them) there were references to development (Af6, Af9, and Af10). Some of the US respondents (NA1, NA8, and NA10) talked in terms of employability, a theme not explicitly mentioned in any other region. A few made the point that much of scientific research is not actually useful and is also threatened by the utilitarian attitudes of policy makers.

When we set the question, we actually had a different point in mind. Our hypothesis was that public attitudes and hence funding are adversely affected by the perception that the humanities do not advance knowledge as the sciences do. Six respondents did take up this hint, and agreed (four of these are among those who embrace an anti-realist conception of the humanities), for example:

> NA1: I think it would be problematic and self-defeating to adopt that language [sc. of findings].... Admittedly, it makes defending the humanities harder if you can't point to important findings or discoveries.

Of course one can say that, if the public think the humanities do not advance knowledge, *a fortiori*, they think the humanities do not advance useful or relevant knowledge for society. But those of our respondents who made the utilitarian point did not make this more complex argument. Their point was simpler, whether or not the public and policy makers think humanities research produces knowledge and findings, they don't think the results are useful to society.

What is the solution to this problem of perception? Although the humanities do produce concrete benefits to society (more often than is often acknowledged), they do it in a different way from some technology disciplines. So we should articulate the specific benefit we do produce, even if it is more gradual and less obvious than in other research fields. Here, it is useful to quote one of the few respondents who struck a more optimistic tone in this part of the questionnaire:

> E2: To be sure, many people see the humanities as impractical and irrelevant. But there are also many people with a profound interest in history, literature, arts, philosophy, etc. who appreciate our work. We need to make a more sustained effort to reach out to our non-expert audiences. In sum, I do not think that the public perception of the humanities is particularly negative in Germany and that we have problems acquiring funding because of negative stereotypes. I realise that many colleagues habitually raise such complaints but there is nothing new about this self-image as underappreciated scholars.

Many humanities scholars already make an effort to reach out, a point we shall discuss further in Chapter 5 on translation, but there is a dimension we feel it important to add here. Before the public can appreciate the full value of the humanities they need to understand more clearly what we do. But how effective are humanities scholars at explaining the outcomes of their research? In their answers to the question about the value of the humanities mentioned at the end of the last chapter, two North American respondents (NA7 and NA10) complained that humanities research can be too esoteric and ridden with jargon. Perhaps we should be better equipped to give crisp examples of research outcomes that support the different roles or values discussed in the previous chapter. Again, we acknowledge that some humanities scholars already do this, often unsupported by their institutions. If this readiness and ability were more widely shared, perhaps it would do something to counteract the negative impression of the humanities as described by one respondent:

> NA11: In America, the humanities are perceived as fluff: in universities, high schools and grammar schools.

Conclusion

Most of the respondents converged on these points:

- They identify socially relevant themes as being prominent in humanities research (though less so among the European interviewees).
- They identify cross-fertilisation, especially interdisciplinarity and collaboration, as a way forward.
- They believe that the humanities produce knowledge, most agree that breakthroughs may be identified but they are divided in their views on the concept of findings.
- They were pessimistic as to how society perceives and values the humanities.

Building on the conclusions of Chapters 2 and 3 it is clear that stereotypes of humanities scholars as removed from the world, only too content to live in their ivory towers and unable to relate to real-world problems, do not conform with how humanists themselves perceive their role and value. While there may be widespread scepticism among academics about how their insights are valued and taken up by politicians, and perhaps society at large, it is clear that many researchers see a social value in their knowledge and want to engage and have an impact on the world. There is a sense of disconnection and lack of bridge-building rather than an unwillingness to engage. Such problems will inform later chapters but first we need to investigate how humanities knowledge is being impacted by digital technologies.

Except where otherwise noted, this work is licensed under a Creative Commons Attribution 3.0 Unported License. To view a copy of this license, visit http://creativecommons.org/licenses/by/3.0/

OPEN

4
The Digital Humanities

In the last 25 years digital technologies have changed the humanities. The question is: by how much? Is the digital revolution transforming the humanities intellectually? Or has it just sped up processes and access in ways that are certainly faster but not essentially different? Are we asking new research questions or are we just using new tools? Furthermore, do the digital humanities require new skillsets, which could cause us to think of universities and research training in fundamentally new ways, or is it sufficient to rely on established ways? This chapter explores these questions.

In the first section we give an overview of the world of professional digital humanists before turning to our interviewee's responses to see how the research culture of the humanities is responding to these new developments. We find that, while digital technologies have made information vastly more accessible, major regional imbalances remain. Furthermore, experts in digital technology face the challenge of explaining the intellectual benefits of new technologies to traditional academics, who are often mildly sceptical. There is also the problem that the present generation of humanists, trained in an analogue world, face the double challenge of training the next generation for the potential of new technologies and of embracing and rewarding new research questions and practices.

The world of professional digital humanists

The digital humanities (DH) cannot be easily defined. Many view DH as a movement within the traditional humanities and social science disciplines, which promises to bring digital technologies to bear on traditional research questions.[1] The same questions that once required a lifetime of manual gathering and processing of data may now be answered within a few weeks, or even a couple days, with the aid of digitised information. Digital humanists have sometimes resisted this definition, however, seeing DH as a more expansive movement and as a discipline in its own right, involving new modes of scholarship and institutionals. Others are resistant to formally defining DH, seeing it as a young and 'constantly changing field, which escapes easy definition'.[2] Some disciplines, such as archaeology and linguistics that perhaps have embraced digital technologies more thoroughly than others, see little or no need to separate out a special digital humanities field. Rather than attempt to define DH outright, this chapter provides a brief survey of professional associations, the location and makeup of DH centres around the world, and a number of common research trends engaging with IT over and above the simple accessing of digital information. It is our hope that this overview will clarify many questions about who works in the digital humanities and what it is that they do.

The Alliance of Digital Humanities Organizations (ADHO) is a global umbrella organisation, which 'promotes and supports digital research and teaching across all arts and humanities disciplines, acting as a community-based advisory force, and supporting excellence in research, publication, collaboration and training'.[3] ADHO is currently comprised of a number of regional professional organisations and has approximately 400 members worldwide.[4] The Alliance supports a number of publications, including *Literary and Linguistic Computing* (LLC), a print journal published by Oxford University Press, and *Digital Humanities Quarterly* (DHQ), a peer-reviewed electronic journal.[5] ADHO organises a number of conferences and training initiatives, including the Digital Humanities Conference, the largest annual international meeting of digital humanists, and a large number of international THATCamps, in which scholars and technologists meet to share ideas and develop future collaborations. In July 2013 THATCamp was held at the University of Buenos Aires with further ones scheduled in the United States, Germany, Slovakia and New Zealand.[6]

While most digital humanists are regular faculty members in specific academic schools, many belong to specialised digital humanities centres. A centre is roughly defined as a group of scholars within a given community or academic institution, who are devoted, at least in part, to digital humanities research. The centre may conduct its own research projects or may provide technical support to academic projects across several schools. The majority of centres are housed in colleges and universities, although some are funded by governments or private initiatives.[7] In many parts of the world, there are large numbers of independent digital humanists, despite there being no unified DH centres. The absence of DH centres is not always indicative of the number of scholars participating in the field.[8]

Table 4.1 summarises the number of digital humanities centres around the world according to information provided by centerNet, a global coalition of DH centres. The list is not complete, but is a good approximation of the reality at the time of compilation in July 2013.[9] The grouping is somewhat artificial in that many DH initiatives are collaborative, transnational and transcultural by design.[10]

It should be noted that a large university like the National Autonomous University of Mexico (UNAM) does not have a single, unified DH centre but does have many 'small personal initiatives'.[11] Recent findings show that there are at least 20–30 self-identified digital humanists working in four Mexico City universities.[12] This illustrates both the relative lack of information about the DH community in Mexico and other parts of the Spanish-speaking world and underscores the importance of looking beyond unified DH centres as a way of quantifying participation in the field. By way of illustration centerNet reports one DH centre in South Africa, the University of Cape Town Center for Educational Technology.[13] It is worth noting that the Rhodes University Book and Text Studies programme has held workshops in Humanities Computing. Additionally, the eThekwini Municipality's Libraries and Heritage Department in Durban, South Africa maintains a cultural heritage project, intended 'to collect and disseminate local content, in English and Zulu'.[14]

There are at least 7 DH centres in Australia,[15] the ANU DH Hub being among the largest, housing five permanent staff members, and nine affiliated faculty.[16] There is a least one centre in New Zealand, the New Zealand Electronic Text Centre. There are three DH centres in Japan,

Table 4.1 Digital humanities centres and individuals by region, July 2013

Latin America	3
USA	60
Canada	19
Europe	65
South Africa	1
Australia and New Zealand	8
East Asia	8

including the University of Tokyo Center for Evolving Humanities, The Ritsumeikan University Digital Humanities Center for Japanese Arts and Cultures, and the International Institute for Digital Humanities (DHII). Taiwan is home to the Nanyang Technological University Research Centre for Digital Humanities (NTU) and the Dharma Drum Buddhist College Library and Information Center. A number of these centres have a strong interest in preserving and disseminating local historical and cultural information.[17] In China, there are several academic departments with a strong interest in DH. The Fudan University Research Center on History and Geography, the Wuhan University History College, the Nanjing Normal University and the Chinese Academy of Social Sciences have developed digital projects concerning Chinese geography and ancient archival materials.[18]

Europe has at least 65 DH centres. The densest concentration of 19 centres is in England,[19] the largest being the University College London Centre for Digital Humanities with six directors, ten staff, student, and liaison positions, ten affiliated faculty, and 13 or more affiliated graduate students. Ireland has the world's largest structured PhD programme in digital arts and humanities in a consortium of six universities, north and south of the border, with more than 60 doctoral students. There are at least 38 centres on the Continent,[20] with strong representation in countries like the Netherlands, France, Germany, Denmark, Sweden, Italy and Austria.[21]

centerNet reports 19 DH centres in Canada, ranging in size from one permanent faculty director, with five appointed scholars (CIRCA) to seven staff and faculty positions and 40 affiliated faculty (DH McGill).[22] As the largest of these, the initiative at McGill is shared between the Faculties of Arts, Religious Studies, Music, and the Library. Its projects tend to focus on textual analysis, knowledge environments, spaces and publics, cultural archives, curation, and visualisation.[23]

There are approximately 60 DH centres in the United States[24] with world-leading facilities, such as the Massachusetts Institute of Technology HyperStudio, the Harvard University Digital Arts and Humanities (DARTH), the Columbia University Digital Humanities Center (DHC), the University of Maryland Institute for Technology in the Humanities (MITH), George Mason University's Center for History and New Media (CHNM), and many other centres, indicating a vigorous growth of this field at most North American humanities faculties.

Research trends

Digital humanists are concerned with a variety of topics and, despite many initiatives to create project databases, the landscape is hard to survey.[25] Perhaps it is useful to identify five major research areas:

- Digital collections, archiving and text encoding
- Reading and analysing electronic texts
- Geospatial and critical discursive mapping technologies
- 'Big Data,' social computing, crowdsourcing, and networking
- 3D immersive visualisation environments

It should be noted, however, that many successful projects either do not fit neatly into this framework or fall into two or more categories.

Digital collections and archives

Projects in this category tend to concern the creation of digital editions, digital corpora and networks of existing data repositories. Many projects of this sort begin by transforming analogue material into an electronic format. This usually takes place through some method of scanning and optical character recognition. Where optical character recognition is difficult or impossible, a number of projects have made use of crowdsourcing, asking users to help transcribe analogue materials. *Old Weather* asks users to transcribe weather records kept aboard US sailing ships from the mid-19th century. User transcriptions are mined to compile data about past environmental conditions, ship movements and the lives of the people aboard.[26] Similarly, the *Oxyrhynchus Papyrus Project*, an initiative at Oxford University, asks users familiar with ancient Greek to edit early Christian and Gnostic papyri.[27]

Other initiatives in this category concern the management and dissemination of metadata, or data about the data of interest. Common forms of metadata include author, title, subject, time and location. Well-managed metadata makes it much easier for researchers to access and analyse large data sets. The Text Encoding Initiative (TEI) has developed among scholars and institutions interested in maintaining metadata standards across projects and disciplines. Many notable data collections, including Tufts University's *Perseus* project, one of the largest digital collections of ancient Greek and Latin Texts, the *Women Writers Project* and the *Early Americas Digital Archive* follow TEI standards.[28]

A major Japanese project is the *Integrated Database of Classical Japanese Texts in the pre-Meiji Period*. This database of documents from Japan's pre-1868 era involves the National Institute of Japanese Literature as the core institute. The project proposes compiling a new database with links to bibliographies, images of original manuscripts and transliterated texts.[29]

Reading and analysing electronic texts

A large number of DH projects concern the presentation, evolution and analysis of electronic texts. Many 'reading environment' projects tend to address the way electronic texts are presented, collaborative reading methods and digital annotation. These projects examine the ways in which interactive digital texts can produce new information and improve existing methods of scholarly debate. For example, *Debates in DH* was originally published as a book by the University of Minnesota Press and recently 'expanded into a hybrid print/digital publication stream that will explore new debates as they emerge'. Readers who visit the website are presented with an online text of the book, which they can mark and virtually index.[30] Text analysis projects use computing technology 'to present, manage, and learn from electronic texts in ways difficult to do by hand'.[31] Common approaches to text analysis include 'stylometry', a method that can be used in determining the authorship of disputed texts, 'content-based analysis', which uses advanced discovery functions to determine the frequency of words and topics within a given sample of text, and 'metadata analysis', which tracks 'information associated with archival material that lists key attributes, such as its author, date, publisher, or general subject'.[32]

A number of projects in this area aim to facilitate text analysis, making it more accessible to researchers. The *Text Analysis Portal for Research* (the TAPoR project) is a gateway for text analysis projects based at McMaster University, in collaboration with five other leading Canadian DH centres, University of Victoria, University of Alberta, University of Toronto, Université de Montreal and University of New Brunswick. TAPoR brings together a number of 'tools for sophisticated analysis and retrieval, along with representative texts for experimentation'.[33] *Textal*, recently released by UCL, is a smartphone application, designed to provide a user-friendly introduction to text analysis. It allows users to create wordclouds and 'explore the statistics and the relationships between words in the text'.[34] *Hermenuti.ca* is a notable collaboration between DH McGill and CIRCA, which has given rise to *Voyant*, 'a web-based reading and analysis environment for digital text'.[35] Voyant presents users with a number of options to read, analyse, and visualise trends in an electronic text. *Wordseer* is a similar project based at the University of California, Berkeley.[36]

Geospatial and critical discursive mapping technologies

Projects about digital representations of space and time often use geographic information systems (GIS) to capture, manage, analyse and display varying 'forms of geographically referenced information'.[37] GIS analysis is especially useful in addressing questions of political boundaries, cultural conceptions of space and time, environmental concerns, and the relationship of historical and literary texts to the physical landscape.[38] It is not surprising that this approach has been adopted by many historians and social scientists. *Hypercities*, a tool at UCLA and USC, rectifies and stretches historical maps to fit digital platforms. Projects like *AfricaMap* (Harvard), *The 'American Century' Geospatial Timeline* (Emory), *Bomb Sight: Mapping the WW2 Bomb Census* (University of Portsmouth), *Digital Augustan Rome*, *The Dictionary of Sydney* (University of Sydney), *Driving Through Time* (University of North Carolina), *Mapping the Lakes* (British Academy), *The Map of Early Modern London* (University of Victoria), *Mapping Medieval Chester* (Kings College London) and V*alley of Shadow* (University of Virginia) attempt to collect, visualise and disseminate historical and cultural information in new and informative ways. A number of similar projects have been developed by literary scholars in an attempt to explore the spatial dimensions of fictional texts. Projects of this sort include *Mapping St. Petersburg* (UCL), *The Digital Literary Atlas of Ireland 1922–49* (Trinity College Dublin), and *Mapping the Catalogue of Ships* (University of Virginia).[39]

Other projects in this vein build collections of complex spatial and temporal data. For example, *The China Historical Geographic Information System* (CHGIS), a collaborative project developed by Harvard and five other universities, is a database of administrative borders in China between 221 BCE and 1911 CE.[40] This data set serves as a starting point for researchers using spatial analysis, statistical modelling and digital visualisations. Harvard researchers claim that 'the advantage of creating the CHGIS, rather than printing paper maps, is that the relationships between the units can be modified and improved whenever new information becomes available and the new "edition" needs only to be posted on the Internet for users to download'.[41] The *Pleiades Project*, a digital gazetteer of ancient places, is another well-known data set, as is the *National Geospatial-Intelligence Agency: GEOnet Names Server* (NGA GNS).[42]

A major geospatial project in Japan is the *Global Integration of Regional Knowledge Resources and Intercommunity Platform*. The core institute implementing this is the Centre for Integrated Area Studies at the University of Kyoto, the Centre for Spatial Information Science, the Japan Consortium for Area Studies and the Japan Organisation of Geographical Sciences. The objectives of the project are to collect, digitise and structure regional knowledge resources, including historical documents and maps, and to construct and continuously run an intercommunity platform for acquiring, managing and retrieving resource information. The project aims to further enhance the development of area studies.[43]

Big data, social media, crowdsourcing, and networking

All DH projects deal with lots of data but big data signifies the problem that occurs when data are so massive and complex that they defy the ability of relational database management systems. Researchers in big data may need to rely on software running in parallel on a dozen or hundreds of servers, in which case the infrastructural and technical demands exceed the typical setup of a humanities department. The technological needs were first realised in fields such as astronomy and genomics, but similar project needs are developing in the humanities. High-volume data streams may occur when sensors are used for geospatial mapping of movements or when capturing text messages from social media.

There are very big problems of research access and data security in big data when applied to social science and humanities. Big data is used for business intelligence to understand customer needs and preferences, and the data is often proprietary market information, which is only shared with researchers under strict rules of confidentiality. Such information may be of extreme interest for understanding human behaviour, communication and perception but is largely not accessible for research. Other fields for big data, such as library information, archival and physical heritage data, are in the public realm and rapidly growing. Crowdsourcing data from voluntary information providers, perhaps gathered by with sensors and cameras, is another vast source of information.

The *Digging Into Data Challenge* was launched in 2009 by the Joint Information Systems Committee (JISC) from the United Kingdom, the National Endowment for the Humanities (NEH) and the National Science Foundation (NSF) from the United States, and the Social Sciences and Humanities Research Council (SSHRC) from Canada. Already in its third round of open calls the initiative has funded path-breaking humanities projects such *Mapping the Republic of Letters*, a product of Stanford Literary Lab, which analyses metadata about date, author, place of origin and recipient in order to create a spatial analysis of 'intellectual correspondence networks' in the 17th and 18th centuries. Another example is the *Harvesting Speech Datasets*, which harvests audio and transcribed data from podcasts, news broadcasts, public and educational lectures and other sources to create a massive corpus of speech. The project will develop new tools to analyse the different uses of prosody (rhythm, stress and intonation) within spoken communication. Other funded projects are *Digging Into Image Data, Structural Analysis of Large Amounts of Music, Railroads and the Making of Modern America,* and *Digging into Human Rights Violations.*[44]

3d immersive visualisation environments

3D immersive visualisation relies on advanced displays, image generating computers, video switching/distribution, and application software that allows users to be immersed in a displayed image. The 3D lab enables neural and behavioural scientists to track individuals as they respond to simulated environments in a controlled setting. The immersive 3D lab also enables the researcher to analyse and interpret complex data. Visualisation enables the research team to create simulations of past heritage sites or future landscapes. It is a field with much crossover between the visual arts, gaming industries and the spatial and cognitive sciences. The potential for the humanities is huge but high infrastructural costs are probably currently limiting the application of these technologies to a few laboratories, which are typically based in computer science departments that collaborate with humanists for their data. Successful projects include archaeological and landscape simulations and conservation of works of art.[45]

Resistance to digital humanities

So far our survey has indicated that the digital humanities is an established field with notable success stories, even if it is unevenly distributed and difficult to track or map. Nevertheless, there is a great deal of more or less implicit reluctance or even some explicit resistance to DH within the world of humanities, of which we need to take note. Strangely, much of this debate is not published but articulated in blog posts and other short web-based forms, which do not encourage the writers to fully argue their case. We have identified four poles around which DH criticism tends to revolve. Not all reluctance is born out of resistance and not all resistance is hostile; so the poles listed here are simply intended to identify the main critique of DH before we turn to our interviews.

Reward structures in academia do not recognise digital publication

One main criticism of the digital humanities is shared by both its supporters and critics. It is well known that the reward structures of academia change very slowly and in most institutions do not favour digital work. Digital modes of representation may therefore put the early career researcher at a relative disadvantage. 'Indeed, this may be [the] outright advice from senior faculty and administrators', as Patrik Svensson of the HUMlab of Umeå University, Sweden, concedes.[46] Reward structures may be changing, but at a very slow pace and there is no simple path to advancement. Given this, many prospective DH researchers who want to pursue an academic career may see themselves forced to compete in two worlds – the digital and the traditional (or perhaps, for want of a better word, the analogue) worlds of humanities at the risk of not becoming really good in either. The proponents of DH may of course counter that such scepticism is true of any interdisciplinary endeavour and that the world would come to a standstill if the boundaries were not crossed by some adventurous pioneers. Nevertheless, the concern about future job opportunities is probably shared by both sides.

Failure to see how DH applies to some disciplines

In general, DH appears to fit better with empirical disciplines whereas some disciplines like philosophy may legitimately find the DH challenge less relevant. Even in this discipline, however, there may be ways to introduce digital technology, as argued by P. Bradley.[47] Again, this is an argument that should cause dialogue rather than opposition.

'Where are the results?' 'Show me a project that does something useful with technology'

However, not all opposition is friendly or well intentioned. These rhetorical questions are occasionally asked perhaps less out of curiosity than defiance. Any mapping of digital humanities, as attempted in this chapter, is unlikely to answer the questions satisfactorily. D. G. Myers puts his challenge to DH this way: 'a mind must interpose between machine and meaning. And this is the scandal of the digital humanities. They have been unsuccessful at their fondest hope – eliminating the mind from humanistic scholarship. ... The confidence that they "will enable us to move beyond the traditional methodologies" might be called the Great White Hope of the digital humanities. It is overweight, overhyped, an expression of superstition and prejudice.'[48] Myers, however, fails to establish that such fond hopes are or have been nurtured by digital humanists and he seems to be fighting a straw man.

The dark side of DH

This is the title of a session at the Modern Language Association meeting in the USA in January 2013. While it was not very clear what the dark side is, the papers presented were based on a sense that the humanities are in crisis and that DH is presented as a way out. The organiser of the panel Professor Richard Grusin stated: 'I would assert that it is no coincidence that the digital humanities has emerged as "the next big thing" at the same moment that the neoliberalisation and corporatisation of higher education has intensified in the first decades of the 21st century.... To hazard a probably ill-advised metaphor, I worry that digital humanities projects might serve as something like gateway drugs for administrators addicted to quick fixes and bottom-line approaches to the structural problems facing higher education today, providing them with the urge to experiment with MOOCs (Massive Open Online Courses) and other online forms of "content delivery", which is how college courses are being increasingly defined by university administrators, government officials, and techno-utopians alike.'[49]

In this case the term DH seems to be short for almost any unwanted development in academic life. The criticism does not seem quite transparent, but it is clear that a camp mentality is easily being fostered on both sides of the debate.

Interview responses

The question remains, however, if the heated and somewhat antagonising discourse about the DH in the documents we have examined exists among humanities scholars at large. To help with the answer we now turn to our interview results. Our main concerns are how much scholars know about these DH developments, how engaged they feel with them and, more generally, what attitudes they hold towards the DH. It is important to stress at the outset that almost none of our respondents had been specifically selected for their interest in the DH.

We asked:

> Is the development of digitisation changing the nature of research practice in your field?
> Do researchers in your field have the necessary skills to make the most out of the digital resources available to them?

Lack of engagement?

The first point to make is that few of the respondents gave detailed answers and discussed the DH with reference to specific projects that had affected their own research or at least impacted their field. In fact, only seven respondents gave any detailed kind of unprompted answer. All the rest answered the question in very general terms.

It was quite typical of respondents to refer to the rather basic point that digitisation has made research more convenient, especially by creating online databases for literature, sources and data. A point made by 34 respondents, including:

> *Af12:* More materials are becoming available in digital format, making traditional research approaches less relevant. Availability of digitised version of documents online has made unnecessary traditional visits to archives.
>
> *As9:* Digitisation certainly makes it possible to view a lot of information in a considerably short period of time which also makes it convenient to look at information not necessarily directly related to one's research topic. The time usually consumed by commuting between libraries can be used for browsing a greater variety of sources.
>
> *As10*: Quite simply, it is much more convenient to check facts on the Internet, which means one is less reliant on one's own memory – and I don't have to make as many trips to the library.

Some confined themselves to talking about accessibility, which we discuss in more depth in Chapter 7. Other respondents said that, in addition to convenience, digitisation might be changing the nature of research, though only one gave details.

> *Au4:* It is now much more common, I think, for historians...to actually go looking for metadata, so looking for statistical sources.... Quite senior historians...are really enthusiastic at the prospect of going and tracking down, for example, weather records from the Philippines, data on rainfall, on wind, on the strength of storms, which have been collected by Jesuit missionaries in the Philippines for a period of several hundred years.

We discuss the lack of take up of a DH perspective among our interviewees below.

Difference in take up between fields

It is clear that there is an uneven take up of digitisation across different fields. Some connected this with the distinction between qualitative and quantitative research:

> *Af7*: History as a discipline is less affected by digitisation because much of the historical research is qualitative and descriptive.
>
> *ME1*: I belong to a field of anthropology that uses qualitative rather than quantitative methods. So although I use the Internet to find

literature, digitisation is more significant for those who use quantitative methods. In these cases, it is changing the nature of research.

Four philosophers from quite different regions (Lebanon, US/Korea, Spain and China) thought that digitisation affected their field less than others:

> ME3: If you're a geographer or a historian, digitisation makes a big difference. But it doesn't in my field (unless you're a historian of philosophy). And I can't see how digitisation will become more applicable to philosophy.
>
> As11: [Is the development of digitisation changing the nature of research practice in your field?] Not in my field, although the greater availability of online journals can only be a good thing.
>
> E3: *[Is the development of digitisation changing the nature of research practice in your field?]* Not in philosophy, though to an extent in logic. To some degree there are significant changes in linguistics and archaeology.
>
> NA13 *(philosophy and religion):*...digital literacy in my field is relatively less complex than some other fields.

But others (three from the Far East and one working on digitisation) made the point in more general terms, or with reference to a different or broader range of disciplines*:*

> As1: Subjects vary as to how well they use digitisation.
>
> As8: There has been a discussion amongst scholars about this issue and it varies depending on your field and different topics. Some lack certain research, which is a vocabulary of how Western notions and concepts became a part of East Asian media and publications. A digital survey may give you more evidence because with digitised material you can do quantitative work. I think in linguistics, literature, history and in some fields it isn't so necessary.
>
> NA12: Students of Japanese, Chinese and Korean are working with philological problems, and it's a long time before they are even getting to DH.
>
> As7: Personally this doesn't affect me so much because I am an actuarial historian and old fashioned. In my field of being a Confucianism specialist, I'm not sure.

A culture clash?

Some of our respondents referred to a culture gap between DH enthusiasts and more traditionally minded scholars. Here, for instance, are some comments to this effect (from India, the Netherlands, Thailand and the UK):

> *As2:* Researchers in many cases do not have the skills to fully exploit the new facilities. But that comes mainly from the inability to break out of the old moulds of scholarship and embrace the new possibilities of digital humanities.
>
> *E4:* Conservative...humanities scholars have been very concerned about digitisation. They and their students live in quite different worlds.
>
> *E13*: At present there is something of a gulf between humanities scholars and those who understand the technology (the techies). They live in different silos.
>
> *As13*: Generally speaking, there are three groups of researchers in view of their use of digitisation: the aliens, the immigrants, the natives. Many of the older generation researchers do not access digital databases on regular basis, the immigrants access them on some occasions, while the natives depend heavily on digital access.

Picking up on the reference to concern in the second extract, note those respondents who saw training as a means to overcome apprehension of or lack of engagement with DH:

> *LA2*: Researchers don't have the skills; we're not adequately trained, not even in archaeology. We're trained to be scholars in the traditional sense, but there's a fear of engaging with technology.
>
> *NA7*: There's an ideological resistance to [digitisation] in the humanities, out of fear that it's going to replace the humanities, but it's just a tool. It can be embraced or rejected as it is useful. There's nothing more fearful about it than that.

There seem to be two different kinds of anxiety being discussed. The first might stem from the fact that traditionalists do not understand the technology involved in the DH, and treat it as a 'black box'; and what they don't understand, they fear. The second might be described as follows. If some of the more extravagant claims of the DH enthusiasts are right, whole swathes of humanities scholarship might have to be revised. The traditionalists fear that their expertise will be devalued.

Others who perceived a culture clash thought that it could be resolved, but only over time:

> NA1: I do think that it's going to take time and a cultural shift for humanists to think of their research as collective, rather than an individual slaving in the archives.
>
> NA2: *[Do researchers in your field have the necessary skills to make the most out of the digital resources available to them?]* The overwhelming majority does not. This is partly attitudinal. Some still want to use their three by five cards. It is largely that everything is happening so fast, and it's hard to keep up. It's almost impossible. [My] university has a special centre on campus that holds classes on new technology, from basic things like PowerPoint to course websites. Most of my colleagues are mostly not into that kind of thing. There is a tension between tech and teaching. The new generation, the junior range and below are more comfortable with it, but it's going to take a while for all of us to be accepting and competent. Simultaneously the tech is becoming more idiot-proof, so it's making it a bit easier.
>
> E4: *[Is the development of digitisation changing the nature of research practice in your field?]* Yes, but the change is slow in coming. What has been fast is the creation of databases over the last ten years, i.e. the immediate use of the quantifying power of the digital humanities. But the meta-discourse about how this is changing the humanities has been very slow, because painful.

Scepticism about the DH

If some of our respondents referred to a culture gap, did any of them show hostility towards digitisation themselves? One, from the UK simply raised the following question:

> E12: We are prompted to ask ourselves both what do we gain from digitisation and the virtual workplace, and what does it threaten to elide or obfuscate?

A few were sceptical as to whether the DH is introducing anything new:

> NA1: I'm not a technophobe, but I'm not the best person to comment on the future of the DH. We have done a number of things in the DH. I wouldn't say I'm a skeptic, but I'm not yet persuaded. ... I don't see yet how it's changing the questions we ask. Sure, new

databases change and enhance the process of research. This may reflect my own limitations or my own slowness to coming to this, but I haven't seen an instance where we're really changing the whole direction of our research.

NA12: *[Is the development of digitisation changing the nature of research practice in your field?]* It seems to be for a lot, but not for others. ... I think the jury's out. From what I've seen, some of this development is like the relationship with the typewriter. For a lot of people, computers are just really fancy typewriters. People doing the same thing they have always been doing, just on a fancier machine. To be honest, the digital humanities hasn't really pervaded this campus.

R7: I would not say that the changes in research practice brought by the advent of the electronic media were enormous. Quantitative data have become more available and easy to deal with (although this process has largely started already in the 60s), but their nature have not changed. Internet as such provides a new and very rich source of data in itself (e.g. using different forms of connections as raw data social network analysis, or latent-semantic analysis), and I expect much work being done in this direction due to relative cheapness of such data, and possibility to make truly global research on their basis from any geographic point on the Earth. But the logic of such research will not be much different from those implementing more traditional data.

R8: [Is the development of digitisation changing the nature of research practice in your field?] It certainly changes the framing. Not sure about the content.

Some acknowledged the convenience of digitisation, but insisted that it cannot obviate older methods:

As8: I think digitising material will provide a lot of convenience for scholars; sometimes you will have to travel a long way to get it and even when you get there, it may be a weekend – you can't conduct the research you want to. Doing research this way may be costly and it is much cheaper to use digital material, but during the final stages of research, we would still want to see it with our own eyes. When you digitise material, you can't always tell by itself – the quality of the paper, colour, texture and size. Often, you'll want to check with the original and you can't simply rely on the digital version.

E2: *[Is the development of digitisation changing the nature of research practice in your field?]* Definitely yes! Libraries and archives in the US have pioneered digitalisation and have made many sources available via online. For an historian based in Europe that makes access much easier, faster and much less expensive. Still, I believe that historians who study the history of foreign countries need to experience the culture firsthand. I have lived more than six years in the US. I do not think that I could write American history the way I do without that experience.

NA10: I think every field is affected by digitisation of knowledge, generally for the best. But I think there's still a lot of value to traditional methods and working into archives.

Further along the critical spectrum, others warned of various risks to the quality of research:

ME2: I'm lucky to be of the generation that has made the transition between the analogue and digital worlds. I'm familiar with analogue research, so I know about and can be critical of the hierarchy of sources available on the Internet. Not all sources are on the same level. It's often difficult to get students to understand that.... some younger researchers lack a critical sense of the sources, because they have not worked enough with analogue material; they attempt to minimise the qualitative assessment of sources.

Af1: Digitisation tends to produce the younger 'cut and paste' scholars, too lazy to do actual under-the-hood, retro research, they surf Google books, cut and slice expressions and segue them into a conference paper.

ME4: As regards research, digitisation does not necessarily save time. The facility of digitisation makes you keep searching, and so makes you avoid the moment when you need to think and write. (It's easier to read on a computer than to think and write.) Digitisation doesn't affect or reduce the real effort required for research. In the end it's got to be your own work.

As13: It seems that researchers read less and have less incentives to work on something really deep or taking a lot of time.

However, it must be stressed that all but one of these also pointed out the advantages of digitisation, so they were by no means purely negative. In fact only one out of our 89 respondents showed outright hostility.:

NA4: I'm a Luddite. I think that DH are essentially bankrupt. Yes, they bring content to people, but I'd never encourage a graduate student of my own to go into the DH business. Our business is to think and reflect on ideas. In answer to the question: what research questions do the DH open up, my response is: what questions are they shutting down?

Beneficial effects: collaboration and the opening up of research

On a positive note, we should record the views of a cluster of respondents, again from very different regions, who talked about the ways in which digitisation is creating more collaboration:

> *AU2:* I think what you have to do is get a collaboration..., to be able to go to digital experts and work with them in common projects where they see some benefit from having you and you benefit enormously from their expertise.
> *As10*: The Internet provides immediate information about what other people's research agendas are and what conferences are happening.
> *E1*: Being able to create sophisticated databases yourself and then being able to share that information with the scholarly community enhances quality and makes our work more efficient.
> *As2*: Access to material on the web, the digital commons initiatives and the facilitation of connections between disparate materials have resulted in both increased research output, new platforms of publication and, more importantly, in new methods of collective, cooperative work.

A few who made this point stressed the international potential of digitisation:

> *E10*: [Digitisation]...helps conducting research in a more comparative manner, and to build research communities, by strengthening the connections between historians from different countries and/or affiliations.
> *Af4*: I have encouraged the use of digital equipment for the recording, storage and archiving of field materials. I am doing the same at the Institute now, seeking well-meaning global partners for the digitisation of indigenous knowledge fields.
> *Af8*: For African and other poor universities digitisation allows scholars to overcome the lack of libraries, to share information and to build global networks, even though there are problems associated with access to ICTs.
> *As14*: It's quite a thrilling time to participate in this sort of global interaction amongst scholars.

> *LA10*: We also have a more fluent communication with researchers from other countries, mainly with the nearby countries. Last year we organised in Uruguay the first international conference about all the realms of philosophy. It was attended by more than 100 researchers from seven countries of South and North America.

Finally, here are some respondents who referred to the democratic potential of digitisation:

> *LA1:* Internet and digitisation changed the picture completely toward a more democratic access.
> *LA10*: Internet changed this situation into a more democratic access. Nowadays we have online access to electronic journals and to relevant papers uploaded by philosophers from important research institutes.
> *Af11*: The development of digitisation ... popularises research outputs that might not be made known to many people in the past due to costs and distance.
> *NA12:* Computational technology then becomes the very condition of how we think about the very questions and problems we ask and attempt to solve in the humanities. Such thinking changes the university as the gatekeeper of cultural ideals and values and the intermediary between these values and the state and marketplace. What we are experiencing now is that professors, administrators, or whomever, but especially students, can access massive databanks of knowledge from anywhere at any time without the professoriate guarding the gates.

Conclusion

In the first half of this chapter we showed that the digital humanities are developing rapidly, both in terms of number of scholars and the means of engagement. Based on our mapping of digital projects, we find that there is a breadth and depth of engagement across the humanities with digital technologies. We are also in no doubt that digital technologies are creating the potential for conceptualising radically new research questions. The DH is facilitating new ways of research organisation as evidenced by the crossover between humanities and computer science. However, it is also clear that there are real challenges to the world of humanities as part of this development. Some problems of access and data security are shared with other sciences while others seem to be peculiar to the humanities. The scepticism and even outright hostility to

DH evidenced by some blog literature might be a unique phenomenon within the humanities.

In the second part of the chapter we looked at responses to our questions about the DH. Based on our respondents' somewhat lukewarm answers, we would say that, however much DH activity is taking place, and despite the funding, mainstream humanities scholars are not very deeply engaged. It is not our role to allocate blame; one could accuse mainstream scholars of not making the effort to learn more and to become more engaged; or one could accuse the DH researchers of creating their own ghetto and failing to communicate effectively with those outside it. On the basis of our interviews, it is certainly safe to say that the main problem is presently one of communication between mainstream scholars and the digitalists.

We have also discussed the possibility of a culture clash. However, we have not found much evidence of outright hostility among our respondents. What we did find were varying degrees of scepticism about just how much digitisation can achieve. But we also found optimism about the changes digitisation might make to the culture of research, in terms of collaboration and openness. Very likely there is a problem of uptake of the DH among mainstream humanities scholars, perhaps involving generational differences, which will take some time to solve. But it would be erroneous to see humanities scholars divided between different tribes on this issue.

Digitisation certainly reduces transaction costs by obviating the need to travel to archives and easing access to rare books, but the humanities do not become digital simply by moving texts from paper to hard disks. So far DH has mushroomed within and all over the world of humanities, while leaving most of the humanities unchanged except for quickening and democratising access.

The real challenge of digital humanities still lies ahead in asking new research questions enabled by the technology, training researchers to identify and utilise the potential, and developing a critical sense of the explanatory power of new technologies.

Except where otherwise noted, this work is licensed under a Creative Commons Attribution 3.0 Unported License. To view a copy of this license, visit http://creativecommons.org/licenses/by/3.0/

OPEN

5
Translating the Humanities

This chapter explores the different ways in which research's insights and results are communicated and translated to beyond university boundaries. First we outline the flow of academic knowledge from researcher to end user. Second, we look into how this translation takes place, according to current national reports, and identify what senior academic researchers and academics in leading positions believe is happening and what they recommend. We find that the knowledge pool of the humanities is tapped in haphazard and entirely contingent ways. The way forward is to ensure that translational practices are valued and resourced adequately. The flip side of that coin is that problems of academic freedom and ethics must be addressed.

Translational research practices

Knowledge, insights and findings are the outcome of research but they need to be communicated to and internalised by recipients before they can be of value outside the researcher's mind. Teaching, publishing, broadcasting, lecturing, engaging with communities, putting knowledge into practice in public institutions, medical care, schools, business, advising on policy and so on are all examples of communication. They may be captured by the concept of knowledge transfer. In many types of research, however, knowledge flows in more than one direction: as the researcher engages with a field, he or she learns from the practitioners; the people who are the object of the research may engage with the researcher and share their insights; practitioners may also criticise and help refine research insights as they are shared or published. In broad terms, these loop-back mechanisms may be defined as knowledge exchange. Knowledge flows may be supported or stimulated by knowledge infrastructure, such as museums and galleries, and best practice as generally accepted by researchers or prescribed by senior academic management or contractually agreed with third parties. Utlimately, decisions to fund or initiate research may be informed by a consideration of the communicability of that research or by end user needs. Such considerations may, for example, inform the research strategy of a museum or an independent research organisation. They may also inform requests for research by funding agencies, either through the prioritisation of a particular theme or by requesting solutions to a particular problem.

To capture the full extent of such knowledge flows we use the concept of translational research practice as a broad term for the flow of research insights from a researcher or a group of researchers to a broader community of other researchers and end users, and the feedback processes that come with the interaction.

The concept of translational research is broader than the more commonly used term transactional research, which we define as the commitment of researchers to bring knowledge into social action, and is therefore a specific form of what we would identify as the role of the public intellectual. Transactional practice is well known from certain types of sociological work, which involves direct interaction with a community to empower a decision process. While transactional practice is certainly part of translational practice, the translational concept is broader since it includes the infrastructural, institutional and funding parameters of research. The translational concept also includes research practices, which are not dedicated to any type of direct intervention. Translational research practice is therefore a concept that is relevant to all of the humanities as regards the flow between the production of research and its appropriation.

All research translation needs to happen through specific channels, and those channels may select what is good and relevant research and therefore ultimately decide what gets funded. Translation channels in the humanities typically involve:

- Academic publication
- Public intellectual practice
- communication to the public via the media (popular books, web, TV, lectures)
- personal interaction with communities, stakeholders and policy makers
- Contractual engagement with public institutions, e.g. schools, museums, archives, public bodies and professional associations
- Entrepreneurial engagement with innovation systems and businesses.

Inherently, there are very real dilemmas and blocks in the flow from academic research to translational practice. Much academic research is driven by the individual curiosity of the academic and translation may generate a clash with outside requests. While academic publishers have streamlined, if not perfected, the production of books and papers, in most other walks of life academics in general and humanists in particular find that translation involves considerable costs in both time and presentation of research output. Indeed, the use of knowledge may potentially compromise the integrity of the academic and there are therefore ethical choices to be made and economic costs involved in translational practices.

Finally, considerations and choices of translational research practice may involve a prescriptive element. So far, we have used the term exclusively in a descriptive way but research managers (dean, departmental chair or the director of an academic unit such as a museum or private company) may prescribe certain translation practices as part of a strategy to optimise the use and impact of research output. Such prescriptive strategies may be based on academic consensus as, for example, some disciplines adhere to a notion of best practice for community feedback or they may be based on a common sense approach to the need to project the voice of the humanities. In recent years, many universities have established humanities institutes and centres to facilitate research, to promote public interest in and to project the relevance of the humanities. Many thematic research centres are similarly established with both a translational and a research agenda.

While a prescribed strategy of translation would be alien to many academic institutions, it is known to come up – often as a surprise – when large financial considerations are at stake. Less controversially, such concerns may also inform or influence individual academic choice at the start of a research project. Many, if not most, humanities projects begin from a need for a better product than the one at hand, such as a critical edition of a manuscript or a need to understand better how society worked in the past. Translational concerns about the end product are likely to inform the design of such projects, for instance when a digital humanist designs a user-friendly interface that allows for multiple layers and feedback. Similarly, new findings or changes to the research agenda often cause the researcher to rethink modes of translation.

Translational medicine

By way of contrast it may be useful to consider translational practices in academic fields outside the humanities. Translational medicine is a term that was increasingly used from the late 1990s to denote – and promote – a transformation of health research through an emphasis on shortening the turnover time and reducing transaction costs 'from bench to bedside' or from bioscience laboratory to clinical practice. Translational medicine is key to the strategy of major funding bodies, such as the American NIH and the British MRC, to ensure that basic research and knowledge at one specialised level is translated to the next, and to develop collaboration from research labs to hospitals, GPs and ultimately to patients. Crucially, this is identified as a bi-directional strategy and so inherently prescribes collaboration between researchers and practitioners. Translational research practices require dedicated institutional support structures and funding models, including entrepreneurship and business.[1] This is clearly expressed in this quotation:

> The ultimate question regarding any biomedical research is whether it addresses a real need (of patients, people or populations) and helps improve people's lives (by preventing, curing, or improving the outcome of disease). To facilitate the 'translation' of new knowledge into health benefits, the scientific community, healthcare providers, industry, policymakers and the community at large need to apply their collective capabilities in a highly collaborative manner, across disciplinary boundaries.[2]

As a strategic concept, translational medicine is not just an analytical tool used to observe actual research practice, it is also a form of rhetorical discourse or an instruction with a view to a particular goal, viz. promoting the flow of knowledge from bench to bedside.[3] The concept also makes clear that parameters outside pure science determine the impact of the findings: 'The success of translation does not lie with scientists, however good their science, but with human motives, individual and corporate, selfish and unselfish, which underpin health care markets and drive market traders'.[4]

These observations may help understand translational research practices in and recommendations for the humanities. Of course, the humanities differ from the health sciences with regard to justification and outcome of research. Knowledge gained in the humanities may have consequences for life and death (for instance, through improved methods of peace negotiations; smart sanctions; social reconciliation after conflicts). However, in medical science the significance is more direct, at least more directly felt, and, humanities scholars disagree about justification, as we saw in Chapter 2. Obviously, the choice of translational strategy depends on the aim. Translational practices will therefore vary greatly between, say, an American liberal arts tradition and a practice that focuses on implementation of research findings.

However, the problems of translation within humanities do resemble those within contemporary biomedicine as they ultimately revolve around human linkages, institutional practices and intertwined communities. The humanities are just as conditioned by the interaction of researchers and practitioners whose training, outlook and institutional context vary greatly.[5] Social learning may be important for the choice of research fields and methods and, indeed, ideological and social pressures can have very negative effects. These are well-known problems but it may be helpful to conceptualise them not as problems peculiar to the humanities but as part of a general translational problem for academic research.

Evidence from interviews

In the following section we look at how senior academics responded individually and in workshops to our questions about humanistic practices of translation. The interview questions were:

> How are you or members of your organisation working with or exchanging knowledge with stakeholders outside academia?
>
> What support systems are in place for translational research?

The interviewee was encouraged to expand and qualify their statements as they wished. The questions are quite open and respondents therefore gave evidence in accordance with their interpretation of the questions. In the regional workshops we were able to follow up on the interviews to get a more consolidated view from participants.

Quantitative evidence

Table 5.1 summarises respondents' experience of and commitment to translational practices. A total of 26 gave very low or negative priority to the questions: 18 did not give a response; three declared they did not understand the question; only five expressed a negative or cautionary attitude to the idea that a university should concern itself about outreach. On the other hand, a clear majority of 62 people gave positive examples of translational practice. Their responses may be categorised at the individual, collegial and partnership levels, and some gave examples of all: 46 provided examples of personal experience; 16 offered examples of collaborative efforts; and 42 stressed the importance of non-university partnerships. There were some clear regional patterns among the interviewees. European, Australian and Asian respondents stressed the importance of non-university partnerships, while African, Latin American and North American respondents gave examples of personal commitment. Out of 16 European interviewees 12 stressed the importance of non-university partnerships, while six mentioned personal experience and only two gave examples of collaborative efforts with colleagues. Only four Asian respondents gave examples of personal experience, while nine gave examples of non-university partnerships, such as with galleries and media. On the other hand, individual engagement was cited the most in Latin America (7 out of 9), Africa (10 out of 13), and North America (14 out of 16). These differences may reflect institutional cultures as well as the lack of institutional partners in some regions. In light of the importance that European funding agencies attach to questions of public impact it is striking that so few examples of personal engagement were forthcoming from European respondents. In general, however, the interviews gave a strong sense that humanists are committed to translating their research and many cite positive experiences of such engagement.

Responses at university level are similarly summarised in Table 5.2. No fewer than 49 respondents offered no opinion on their university's dedication or lack thereof, while 24 noted strong institutional support for translational practices, ten noted institutional indifference, and only three felt that the university actively discouraged researchers from engaging in translation.

A total of 11 out of 16 North Americans confirmed that there is institutional support for translational practice, while only 17 of the

Table 5.1 Translational practices among respondents

Did not respond to question	18
Did not understand question	3
Negative or cautionary remarks	5
Positive evidence	62
– individual commitment	47
– collegial efforts	16
– non-university partnerships	42

Table 5.2 Respondent views on universities and translational practices

	46
Institutional commitment	28
Institutional neutrality	12
Institutional discouragement	3

72 respondents from other continents were affirmative. This pattern probably reflects the strong role of humanities centres in the US and Canada and a strong culture of institutional engagement with alumni and communities.

In general, it may be fair to say that the figures indicate that most respondents, especially outside North America, believed that their own university offered very little support for translational activities. Respondents were divided between a majority with individual experience of translational practice, and a minority who gave little weight to such practice. The interviews give evidence of a richness of experience and a variety of concrete engagement. The following examples, by necessity, draw more on interviewees who expressed a positive interest.

Educating role

Undergraduate teaching is explicitly excluded from this report and was therefore not identified in the interviews as a translational practice. Most interviewees identified the translational role of the humanities as one of educating and reaching out to the public by means of open lectures. Open lectures can be standalone events or serialised, sometimes building up to a coherent programme from several months to a full year. One director of a humanities institute (E9) was clear that public engagement was a core activity. Similarly, a dean at the same university stated that

> *(E11)* Knowledge exchange and public engagement is an enormous issue for us. We have a college knowledge exchange office and manager and every school has an officer engaged in supporting knowledge exchange and – we hope – also a part of its research office dedicated to that work.

The director of a specialised research institute expressed the same opinion:

> *(E2)* The ... Centre sees itself as a public resource and forum for all issues that have to do with [our field]. We offer many lectures that are open to the general public; we interact with the media and contribute to non-scholarly publications (magazines, weeklies) as often as possible. I have written books for general readers; I participate in teacher training and give public lectures.

Similar views were expressed by the director of a Latin American research centre, *LA2*: 'Translation is very important to my field and in my university. [My university] takes a big stand on the popularisation of research.' From Asia, As1 stated that public lectures and seminars were a key component of the centre for advanced studies at his university.

However, many stated that support for even such basic outreach activities was undeveloped,:

> *(As12)* Support systems for translational research are still very limited. There has been no national support for institutions for translations or translational research.

That interviewee personally took a leading role in developing projects with local museums nationwide. Some interviewees with no management role subscribed to the same opinion. A professor from Australia wanted see public outreach developed even more:

> *(Au1)* There's not enough of this in Australia. A lot depends on your field: the fine arts do work well with galleries and museums, well, as do local historians to an extent. But international historians are less 'out there' (except on radio and occasionally TV). And there's not much in the way of support systems for outreach.

Some European voices echoed this sentiment. E3 reported that the university had no funds or policies for translation practice, and another lamented the underdeveloped state of translation:

> *(E6)* This is certainly an underdeveloped field. The transmission of insights from research is often indirect and invisible as such, as e.g. when members of our faculty writes newspaper reviews of books,

plays, art exhibitions etc. Other and more visible examples are cooperation between historians and local communities on writing local history, or cooperation between linguists and local communities on local place names, often funded by the local community. There are no permanent support systems in place for this kind of community related research.

Finally, African humanities are particularly deprived of support structures. One African interviewee, Af5, said that 'there is not any support for translational research that I know of. Anything done along this line is born from one's own initiative and commitment'.

As we shall see below, the evidence of the interviews indicates that direct community involvement rather than public lectures are preferred by many African scholars. It should be noted though that South Africa has excellent support for elite universities, including new humanities centres.

Several interviewees mentioned the particular importance of outreach to secondary level teachers. They will often be graduates themselves, have a special interest in university research, and want to convey the newest ideas to their students. One professor stated:

(E15) In my field translation mainly happens in three ways. (1) The university classicists keep in touch with 'real life' through high school teachers by keeping them in touch with their research. This happens via conferences both biennially on the national level (with 1,000 and more participants), and much more often regionally and locally. (2) There is clearly a market for publications written by specialists for a wider public. The format of these publications ranges from relatively voluminous books (often with lavish illustrations) to small booklets which inform concisely (circa 100 pages) on a specific topic (as in the series *Wissen* of the Beckverlag). (3) There are the Volkshochschulen (programmes of adult education) sponsored by individual cities, providing evening classes on a wide range of topics including those concerned with classics, as Latin, Greek philosophy, Roman Germany or whatever.

A similar broad range of outreach activities was identified by E8. He gave as examples a foreign language summer school, public performances of folksongs to maintain their presence, a folksong competition in an island community, public lectures, public readings and media consultations. A Russian interviewee, R5, similarly identified workshops for teachers, journalists, and museum researchers as a regular outreach activity.

Interviewee E1 indicated some frustration at the limited extent to which the humanities have developed translation as the third task of the university, after teaching and research. The humanities have 'not really [developed] in the same way as economics or medicine. In the end, it ends up with third task examples that you tell the public about'. However, many interviewees did give examples of humanities going beyond public lectures.

Community engagement

While African universities generally suffer from lack of infrastructural support, the interviews did give striking evidence of individual engagement. One professor listed a number of vibrant health research projects, including in the behavioural sciences, that involved working with and learning from local communities.

> *(Af3)* ... we teach, train, and undertake research with local communities as we address their primary health needs. Translational research is supported through the office of the deputy vice chancellor in charge of research and extension, through annual conferences, and through community engagement and outreach work. There haven't to date been specific humanities knowledge exchange programmes, but [the university is] increasingly seeking to develop these as they continue to review their programmes. In [the interviewee's department] for example, there is a programme on youth and development where students work with young people in the community.

Another interviewee stated:

> *(Af5)* in my case I often organise information-sharing rallies at my research sites close to the conclusion of my research where I inform them of what I have found and what that means in terms of science. Thereafter, I make publications in simple language and take them back to them. Finally, all tangible materials retrieved from the field work are submitted to the Antiquities Department as required by law. Some of these may end up in museums. In addition to these basic steps, feature articles in local magazines, commentaries on radio and TV, etc. are used. This is done by most researchers, archaeologists and non-archaeologists.

Af7 stated:

> In the recent past the University of Zambia has introduced a public forum at which stakeholders, including government, are invited to public displays and dissemination of research work. This process is expected to open avenues for translating both humanities and science researches into end user products.

The interviewee also stated that a regular methodology was the practice of going back to communities where fieldwork was conducted and reporting results to them as producers of the primary data.

However, most African interviewees noted an absence of support for any kind of translational practice. Af1 stated:

> down here 'social impact' does not amount to much since the arcane findings of our research are only valued in obscure foreign journals – especially if the research contains a title no one really understands! The government could not be bothered – despite [country] having numerous research institutes.

Af2 noted that translational activity is patchy in Africa:

> it happens if it's part of funding requirements, or if an individual researcher happens to think it's important for them to take their research back to the community. The support systems are also patchy, though there are some institutions who have a history of taking research beyond the usual academic boundaries.

A more optimistic note was expressed by Af13:

> Cultural production has also been an important site of experimentation with new ideas and indeed understanding the continued transnational dialogue that has been going on in this continent for generations. I think this dialogue has contributed to what now passes as a common human culture and the ideals of a common humanity that we are all striving for.

Community engagement is typical of much anthropological, archaeological and even historical work. One historian, As15, stated that, after publication of a dissertation as a monograph, engagement with the community has continued, and indeed one monk 'now uses my book to train young monks'. Similarly, a Brazilian archaeologist reports:

> (*LA2*) We're engaged in 'public archaeology', where the focus is on work with the community (e.g. through museums). To give an example. We worked with a community of Indians in the Amazon Basin. We studied artefacts from the region, but then donated them to the Indians and also had a dialogue in which we exchanged our different interpretations of the objects.

A different take on community engagement was noted by As14, who reported that the university provided free public music concerts and

> will send scholars or students to villages and towns, especially aboriginal villages. They'll talk to people about general problems and they'll speak to students to get them excited about the issues in the humanities and sciences.

Many North American humanities centres have extensive community involvement. NA9 reported that the centre

> has exhibitions, public readings, poetry readings all the time. We are really engaged and very active in the community. I'm atypical, I would say. But remember that this isn't just a place for literature, we have a very good collection of photography and film. Public engagement is in the mission statement of the [...] Centre.

NA10 stressed that

> our humanities institute has always put a lot of emphasis on the public humanities, on building bridges between the public and the university, on recognising the kind of thinking that is going on in the public. So, rather than a knowledge transfer or translation model, it's a more synergistic model. And there is absolutely not enough support for this work because of the recent downsizing. That's true, I think across the board. This kind of work is categorised under service and it's seen as supplementary rather than as basic.

By contrast, community engagement was not mentioned by European interviewees with the exception of E10 who stated that 'historians and researchers of literature rarely meet stakeholders of the university, while it is more common in fields such as sociology and psychology'. The focus of European respondents was much more on institutional partnerships, as we shall see below.

Social media

Social media, such as Twitter, YouTube, blogs, LinkedIn, academia. edu and Facebook, are increasingly used by individual academics. For instance, one of our African respondents maintained a blog linked to a number of social media:

> *(Af1)* I am engaged in community work dealing with the digital preservation of Arabic manuscripts, musical performances and the film industry. I have a website and a production company (visually ethnographic, part of the website). I use these platforms to interact with the community of writers, local scholars, practitioners to find ways of improving practices at all levels.

A similar use of social media was reported by one of our Indian respondents (As5). Research centres are also increasingly using social media, as reported by an American interviewee (NA1), whose centre, in addition to live streaming public lectures, uses social media to create attention. Another American (NA6) had started a research project to showcase humanities research, building on digital resources.

The use of social media for academic purposes is seen as both critical and contentious in Russia where the use of Facebook has become an important tool, not least for academics living in provincial Russia. Often, the success of academics seems measured by the number of public interviews and their visibility in social media. This was confirmed at our Russian workshop as well as in individual interviews. While one respondent (R6) maintained his own blog, he warned against the dangers of overgeneralisation/oversimplification when using fast electronic media. In general, however, he believed that most academics have little time for social media. This sentiment was shared by another Russian (R8) who felt that 'research suffers from overtranslation and media misuse as salon science'.

Although the use of social media for academic work is under-researched, it is conceivable that it provides a fast and much more personal way to engage with user communities and build support for particular research. But it also carries opportunity costs in terms of sacrificing research time. Conventional publicity should still remain pivotal in academia.

Engagement with media

The role of intellectuals in media was mentioned primarily in the interviews with Asian scholars. One respondent (As8) mentioned that one of the key performance indicators of Japanese universities is 'the frequency at which scholars talk to the media'. At our East Asian workshop, another Japanese scholar reported that his institute was under too much pressure to disseminate research rather than to facilitate new research.

The interviewees indicated that the role of academics on Chinese and Taiwanese TV is very different. Interaction with mass media may take on quite innovative forms in Taiwan, such as the development of animated cartoons to convey philosophical points. This experiment has been successful and did not lead to oversimplification (As14). However, with the growth of private TV and radio in these countries academics have been cast as entertainers and the level of public discourse in these media is often so low that 'they think of professors that engage with media as a bad thing'. A professor from China corroborated this statement:

> *(As10)* There is not much translation here. When it is done, it's done by scholars who aren't so good. The good ones stay away from it. [My university], which is a top university, does not encourage it, but universities of lesser rank do, especially through TV and newspapers. But scholars who do this kind of thing tend to get looked down on.

But a scholar from Taiwan took a more conciliatory view:

> *(As14)* In my country there's a strong tradition of scholars writing articles in the newspapers and magazines, even appearing on television talk shows. Literature professors, history professors and even philosophy professors look at some current issues and current problems in society through the lenses of their humanities study. I think that if people watch these shows then they do get some impression or they do feel moved by the insights of these professors. It's just that nowadays there is cable television and there's the Internet, so it's much harder for anyone to make a strong impact through one channel anymore. In the old the days there were only three television stations and no Internet so if the professors came on the air they could reach several million people. But now there's too much sensationalism in the media presentations. The reality shows distract people from the reality of what is going on in society and the world.

In the East Asia workshop it appeared that there has been a rediscovery of the humanities in South Korea over the last few years. There are public lectures and companies have new employee orientation sessions with lectures demonstrating how creativity and innovation come from the humanities. The view promoted in the workshop was that in South Korea humanities are better represented than in the US.

Political role

A number of interviewees, nearly all from Latin America and the MENA region, took a very different position. They often stressed the political role of the humanities, whether potential or actual. Seven out of nine Latin Americans gave examples of involvement with political processes, like LA3 who stated that the university

> has had a considerable impact on Peruvian society; at a certain point, we got used to taking institutional and public stands on fundamental aspects of our national life. The group of academics and intellectuals that were a part of the Truth Commission – which investigated the crimes and violations of the period of the Shining Path, a terrorist group that unleashed a civil war in the 80s and part of the 90s – has been extremely important in that respect. Our professors continue to comment in the media, taking positions on various themes that affect our country. This has generated strong criticism from the most conservative sectors in our society, and it has even reached the point of open conflict with [the most conservative] sectors of the church. [...] Also, some members of our community participated in the construction and implementation of what is called the Museum of Memory, which remembers the victims of [the civil] war and documents the human rights violations committed by the [Shining Path] terrorist group and also by the [Peruvian governmental] armed forces.

In the same vein, LA4 from Brazil gave examples of direct engagement with the political process of developing a new law on migration and collaboration with artists on an exhibition on human rights. Our Latin American workshop gave evidence of this political role, which is further discussed in Chapter 8.

In Turkey, ME2 identified a similar critical role for the university, and the humanities in particular, and specifically mentions a 2005 conference:

> which was organised with a conscious political agenda. And we did have an effect; you can now talk of the Armenian genocide, without using the word 'alleged' in front of it. This is an example of very wide social outreach. At another level, you can reach out to people with

popular history books. But you need to distinguish between those who draw attention to a particular issue on the basis of little historical knowledge and scholars who maintain the ethical and methodological standards of their discipline while still popularising their subject. We do this to an extent, but not as much as we should. But in Turkey the nationalist culture (i.e. the nationalist reconstruction of history) is a problem: what people read is what confirms their beliefs. We need to do more to break the comfort zone of popularism. Instead we have a tendency to preach to the choir. [...] Among my peers, very few have tried to change the way history is taught in high schools.

Asked about the role of humanities ME4 saw a potential policy role for them:

In Tunisia, the humanities and social sciences are not used in policy making (as is agricultural science, for example). The humanities are actually disturbing to policy makers. So there are almost no links between social demands and SSH researchers; very few get commissioned to work on social policy. But linguists can help in policy, and elsewhere there are links with policy makers, e.g. the use of applied linguistics in educational policy, or in language policy in the context of immigration (which has happened in Holland and the UK).

Such use of linguistics for language policy is also mentioned by As12 for Mongolia and ME3 affirms his engagement:

Yes, I am engaged in outreach. My main link is with regions beyond Lebanon. For instance, as a result of my research on global poverty I work with NGOs in Africa. More generally, in areas like secularism, liberalism and gender equality, research that has been discussed within academia is now having an impact beyond it. In the Arab region, we're now in a moment of reshaping, and ideas that have been for a long time discussed in the humanities are beginning to have an impact. The best example is in Tunisia, where there is a much more mature level of discussion than elsewhere in the Arab world.

It is by no means easy to take this position in all Arab countries as evidenced by ME1:

We need to define who the stakeholders are. As regards policy makers, there's no communication between them and SSH researchers in Jordan. So it's very difficult for researchers to have any influence here. To do so, you need to use traditional strategies, i.e. tribal and personal connections. Concerning society itself, it's not easy either. The problem is that Jordanian people read very little. So, like other Jordanian researchers, I publish in Western countries. In fact, although I receive an invitation from overseas every six months or so, I never get one in Jordan. Reading is just not a habit here. However, I have been invited to talk on Jordanian TV. Also, one thing I'm proud of is a project I did with school pupils (ages 12–16). This concerned increasing their understanding of an archaeological site in north Jordan of which the local people were unaware.

Russian interviewees indicated that humanities topics, while generally considered non-political, may be drawn into public debate and indeed raise political concern and even cause political intervention. R2 stated that 'the topic of religion in its connection with history and national identity is too sensitive for Russian society today' and therefore prefers to keep research away from public attention. A particular trait of some leading Russian universities is that they host think tanks to apply research on policy issues (R7). Our Russian workshop confirmed that there is a tension between academic independence and authoritarian interventions, which is especially evident when universities compete for government funding. Special think tanks funded by government have become important assets for top universities in Moscow and St Petersburg in the last decade but are also very vulnerable to changing political circumstances at the very top of government. At a lower level, humanities research has been useful for governors across Russia when they apply for funding to generate foreign tourism. On the other hand, there are very high-profile cases of academics working with journalists and the public to prevent the destruction of historical sites.

African interviewee Af4 deplored

> the striking disconnect between researchers and policy makers. In fact, they are rivals and do work at cross purposes. This is a tragedy as much useful research findings end up in the garbage bin or on the idle shelf. Civil servants often see academics as threats and do not understand why they should be better paid or funded.

However, some parts of the humanities in Africa do get the attention of government. Af7 mentioned that 'the latest institution to come up with a research unit is the Zambia Police Service. The researchers are engaged to conduct research in the field of security and facilitating the operations of the Police Service.' Af11 was called on to translate historical documents in indigenous languages into English to settle a dispute.

While many Western European academics did have a role in politics, it is striking that few identified a direct political role for the humanities. E9 was the most explicit:

> One of the research themes of our institute is about the academic and the civic, about how universities have an impact on and are impacted by their local communities. As for public policy, networking tends to be very much a social science thing, though they hold meetings at the Institute. But on our advisory board we do have civil servants....

Such a role was also identified for leading humanities academics in Estonia (E7):

> Quite many members of our faculty belong to various decision-making bodies on national level (a big university in a small country). Many of us are members in different academic societies, belong to advisory boards at different ministries, etc..

A more negative view was that of E4 who saw a contradiction between translation in a broad sense and that of policy advice. While the interviewee personally believed strongly in the usefulness of broad outreach, most colleagues thought that 'the only acceptable form of translation would be influencing public policy makers (the contemporary equivalent of advising the King). Anything else is considered vulgar.'

North American and Asian scholars rarely mentioned a policy role for the humanities. One respondent from Taiwan (As7) mentioned that some scholars have a direct role in political life, but added that they tend to be drawn from the social sciences. NA10 stated that policy advice was a potential role for non-academics: 'The non-profit researchers we work with may have policy recommendations [and] they may work with our faculty to come up with those.'

Engagement with businesses and the innovation system

Humanistic entrepreneurship was mentioned specifically by only four people, two of them stated that it rarely happens, the two positive comments were from Chinese respondents. As16 mentioned that his department ran a programme every year for business entrepreneurs and most members of the department participated. It regularly attracted about 30–40 people, mostly senior businessmen. As11 stated that the best use of philosophy was by philosophers in the medical school working on bioethics (e.g. regarding stem cell research).

However, E13 may have reflected a more general view by stating that 'the humanities haven't really cracked open the business sector'. In a more negative sense, this is confirmed by E4 who stated that her university 'has a knowledge transfer office, but its Director only considers translation in a neo-liberal way. He has no time for the hardcore humanities (only the digital humanities).'[6]

One respondent emphasised the benefits of working closely with private benefactors and the public support system for innovation:

> *Au2:* Our organisation is very actively concerned with stakeholders outside of the university, to a degree that in the humanities it would be very unusual in Australia. It's a specific policy of ours and it's something that we have decided we want to do. And it's also been influenced by the fact that these grants that I've been getting through the government system of these linkage grants, which are with industry partners, have proved to be so much more gettable and so much better value for money and so much more fluid in terms of open to open-minded research that we use that as a model in my particular institution as a desirable thing. And it's also true that we have one or two quite significant business patriots who are loyal to us and work with us and help us in that way.

Engagement with public institutions

Collaboration between humanities and arts practice was emphasised in interviews with UK academics. E12 stated that 'there are numerous collaborations between members of the school and non-academic stakeholders, from links between our creative writers and theatres, book festivals and publishers' and went on to give examples of working with other public and private parties. E9 similarly reported 'very active creative partnerships' with galleries, cinemas and an international arts festival.

An Australian view (Au1, already quoted) was that 'a lot depends on your field; the fine arts do well with galleries and museums, as do local historians to an extent. But international historians are less out there (except on radio and occasionally TV).' Russian interviewee R3 reported that we are developing cooperation with the museum in honour of Astafev where a part of the heritage of the writer is being preserved. Fellow linguists are studying the language of indigenous peoples of Siberia, corpus linguistics with the help of dialect material (the language of the indigenous population of Siberia), the latest initiative is supported by the fund in honour of Prokhorov and the regional museum.

During the Russian workshop several examples were given of Moscow art galleries working with academics to develop educational platforms and organise cultural events. African respondent Af11 had been invited by the management of museums to hold seminars, which in turn helped in the running of the establishment.

Conclusion

Our interviews and workshops brought out that humanists engage with the world in many ways beyond the traditional academic practices of teaching and scholarly publication. However, most examples concerned a one-way rather than a two-way communication of knowledge, thus not very often being truly translational. Furthermore, it is clear that much of this activity depended on the individual and that very little institutional support was in place. Indeed, many colleagues will be sceptical or even disdainful about such practices and it is unlikely that time invested in translation is matched by career progress. As a concept translational humanities may benefit from the insights of translational medicine, but in practice the two are worlds apart. Perhaps As13's response summarises the sentiment of those who take a positive view of translational practice:

> When it comes to translation, I feel like a sacrificial lamb. I have to sacrifice my own research. It's time consuming. It's difficult to create a team and sustain it. It does not benefit my research career but it does give me a sense of pride.

Evidence from national reports

We have found relatively few national reports on translational humanities – or on any subset of this phenomenon. While funding agencies, ministries and councils are concerned with how and why they spend their money and therefore report on humanities research objectives, they are much less inclined to investigate the translation and use of the knowledge produced. Questions of translation may get a fleeting treatment but reports rarely provide data that lend themselves to wider comparison. We limited ourselves therefore to those few reports from North America and Africa that did provide a baseline for future comparative study.

United States

The Association of American Universities (AAU) conducted a survey of outreach activities in 2002, published in 2004 as part of a more general report.[7] This survey is clearly dated but remains the most comprehensive source available. It looked at the outreach activities of over 40 universities. In 2012, in an effort to update the information, we revisited the websites of the universities concerned to see if the outreach activities were still ongoing and in what ways they had developed. Outreach was clearly a different concept from the translational model that we prefer and may be used only as a proxy for those translational activities that deal with dissemination and some exchange activities.

It is useful to look at an example of outreach in the US context to see how the concept is defined. At Ohio State outreach and engagement are defined as meaningful and mutually beneficial collaborations with partners outside the academic community, such as those in education, business, and public and social service. The university identified outreach and engagement as:

- That aspect of teaching that enables learning beyond the campus walls
- That aspect of research that makes what we discover useful beyond the academic community
- That aspect of service that directly benefits the public.

This definition puts the emphasis on teaching services to the community. Knowledge transfer rather than knowledge exchange is clearly identified as the primary function. A similar picture emerges from the responses by the 40+ universities that informed the report. They framed the activities in terms of: publicising the humanities; involvement with policy; outreach to K-12 schools; collaboration with state humanities councils; and outreach efforts to the community. Most of the activities identified were public lectures, adult education and broad arts programmes, while other outreach activities were festivals, TV and other media services, writers' workshops seminars and community engagement. Only a couple of universities identified involvement with policy development and human rights. The liberal education focus led to an emphasis on outreach to high schools in US; and outreach to K-12 schools (upper secondary level preparing for university) was identified by many universities.

University faculties in the US are generally evaluated on research, teaching and service, often based on a roughly 40–40–20 split. While about a third of the AAU universities considered outreach activities only minimally or informally, others had increased the recognition given to such efforts and viewed them as important. Even among the latter it remained clear that those efforts would not, by themselves, lead to tenure. Research, publication and teaching remained the primary criteria upon which tenure was based. Moreover, although most universities considered outreach projects as a part of the service component, this was not universally true. A few AAU universities still construed service primarily as service to the academic community. Outreach programmes, however, can do a great deal to communicate the value of the humanities (and of the institution) to the surrounding community. Finally, it appeared that most outreach activities were conducted by tenured faculty. Indeed, one university specifically discouraged junior faculty from outreach activities in order to give them time to establish themselves in their disciplines. At that institution, senior faculty led each of the university's major humanities outreach initiatives and were rewarded for their efforts through pay.

Africa

In March 2009, the British Academy published a report about research collaboration in the SSH between the UK and Africa.[8] It was described as 'the culmination of a two-year process of reflection and discussion among UK and African scholars across the humanities and social sciences' and presented 'a series of frameworks derived from the collective ideas of some 60 scholars and research leaders, who met in Nairobi in September 2008, which aim to address the challenges facing Africa–UK research collaborations in the humanities and the social sciences, and to formulate practical solutions to these'.

In general, the report argued that many of the barriers to research were organisational and managerial rather than simply financial. New money for research was only provided if there was confidence in the ability of institutions to manage it and to deliver good research. In this context, questions of translational research practices are important for the future development of a healthy research environment in the humanities.

The issue of translation featured in the report in two ways. First, in many African universities there was often little or no time allocated to research and any research or writing had to be squeezed out of a researcher's own time. Rates of publication were therefore currently low across the continent, and the report found that early career researchers needed support and advice to negotiate the peer review and publishing chain. But it also found that they needed support to understand how to communicate their research beyond the academic world. In advocating the need to develop platforms for public engagement and discussion, it argued that departments and research networks can do much to support this by hosting public discussions of research and through encouraging scholars to write for newspapers and non-scholarly publications, online and offline, with due recognition for this work.

The second reference to translational research in the report concerned academic consultancy. It was interesting that in some African countries, scholars in the SSH were able to do consultancy work. In one sense this was a success story from the translational side of things. But, according to the Report, this phenomenon also gave rise to concerns, because such work was not done for the benefit of the university to which the scholar belongs, but 'on the side'. So the report recommended that African universities seek to incorporate consultancy formally within departmental research programmes to encourage academics to contract their expertise through their institutions rather than independently. Research management offices might be a way to further such a process.

Canada and the UK

Chapter 2 brought out that few academics would argue the case for the humanities on the grounds of their economic contribution to society, and this chapter confirms that very few mention academic interaction with businesses and the innovation system as part of their translational practice. Yet, there is solid ground for arguing that the humanities contribute in a major way to the economic wealth of modern society. If this is correct, we are faced with major questions as to why academics do not perceive their role in this way and how, despite their lack of engagement, they nevertheless play a major role.

The research councils of the United Kingdom have taken a lead in recent years to advocate and measure the impact of research in broad societal terms. However, in 2008 Research Councils UK decided to abandon its effort to develop a universal algorithm to calculate the economic impact of all types of research, because of the difficulty of the task. Later reports on the societal benefits of humanities indicated that, while it is comparatively easy to measure effort (outreach and other translational measures), it is exceedingly difficult to measure impact.

In 2008 the Impact Group of the Canadian Social Sciences and Humanities Research Council published a report on the economic role and influence of the social sciences and humanities. The report concluded that

> academic knowledge – whether from SSH or STEM – is not a principal input to the economy – or at least not a direct input to the economy. Yet, [...] embodied knowledge (technology) and tacit knowledge (know-how) are all important inputs to enterprises. The discrepancy, if any, we believe is due to the fact that 'raw knowledge' knowledge that arises directly from research – does not become useful to business enterprises until it is expressed through publications/conferences, technology, or people (employees, consultants, etc.). The fact that enterprises tend not to use 'raw knowledge' as it comes directly from academe, should not be confused with the fact that the same knowledge can be of immense value when it reaches enterprises through other sources, often when those sources (e.g. students, consultants) have added value to the raw knowledge.[9]

This line of reasoning highlights the importance of understanding what goes on when research is translated. Unfortunately, the report goes on to say: 'This discussion highlights the importance of so-called "knowledge transfer" activities in an academic setting, a topic that is beyond the scope of this paper' (p 32).

Despite the difficulties the report made a bold general assessment of the economic value of STEM and SSH to Canadian industries and concluded that, while STEM are of very high importance to the GDP of the goods sector, the economic value of SSH to the services sector is of the same magnitude. A similar conclusion was reached by a study of the value of STEM and SSH graduates to the goods and services sectors in Denmark[10] and an analysis of the careers of Oxford University graduates reached a similar conclusion.[11] In the US some useful data has been collected on the employment of humanities graduates.[12]

While these results are interesting, they highlight the need to understand what actually goes on when academic research is translated to wider use – not only for economic but also of social and cultural value. The Canadian report notes that

> vast parts of our economy are in the business of creating or trading in products and services that rely directly on the social sciences and humanities, or are otherwise essentially SSH in nature. About

two-thirds of all industry sectors can be described as 'SSH industries' – industries whose primary knowledge input comes from the SSH or that sell SSH-based services (e.g. banking) or goods (e.g. television programs). And, SSH industries employ about three-quarters of all workers. [...] And yet, there is virtually no literature on the economic role and influence of SSH. It should therefore not surprise us that to date, public policy has devoted little attention to the importance of SSH for innovation and competitiveness.

Other evidence

There is much evidence for exemplary translational humanities that we have not been able to draw on for this report. The humanities are fortunate to have a large number of outstanding communicators. Anyone doubting the value of seemingly exotic topics should be persuaded by TV ratings that the humanities certainly have a large audience.

The humanities are inventing new ways of communicating with the public and politicians. The annual summer Swedish gathering of researchers and politicians in Almedalen, Gotland, is a great example of how new ways of interaction may help accelerate knowledge exchange in a radical and very direct way – and with close media attention.[13]

New ways of training humanities graduates are being tried out. The Danish industrial PhD programme, which allows humanities graduates to combine university research with practice-based learning in private companies, is a model that is now being introduced in other European countries and at the EU level.[14] In many cities new ways of grassroots engagement with humanities scholars are being played out – ranging from Ignite sessions, which force scholars to present their research in entertaining and flashy ways, to academic engagement with urban communities who are not usually exposed to academia, such as the Irish DublIntellectial.[15]

Conclusion

Observations about translational research practice are of relevance not only to the study of large research teams with considerable division of labour and substantial funding, but they are also important for understanding the role of academics working on their own, the lone scholar model, with no more institutional support than a salary, writing tools and a library. Of course, some humanists may choose to largely disregard questions of translation and simply write papers and books for an anonymous market. On the other hand, many others do think carefully about the use and distribution of their knowledge and by so doing reflect on their translational practice.

In this chapter we used various sources to get a glimpse of the wide variety of translational practices that happen in the humanities, and we discussed some of the problems involved. In the end these can be boiled down to two.

The first is one of practicalities. The humanities seldom have the financial overheads to pay for transaction costs. A humanities scholar typically needs to cover all the roles of basic scientist, entrepreneur, fundraiser, communicator, activist and lobbyist. If you are not able to play all parts, it is likely that your research will have less impact, therefore translational practices are of utmost importance to senior academics. However, translation may be a drain on academic energy and acuity. Too much focus on translation may have a damaging impact on the junior researcher who needs to build an academic career on the basis of their own research contributions before they start engaging in translation.

The second problem concerns academic integrity. Researchers involved in translation need to strike a balance between being sensitive to the knowledge needs and expectations of the user and sufficiently insulating their research from prescriptions at the receiving end. The former implies the need for channels of communication between researchers and end users. This necessarily exposes the research to a feedback loop, which may impact the design and possibly the outcome of the research itself. It is therefore of the utmost importance to identify and develop checks and balances in the research process to limit bias.

So, while there may be substantial funding benefits to researchers, who have an eye on translational practice, there are inherent dangers as well, which may divert attention or, in the worst case, compromise the research itself.

A full understanding of translational research practice involves sensitivity to risks and opportunities from academic management and researchers. There are real dangers of goal conflict, which need to be borne in mind. Management may need to implement smart sanctions to encourage well-functioning translational practices. If we agree that the humanities may provide socially valuable knowledge, questions of academic freedom of ethics follow. Such questions are often overlooked but need to be more directly addressed in any evaluation of humanities research practice. The solution is not to abandon translational practices. Society already suffers huge opportunity costs by not developing translational humanities. That is, the humanities represent an enormous knowledge pool that today is tapped only in haphazard and entirely contingent ways.

Except where otherwise noted, this work is licensed under a Creative Commons Attribution 3.0 Unported License. To view a copy of this license, visit http://creativecommons.org/licenses/by/3.0/

OPEN

6
The Culture of Humanities Research

Introduction

Setting the scene

This chapter covers a cluster of issues to do with the culture of humanities research. We found broad institutional and technological changes are affecting the way the humanities operate:

> *Internationalisation*: there are more global networks, international collaborations and funding opportunities; increasingly, research is happening outside national and regional boundaries.
>
> *Interdisciplinarity*: there is an established trend for major funding bodies in Europe and the US to insist that projects be interdisciplinary, involving the collaboration of scholars from different fields.

These phenomena are not new. Many researchers will say their fields have always been international and that interdisciplinary research has been on the agenda for decades. Nonetheless, because these developments are now quite established, there are questions about how they are affecting the culture of research. How are scholars reacting to them? Is there resistance? If so, what are the reasons and what forms does it take? While we conclude that interviewees broadly embraced the opportunities of global and interdisciplinary research, these come with challenges of language, power, finance and culture that are little understood, even within the research communities themselves.

We are not directly concerned with developments which might arise in the future and which might in turn affect or even transform the nature and culture of humanities research. For instance, many argue that traditional publishing methods, such as the scholarly monograph, will soon be outdated and that traditional hard copy journals will also disappear eventually. If such things do happen, they will change the nature of research. Similarly, the emergence of MOOCs as a form of teaching might challenge the traditional university model and, in turn, the way research is done. But to discuss these issues we would first need to gaze into a crystal ball to make appropriate predictions and then to conjecture their effects on academic culture. This is a perfectly valid exercise, but beyond the scope of this chapter. Instead, we begin with transformations that have *already* taken place and ask what reactions they are already producing.

As in other chapters, we make use of our interviewee's responses. The questionnaire included these topics and many of the responses were extremely detailed, giving us a rich source of information on which to draw. We shall also use reports and opinion pieces concerned with the issues.

Attitudes to publication

Before we go any further, we need to start with a fundamental feature of all humanities (and indeed any) research, publication. As we shall see with interdisciplinary research and internationalisation, current publication practices have a fundamental influence on the kinds of research carried out.

In our interviews we included a section on publication:

> *How do publications affect the way research is done, in particular through the assessment criteria they provide for hiring and promotion? What effects do the demands of getting published have on the work of younger researchers?*

The answers to this question were wide-ranging but we should emphasise one very basic (and unsurprising) result. The majority of the respondents affirmed the importance of publication to hiring and promotion. A few, notably in India, suggested that the publication requirement is not as yet entrenched. But otherwise, the phrase 'publish or perish' would be an entirely apt way of describing the responses.

The majority of respondents also had some critical remarks to make about current publication regimes. The most common was that they privilege quantity over quality. Some respondents made the closely related point that the requirement for publication at regular intervals deters scholars from embarking on bigger projects, and so prevents longer-term planning and gestation. In reply to our question about younger scholars, many respondents (notably in Africa and the US) complained about the pressure put on scholars at the beginning of their careers. Another interesting theme that was occasionally detected was corruption in publication practices. Some respondents in Asia talked about people paying others to write papers for them, or using their influence and networks to get their name on a publication, even if they were not the authors. In Russia, some workshop participants said that, although nominally there was a system of peer review, in practice it was more or less non-existent. Very often, a paper was published because the author was able to pay the publisher.

This is just a glimpse of some of the views expressed in answer to our publication question. However, for the purposes of this chapter, we need to underline the great importance of publishing in humanities research for two reasons. First, current publication trends also favour the internationalisation of research, which may lead to a certain homogeneity. This was a concern noted by a number of respondents, and we is discussed in the internationalistion section of this chapter. Second, publication regimes may tend to favour monodisciplinary research, which creates a problem for those who wish to promote interdisciplinary work, given the sheer importance of publication for a scholar's career. We discuss this in the interdisciplinary research section.

Internationalisation

In the interviews we asked:

> *What effects is internationalisation (e.g. in recruitment patterns, institutional collaboration, networks) having on research and research activity?*

This question drew a wide variety of responses, describing different ways internationalisation takes place and its different effects. Since we are surveying respondents' views on internationalisation, it may be helpful to recall the discussion of research themes and topics in Chapter 3. In the context of the current chapter it is interesting to ask whether a respondent mentioned themes that were limited to their own region or not. Out of 89 respondents, roughly one third mentioned only regional themes, while two thirds included international themes. The North American results were particularly striking since almost all were international in focus. One respondent (NA9) explicitly commented on the way research has become much more internationalised over the past few years. One interesting answer, which occurred a few times in quite different regions, is that internationalisation is not particularly new. Scholars have long been international in their choice of topics, in what they read and refer to, and in the conferences they attend.

What is new, however, is the growth of international networks, funding initiatives, publishing and ranking systems. According to many of our respondents, all this brings with it the risk of homogeneity. This, at least, is the view of around half of the Asians we interviewed, as well as half the Africans and half the non-Anglophone Europeans (excluding the Russians). Only one Anglophone scholar referred to the issue (an American working frequently in Asia). Although this does not constitute a majority it is still a very significant minority, not least because this same message is consistently voiced in quite different parts of the world.

In what follows we shall distinguish three different forms of internationalisation, which are thought to lead to homogeneity: networks, publishing and ranking.

International networks

Let us start with the increase of international research networks, collaboration and overseas funding. One respondent from Norway noted the phenomenon, but remained neutral about its effects:

> E6: The main national funding body, the Norwegian Research Council, puts great stress on internationalisation when applications are evaluated. This means that projects which can show that they are part of international networks, have a greater chance of being funded, other things being equal.

But the following respondents were far from neutral. They all thought that such internationalisation leads to the Westernisation or Northernisation of research agendas, even though it has other benefits:[1]

> ME1: In addition to EU projects...there are many cooperation agreements between Jordan and Western universities, for both faculty and students. Since 9/11, Western countries are getting more interested in the Middle East, and a lot of people are coming to Jordan. Also, some agencies are working in Jordan, e.g. US agencies and the Japanese International Cooperation Agency (JICA). In most cases they determine the research topics and impose them on us

(e.g. democracy, women's rights). So, although internationalisation is increasing, there's a lack of autonomy for us in the selection of research themes.

As4: Internationalisation of research and research activity brings in both competition and collaboration. Both are important factors for the generation of new findings. However, because of the increased competition from the non-native species, some research fields may not survive and may become extinct eventually. From the view point of preserving cultural heritage, it may be beneficial to preserve these endangered species.

ME2: At present our vision of internationalisation is still too Western, which makes it difficult to confront problems about the East, especially the Middle East. ... As regards its effects, internationalisation pulls research in a Western direction, i.e. towards the EU and the US.

ME3: In general, the existence of an international market homogenises research. On the negative side, this leads to fewer surprises, but on the positive it means people communicate better.

Af3: a negative effect [of internationalisation] is the increasing dominance of research and HE agendas by northern universities. Universities from the North are increasingly becoming powerful and dominant in the running of research affairs of universities in the South. The danger of research imperialism is rife.

Af5: in poor countries like Tanzania research funds are almost exclusively externally sourced. Such funds often come with an agenda. So researchers may be forced to work on topics that may not have relevance to local communities.

Af6: it is not difficult to see how internationalisation leads to colonisation of disciplines/spaces when there are unequal structures, particularly in situations where the collaborations are tied to funding availed by collaborating institutions/partners in the West. Even in intra-Africa collaborations, I have found that some of the top-rated universities (e.g. UCT, Stellenbosch, etc.) have some departments that are basically colonial, structurally and conceptually, as evidenced by the courses taught there and, obviously, when one is involved in collaborations with colleagues from these spaces, the undertaking is not really one of mutual equality but one where a colonial department is striving to reproduce itself on (or drive the agenda of a relationship with) a poor and supposedly naive department in another African university, teaching courses that are structured/conceptualised within postcolonial approaches.

> *Af13:* Internationalisation has been crucial in shaping and improving disciplinary discourse, and in improving the pool of postgraduate students. Cutting edge research has taken place in contexts where researchers deliberately seek to encourage transnational collaboration. The danger though has been a process where (South) Africa is seen as a site of theoretical experimentation when theories emanating from the North are used indiscriminately and unmediated by local conditions. A form of intellectual mimicry is the result.

Internationalisation in publishing

It is not just internationalisation in the form of international networks that may lead to homogeneity, some respondents also pointed the finger at publication. The underlying concern could be expressed as the following argument: [a] publishing, especially journal articles, is key to professional advancement; [b] the more prestigious the outlet, the more useful the publication will be to a scholar's career; [c] but, typically, prestigious means an international and English language journal; [d] the sorts of themes (and criteria) appropriate to these journals tend be Western in focus. The upshot of [a]–[d] is that institutional conditions militate in favour of Anglophone homogeneity.

> *As1:* Internationalisation is useful...But the English language has become the common language, and when it comes to research about a non-Anglophone culture, especially about Asian culture, there's an adverse effect, which results from the difficulty of expressing oneself in this common language. The standard of research has dropped and research has become isolated.
>
> *As10:* Internationalisation is increasingly important, and this is not always for the best. As evidenced, for instance, by the pressure to publish in international journals. This forces me to choose Western topics and play by Western rules.

The European responses were interestingly mixed on the issue. Although some were more positive (as we shall see below), others saw the downsides of internationalisation in publishing:

> *E2:* The need for internationalisation has a profound impact both with regard to the choice of research topics and the need to enhance our international visibility. At a practical level English is becoming the *lingua franca* in the humanities as well. The German

competition for excellence required that all project applications had to be submitted in English.... There are many colleagues who insist, rightly so, that teaching and writing in their native tongues are indispensable to grasp the full meaning of their work.

E3: [Publications and career development] are affecting [research] very much now, though not in recent times. In Spain, there are fewer publishing houses than elsewhere in the EU (e.g. France). So, because of the small number of outlets, in the past there was less pressure to publish. But since 2000 there is more expectation from the EU for us to publish, especially in English. This forces us to play by foreign rules and risks undermining what is distinctive about our research (e.g. in Catalan).

E5: *[How has publication changed the way that research is conducted?]* Well that's very easy; it affects it a lot. In particular with my young researchers I can see it clearly and it affects them dramatically. There are two real effects: one, no national publications, everything is in English; two, no monographs but everything passed down in articles because that is what count in the publication assessment system. Then of course, this is a huge challenge to many traditions within the humanities itself, not to mention disciplines such as history, anthropology and even media studies for that matter.

E14: Internationalisation, when it allows comparison, is basically good. The problem with internationalisation is that it is more and more homogenous and it tends to be more of an Americanisation. This is worrying for sure. The fact that we have to publish in English rather than in our mother tongue, which everyone masters better than the other languages one may speak, is a big issue. It also affects cultural diversity, which is essential for the humanities, and important as well for sciences. If internationalisation is becoming too homogenous, there would be only one kind of network, and then one kind of research. We will lose our rich diversity.

Three African respondents drew the contrast between local and non-local outlets (two merely registered the phenomenon, one was openly critical):

Af1: This university has strict promotion criteria based on publications. Without this minimum number of publications, a person does not get promoted. *[Does this specify types of publication: journal article/book; so-called 'international' versus national or regional journals etc?]* Definitely. An international journal is interpreted as any journal published in the Americas, Europe and some parts of...Asia...

Af5: University policy on publication avenues:...for promotion, academic researchers are required to publish in world-recognised journals almost all of which are in foreign languages and for sure, not found in local circulations. Hence, whatever is published there does not reach the mass of Tanzanians. It is a pity! Given the chance, I would put a condition that one must publish in local journals and in a local language (say Kiswahili), along with the international avenues, in order to get promotion.

Af4: All researchers need avenues and outlets for publishing research results. This is even more urgent for younger researchers. Local journals are not always as viable as world-class journals and books which accord visibility and comparability. This is emphasised for promotion in my university.

International ranking systems

Another issue that concerns is the perception of international ranking systems. In a different section of our questionnaire, we asked:

What effects do ranking systems have on research, on the behaviour of researchers and on the management of research in your area? (Give examples to illustrate your answers.)

This question drew a wide variety of responses. Although we shall not analyse them here, we can say that over half the respondents were, in some way, sceptical of ranking systems (respondents from Asia and the US were the most negative). Some were sceptical in the sense of denying that ranking systems had any significant effect on research activity. Others thought that they did, but were sceptical about the alleged benefits of ranking. Some respondents were more positive and thought of international rankings as a means to challenge bad research practice in their region.

For the purposes of this chapter, the important point to draw out from our respondents' concerns how ranking systems tie up with internationalisation. Here are two extracts:

E7: What is demanded, that will be received. During the past five years the share of ISI and ETIS 1.1 articles (in journals with highest ranking according to our national assessment system) has remarkably increased in the humanities (from 5% of all publications in 2008 to 15% in 2011). At the same time, articles in domestic issues are steadily decreased in number (from 85% to 75%, while the number of monographs has stayed on the same level, instead of increasing). As the monographs published by national publishers are not valuated as high as the articles in international journals, the researchers are not enthusiastic to write them.

R1: University ranking does affect research in my university since its global aim is to get higher in international rankings by means of stimulating publications in international journals that are included in bibliographic databases. That orientation stimulates publishing in English and disqualifies publications in Russian.

These comments are neutral and do not actually criticise the system, though they point to a link between ranking systems and publishing in international journals (with language implications). But three respondents (working in East Asia, Latin America and Africa) were explicitly concerned:

As14: ...citation indices are mostly based in the United States and this is creating American hegemony and favouring contributions based on American views and research paradigms....East Asia has its own distinctive cultures and its own ways of looking at and analysing things, and this is systematically diminished by the current ranking system.

LA4: International rankings have become an obsession of the university in the last few years....The downside is that many areas of research, like Brazilian political thought, that are very important locally, get underevaluated because they have low potential for international diffusion.

Af10: Rankings also have the tendency to ignore research reports in journals which do not originate from the global North. This depresses the development of publication outlets (within Ghana, and the region as a whole) that may have more regional and continental relevance.

The problem could be put as follows. The most prestigious rankings are international, and it is these that will attract the interest of academic managers. The danger is that the criteria of success tend to be set by Western universities, especially those in the US. So when an academic manager forces humanities researchers to 'chase' rankings, they are in effect asking them to make their research fit Western standards. Yet again, this has the effect of homogenising research.

Redressing the balance
In contrast, some respondents positively embraced internationalisation, whether in the context of networks, funding opportunities, publication or rankings. Some were unreservedly positive about the effects of internationalisation in general:

> *R2:* I have no doubt that internationalisation is very good for the quality of the research.
>
> *E10:* In many respects, internationalisation encourages research by accelerating the exchange of knowledge and methodologies between scholars of different affiliations. It is also good by favouring the creation of international research networks.
>
> *Af11*: Internationalisation is the best practice in research activity. This is germane to getting quality delivery of knowledge and it is also important in knowledge transfer. There must be institutional collaboration and networks for proper knowledge transfer, especially as the world has become a global village.
>
> *Af12*: Internationalisation is good for research. Indeed, institutions are actively encouraging efforts that promote internationalisation in terms of research collaboration and interdisciplinary work between researchers from collaborating institutions.
>
> *R4*: I think that internationalisation has big influence, especially in Russia where scientific institutions in times of the USSR were ideologised. Their activity was complicated by all sorts of political and social obstacles: the restriction to hire Jews, non-conformists and other groups, difficulties in career development for the non-party people, sometimes for women, etc. In modern Russia most of these complications are removed, but scientific institutions are weak and not well informed. Internationalisation is an important way of maintaining the intellectual potential of Russian science. Unfortunately, in Russia now the political elite thinks of internationalisation of science as something suspicious. The country's leaders in their public statements speak disapprovingly of those in Russia who receive foreign grants for research and advocacy work, allude to the fact that these people are not loyal to Russia and 'betraying' her for the sake of foreign interests. This 'demonisation' of those who receive grants may harm cooperation of Russian humanitarians with international scientific institutions.

Two Europeans (from Sweden and the Netherlands) actually encouraged publication in English:

> *E1*: If we take the language issue, then we should continue to publish more in the big languages and, of course, English is the biggest. If we think we have reached interesting results then we should be encouraged to spread these results as widely as possible. And I also think that precisely because people in the humanities are often subject to critique, we need to stick together globally.... There are many strong reasons for having a high international profile and therefore publishing in English is one way to go.
>
> *E4*:...methodological nationalism is a reaction to globalisation.... those who subscribe to methodological nationalism think that writing in English only allows you to approximate to the real thing in terms of national culture. So they assume the best work has to be... published in local rather than international journals.[2]

In general, it was interesting to see that not one of our Russian respondents (nine in all) had anything negative to say about internationalisation;[3] either they were neutral, or they were positive and lamented the lack of it. Similarly, none of the Indian respondents mentioned any downside to internationalisation.[4] One was particularly positive:

> *As3*: Whatever internationalisation there has been for research collaborations and networks has been fruitful for research activity in Indian universities.

On the language issue, we should note that there is a report on the humanities in India (sponsored by the UK's AHRC, but written by the India Foundation for the Arts), which does criticise a bias towards the use of English, to the detriment of regional research, though of course the explanation for this reaches back to India's colonial past rather than present-day globalisation.[5]

Conclusion

Clearly this is an important issue over which scholars are divided. Our purpose is not to take sides, but to draw attention to the seriousness of the problem and recommend that international funding bodies take note, with a view to more extensive consultation. This is a particularly acute dilemma for the humanities. As some respondents note, it is of the nature of the humanities to work closely with the nuances of particular languages and cultures. So perhaps there is something in the claim that research can be endangered by increasing Anglophone homogeneity, in a way that STEM subjects are not. However, comparative research depends on a *lingua franca* between researchers. The warning against 'methodological nationalism' (E4) is particularly salient in this regard. At the same time, the humanities are especially at risk of running into conflict with their own governments, or at least suffering neglect, and hence they benefit hugely from international support and collaboration. This dilemma cannot be swept under the carpet.

Interdisciplinary research

What is interdisciplinary research?

In this section we make extensive use of the responses to Section 4 of the questionnaire:

> *Is your own research monodisciplinary or interdisciplinary?*
>
> *What are the benefits or disadvantages of each type of research?*

The overall response to the first question was quite striking: of 89 respondents, 63 were interdisciplinary, and only 13 were monodisciplinary.[6] So far, so clear. But in the course of describing their research as interdisciplinary or otherwise, some respondents reflected explicitly on how to define the term and a number of others revealed their implicit assumptions about the nature of interdisciplinary research. This material is quite complex and we need to analyse it in order to make sense of their responses to the second question about the benefits or disadvantages of each type of research.

Looking at the results as a whole, we can make the following distinctions:

(A) Taking the term interdisciplinary to apply to an individual researcher, one could mean at least three things, presented here in order of strength:

1. *Communicating with other disciplines:*

   NA5: My conception of interdisciplinary is that it is one person whose work is addressed to multiple communities.

   E9: [Interdisciplinary research] could simply involve bringing two disciplines into conversation with each other.

ME4: In my own work, I pay attention to language, not to describe the formal aspects of language as some linguists might, but to see how certain linguistic phenomena might be interpreted in a social context. I point out certain things that a historian or sociologist might not have noticed, but I don't start from a historical or sociological theory. So my own way of being interdisciplinary is to notice a difference in a linguistic term, but hand over to the historian to interpret the fact, to make something out of it. I don't attempt to become a historian or a sociologist, but my work complements theirs. Based on my particular expertise, I try to make people in other disciplines notice things.

2. *Borrowing the methods, etc. of other disciplines:*

R2: My own research is interdisciplinary as I use historical sources, methods and approaches, alongside with anthropological ones.

E9: [Interdisciplinary research] might involve one discipline using the tools and vocabulary of another (something often frowned upon, as it may involve one discipline misunderstanding the tools of the other).

3. *Mastering other disciplines:*

NA3: True interdisciplinarity is so very hard to do. True interdisciplinarity would require a thorough knowledge of more than one discipline.

NA11: I think the word interdisciplinary is a misnomer. I think there is almost no good interdisciplinary research. I think there is good multidisciplinary research. You have to be strong in a discipline working with other people who are also strong in a discipline. Really interdisciplinary people are rare.

E1: I would say that my research is mainly monodisciplinary, it's comparative but it's not really interdisciplinary. As I said, you have to demand more than what I do in order for something to be really interdisciplinary.

As10: The disadvantages of interdisciplinary research are that it is difficult for one person to master more than one field.

(B) Taking interdisciplinarity to involve two or more researchers it could mean collaborative interdisciplinarity (multidisciplinarity):

NA6: A lot of my research is fairly interdisciplinary these days, though I have rather tough standards you have to meet in order to call yourself interdisciplinary. I think we're well beyond the era in which borrowing methods and discourse from other disciplines makes one interdisciplinary. The bar that I would set today is that you have to be working with other people in different disciplines on common projects.

NA10: Interdisciplinary work is almost by definition collaborative, because it's very hard for people to control knowledge within one discipline, much less many.

As8: Even in the single field of linguistics and culture, you may see a single scholar, or indeed scholars from a single country, with a different source of language and materials/resources that are oftentimes different. They have to work together and conduct collaborating research.

E13: I'd divide [interdisciplinarity] into two types: soft and hard.... Hard interdisciplinarity involves specialists from different disciplines gathering together over a common object or text. As a result, their own individual ways of operating have to change.

E2: Of course the term interdisciplinary is vague. Do we mean that scholars of different fields collaborate and that each brings in a specific expertise? Or do we mean, as some people claim, that we need to dissolve the disciplines altogether?

(C) Post-disciplinarity:

The last extract suggests a different concept altogether, also alluded to by another respondent:

E9: I've heard the phrase post-disciplinarity used. I'm not sure I understand it, but I don't think interdisciplinarity will or should take us to a point where disciplinary boundaries actually vanish.

We shall leave post-disciplinarity on one side, since it was only of marginal interest to our respondents.[7] By contrast, collaborative interdisciplinarity is extremely important to the humanities, as we shall see in more detail below. For the purposes of this chapter we shall refer to it as 'multidisciplinarity'. One point should be uncontroversial: a multidisciplinary project will require individual researchers to be interdisciplinary in the first sense mentioned above (A)1, and to an extent the second (i.e. using the sources of other disciplines). But it surely does not require the third, (A)3, a strong sense of mastering another discipline; indeed the function of collaborative projects is precisely to avoid requiring individual researchers to be interdisciplinary in this way.

The value of interdisciplinary research

Next we turn to the value of interdisciplinary research. Many of our respondents claimed both advantages and disadvantages for it:

Advantages

    1. *Interdisciplinary research is broad and synoptic.*

This point was made by seven respondents, Af1, Af6, As1, E4, E10 and:

> *Af3:* Interdisciplinary approaches are more holistic, and so address issues more comprehensively.
>
> *NA2:* It is essential that you simultaneously have specialists and that you have people trying to make sense of the bigger picture.

    2. *Many complex research questions simply require interdisciplinary research.*

Here are the most explicit statements, though the point was made implicitly by many others:[8]

> *ME4:* The problem of monodisciplinary work is that the humanities are essentially plural; there is a complementarity between humanities disciplines.
>
> *E5:* The complexity of the empirical questions simply demands that more researchers from more diverse backgrounds come together to answer the question, that's one trend.
>
> *LA10:* Monodisciplinary research is necessary for improving the technical tools of the trade in a specific field. Multidisciplinary research is necessary because almost all humanistic questions have to do with more than one discipline.

    3. *Interdisciplinary work is much more likely to throw up innovative methods and results, and to open up new horizons.*

This point was made by 13 respondents, As4, As6, As9, As10, Au2, E15, ME3, ME6, NA 8, NA16, R5, R6, R9 and:

> *E12:* The benefits of such work are huge, with each collaborator having the chance to discover not only new materials and insights,

but whole new paradigms to bring to bear on the topics under discussion.

4. *Interdisciplinary research facilitates translation by enabling humanities scholars to link up with researchers in other disciplines, e.g. medicine (resulting in bioethics), and through that discipline allow its own results to feed through to society at large.*

This point was made by 8 respondents, Af11, As13, ME3, R6, NA8, R6 and:

> *E6*: for the humanities as a field it is important to engage with other disciplines, both within the humanities and with fields outside our own. We need to establish and communicate to the outside world the importance of the humanities for the social and economic development of the society we are a part of, and we must encourage our own researchers to take up these challenges in their research.
> *Af9*: Interdisciplinarity lends itself to application beyond mere publication. Monodisciplinarity [is] limited in results uptake...
> *ME4*: We'll always need monodisciplinary research. And I don't use interdisciplinary work to find theoretical research questions, but to find applications.

5: *Interdisciplinary research helps one better understand one's own discipline.*

This point is worth highlighting. It was made by only three respondents, but they came from three very different countries (Canada, China and Romania), working in literature, history and philosophy:

> *As11*: Interdisciplinary research is good when it arises from deep reflection on the boundaries of one's own discipline and on the limitations that these boundaries may impose.
> *E10*: Interdisciplinarity is very useful...in facilitating the understanding of one's own topic from different points.
> *NA14*: [Interdisciplinary research is] a good way of knowing what your discipline does. My own assumptions become clearer to me.

Disadvantages

Our respondents also emphasised some risks of interdisciplinary research:

1. It may lack sufficient rigour.

For several respondents, scholars need to be trained within a well-contained field with its own standards and methodologies. Put simply, their concern was that too much pressure for interdisciplinary research causes scholars to become amateurs. In some responses the solution seemed to be to let scholars master their discipline before they reach out to others.

This point was made by 19 respondents, As6, As10, Au4, E2, E9, E14, LA2, LA4, ME3, ME4, NA1, NA3, NA4, NA14, NA16, R5 and:

> *R1*: I think that the most important disadvantage of the interdisciplinary research is that there is a risk of remaining an amateur and missing some important nuances of some of the disciplines involved.
>
> *E8*: There is an increasing threat to monodisciplinary research. People need to be deeply trained within a single discipline; there is a need for rigour. In the past rigour was exclusive, e.g. in Celtic studies medievalism was considered top of the tree. But there is a need to have intensive monodisciplinary training and then branch out.

2. Interdisciplinary work can be extremely time-consuming, starting from the basic information exchange needed at the outset, and then involving possibly years of hard work, often for an uncertain outcome.

This point was made by 7 respondents, As8, E1, E10, E12, E14, NA8, NA15, R9 and:

> *Af3*: [interdisciplinary work] is difficult to carry out because it brings much greater complexity. It also requires that people from different disciplines work together and this isn't always easy. The advantage of monodisciplinary work by contrast is that it is much easier to carry out, involving a single perspective on an issue.

It is important to consider these objections in the light of distinctions between different ways of being interdisciplinary. If what is at issue is interdisciplinarity in the strong sense of A3 above, the first criticism has considerable force. But it has much less force against A1 and A2. Multidisciplinarity seems to get round the objection that the whole point is to allow scholars to remain masters in their field while still working with other experts from other fields on a collaborative project. However, this form of research is still vulnerable to the second criticism that the work involved is not that of mastering a new field, but of nurturing contacts, applying for project funds and running such projects, as well as having sufficient familiarity with the other disciplines to make the collaboration work, as in the interdisciplinarity of types A1 and A2.

Institutional tensions

These points help to set the stage for the key issue we wish to take up. There is no doubt that senior academic administrators and funding bodies often set a high premium on interdisciplinary research. In many countries and regions, funding schemes prioritise interdisciplinary and collaborative research. Some of the most prominent examples include the Mellon Foundation (USA), HERA (Humanities in the European Research Area), the Volkswagen Foundation, the AHRC (UK) and the NWO (Humanities) (the Netherlands).[9]

Turning to our interview respondents, we can present some extracts that make a version of this point:

> *As8*: *[Where is the push for interdisciplinary research coming from?]* When applying for funding there have been new categories created which encourage people from different disciplines to come together and use interdisciplinary methods and skills. There is always a category which encourages this.
>
> *As10*: Administrators do encourage interdisciplinary work. The reason perhaps is that they want to encourage important breakthroughs, which they think will come from interdisciplinary work. Perhaps the model comes from the natural sciences.
>
> *Af12*: *[What themes have been dominating your own field?]* Most [history research in Nigeria] in recent times has become interdisciplinary, veering into engagements with the social sciences mostly. Attempts to engage with the mainstream of funding [e.g. to access available funding] have encouraged many emerging historians to veer into the social sciences.
>
> *E6*: My own research is monodisciplinary and will probably remain so until I retire...But as a dean I strongly promote interdisciplinary research. Monodisciplinary research will surely be important also in the future, but for the humanities as a field it is important to engage with other disciplines, both within the humanities and with fields outside our own....This presupposes cooperation with people from other fields. I think this development is under

way. An example, when the [National] Research Council posted funding of new centres of excellence in 2011, four applications were sent from my faculty. All of them were interdisciplinary, involving researchers from other faculties. Five and ten years ago, this was not the case.

E11: There is, if there ever was, no longer a bright line with the humanities and the social sciences. There are many examples of interdisciplinary collaborations across that divide and many with the sciences and medical sciences, medical humanities for example, or areas where landscape architecture interfaces with educational sciences and engineering. They are too numerous to mention, but they tend to be the areas which, anecdotally speaking, seem to attract the most funding, because that really is what the big funders are interested in now.

Af2: Interdisciplinary research tends to be pushed by funders. Where there is strong university leadership, it tends to focus on attacking important social questions.

Af7: My own research has tended towards interdisciplinarity because research that is monodisciplinary is not attracting funding.

On the other hand, some interviewees reported a strong resistance to interdisciplinarity among researchers (perhaps mainstream academics?):

Af1: *[Do you think this view on the benefits of interdisciplinarity is shared within...your networks?]* An emphatic NO, NO! Things around here tend to be trenchantly old school. You have your nice little cubicle.... You stay, and don't stray, in the cubicle.... I am an outlier – or better, a loose cannon – who broke down the walls of my cubicle. Still receiving flack though, because other members of the Cubicle (note the capitalisation!) are scratching their heads wondering why I have to leave the nice Cubicle.

E4: There is currently a lack of interdisciplinary engagement between my field and the social sciences. I was trained to respect the present, not like most humanities researchers, who revere the past. The social sciences also respect the present, but they study it by pursuing an obsession with quantitative data.... The general lack of interdisciplinary energy is the biggest problem for European universities. Until we change, we'll be inward looking, self-replicating, medieval corporations who pretend that we're socially relevant.

As7: The worst thing I suffered over the past ten years is the inertia of each and every discipline. In economics a professor does not need to communicate with a political scientist because this won't help them get published in the SCID journal. Even within the discipline of economics, those who are doing macroeconomics don't necessarily need to communicate with microeconomics. This is just no good. This is the number one challenge. This is the reason why I hold this interdisciplinary conference. It is very difficult, especially with Chinese academics. This type of interdisciplinary inertia is very strong. I've been striving to hold this ocean of inertia and I don't want to drown in it! [*Also, from answer to publication question*: They have no choice but to conduct research on smaller areas within disciplines.]

R6: For Russian humanities, though, [interdisciplinary] approaches are still novel, largely due to the fact that most researchers are locked into discipline-specific departments.

Some respondents went a step further and said that monodisciplinary attitudes manifest themselves in institutional ways:

NA7: The disadvantage for doing interdisciplinary work, especially for young scholars, is that professional life is still very much embedded within disciplines. And so you don't get credit for multi-authored publications, for example.

NA10: There are many challenges of interdisciplinary work. Many of the professional rewards are within disciplines and departments. Interdisciplinary work can be easily marginalised...

R9 (an environmental historian): Many disadvantages concern the position of an interdisciplinary researcher to find her/his place in the professional community. You are not a biologist any more, but for a long time even after getting a degree you are not considered to be a professional historian. It happens because you have no connections, you do not have a prominent teacher in your main field, thus you are not belonging to any group of disciples. This is particularly important for the scientific community in my country where many people have their own professional genealogy, being a disciple of a disciple of a famous intellectual.

If these sets of remarks are representative, there is likely to be a tension between funding priorities and more traditional attitudes and, indeed, we did find some respondents reporting such a tension:

NA5: Deans are very interested in interdisciplinary research. Deans want to be cutting edge, and that increasingly means interdisciplinary research. Often [they are] trying to recruit people whose academic and intellectual home is somewhat split between two fields. Generally, we think that's exciting and a good thing, but it also means that it's a challenge for universities and departments when it comes to evaluation and promotion. This is increasingly problematic and becoming more acute.... My conception of interdisciplinarity is that it is one person whose work is addressed to multiple communities. When that is the case, it may be hard for those communities to feel like the person is fully theirs. Sometimes the closest fields have the most difficulty agreeing on standards of excellence and what is authorship. That can be dangerous for junior faculty. [It] requires that junior faculty must be very proactive, making sure they are communicating with their groups [and] must have a disciplinary home, a core discipline. If you veer too far from home, that can be dangerous.

E5: On the one hand, the interdisciplinary trend is, in some parts of the competitive stream, encouraged; that's the ERC trend, the European Science Foundation trend (essentially the ERC trend) and also in some parts of national funding. For example, our government in Denmark strongly encourages interdisciplinary research and, in a recent evaluation of the research council system that was published a few years ago, it was one of the major recommendations. So that's one trend. You have goals that prioritise interdisciplinary research and on the other hand you have very strong gearing of governing publications that have a very good track record, have a very high gate impact factor, and so forth. And that sort of pushes research towards overspecialisation.

E14: Some will promote interdisciplinary research.... But research is mainly monodisciplinary in our humanities faculty although politics and the rectorat tend to encourage interdisciplinary research.

The basic issue is that the institutional incentives may be working in contradictory directions. When it comes to individual hiring and promotion, publishing monodisciplinary books and journals is paramount. But, at the same time, some funding bodies and senior academic administrators are promoting interdisciplinary research. This tension can manifest itself in a number of ways.

Career advancement:

There is a possible tension between the promotion of interdisciplinary research projects and publication regimes. As we have seen, a scholar's publication record is key to their hiring and promotion (and tenure, where applicable). The more prestigious the outlet, the more useful it is for these purposes. The issue is, are the most prestigious journals monodisciplinary? To settle this question definitively one would have to conduct a wide-ranging survey of humanities journals. The purpose of this chapter is to raise the question, and to suggest some anecdotal evidence, that monodisciplinarity does put a scholar at an advantage in terms of career advancement (through publication).

The problem would affect researchers at different stages of their career:

> *Early career*: consider someone who has been recruited as a postdoctoral researcher on a funded interdisciplinary project. Their PhD has been monodisciplinary, but being a postdoc on such a project is their only (or best) career option at the next stage. Since they will have to publish in interdisciplinary formats as part of the project they will not be well placed at the end of the period to apply for permanent academic positions if the greatest prestige still goes to peer-reviewed papers in monodisciplinary journals.
>
> *Tenure*: take a scheme where a university actually establishes interdisciplinary tenure-track positions (there are some initiatives of this nature in the US, for instance). The search committee will typically consist of members from different departments who will have to agree on a single candidate with good interdisciplinary credentials. At least from the hiring point of view this is not a handicap, but an advantage. But as one looks ahead to promotion and tenure, problems loom. Typically, the position will be located in an individual department. When it comes to the tenure decision, the department will decide according to the usual criteria. Here again, there is a risk that the bias towards monodisciplinary publications will put the candidate at a severe disadvantage.
>
> *Senior researchers*: the incentive to publish monodisciplinary research will also deter well-established scholars from engaging in interdisciplinary research. Their promotion to more senior levels, such as named chairs, could be set back by the time taken putting together funding proposals and seeing them through.

An additional problem, which affects all stages of academic promotion, concerns letters of recommendation. Promotion depends on strong referees and readers (whether chosen by the candidate or not), but there could be a problem if the more trusted and respected readers are themselves monodisciplinary researchers. When such a scholar writes a promotion report on a candidate who has done interdisciplinary work, they might disclaim knowledge of some aspects of the research ('it's not really my field'), and thereby sound lukewarm.

Multidisciplinary edited books:
A related problem is that funded research projects of this kind are typically expected to produce multi-authored interdisciplinary books. But who exactly will read them? If most scholars remain in their disciplinary silos, they may look on the papers in such volumes with disdain. The papers are written to be understood by people outside the field, and so won't deserve the respect they would have if written for specialists.[10]

Conclusion

There is a fundamental question to be asked: what is the source of the institutional pressure for interdisciplinary research? Is it based on sound intellectual reasons, or do institutional leaders think that the humanities should imitate the natural sciences (where interdisciplinary research is much more common)?

> *E5*: ... [the enthusiasm for interdisciplinarity] is not founded on any kind of solid evidence, it's founded here on suspicion or presuppositions that interdisciplinarity is good. I haven't seen robust or empirical evidence that this is the case. But on the other hand, I haven't seen robust evidence that delivering very narrow specialisation produces better research results. I suppose that at the end it's very difficult to get robust data on one or the other.
> *E13*: As a general point, I don't think interdisciplinarity should be seen as good for its own sake.
> *NA1*: I do think that interdisciplinary has become a buzzword. Sometimes it really lacks a certain heft.

On the other hand, one can also ask why the most prestigious publication outlets are monodisciplinary (if they are)? Is this merely a historical contingent fact?

There needs to be further discussion about the merits and best practices of interdisciplinary, comparative and multilingual research. Beyond that there needs to be a review of the underlying institutional incentives for research, and those who promote interdisciplinarity need to do more to use their influence to reform appointment and promotion procedures.

Though this is already an acute problem in Europe and North America, there is every indication it will affect other regions as well.

Finally, we would like to state a little more explicitly where we ourselves stand on the nature and value of interdisciplinary research. We have seen how our respondents discussed its advantages under several headings. One of these was that many research questions simply cannot be addressed within an existing discipline; they require us to trespass across existing boundaries and create interdisciplinary projects. We strongly agree. Disciplinary boundaries should not be allowed to impose constraints on the kinds of research questions we pursue, and we should not be put off asking a question because its answer lies in a discipline other than the one we work in. It is the research question that should have primacy and the academic system, including institutional arrangements and individual incentives, should be set up to reflect this.

It would take us too far afield to examine the nature of interdisciplinary research in any detail, especially the well-known question about the contingency of disciplinary boundaries and the extent to which they are the result of historical circumstances and whether they fashion reality at its natural joins? But *prima facie*, it is not difficult to see how important a role contingency plays in the formation of disciplines. One can easily imagine how some disciplines (or sub-disciplines) arose because an individual researcher, or group of researchers, became curious about a set of questions. If these researchers have the appropriate entrepreneurial skills they might manage to draw other people's attention to their activities and succeed in institutionalising their curiosity. As soon as this happens a discipline has been established. Once in place, the discipline will attract the interest of people who consider their interests to be very similar to the now institutionalised curiosity of those who founded the discipline. Professional expertise evolves. But then someone may appear whose own intellectual curiosity does not fit within the existing discipline; they pose broader questions than it is able to answer, and so trespass across its boundaries to draw in knowledge from other disciplines. If this researcher shares similar entrepreneurial talents with their forerunners, they too will institutionalise their curiosity, and their interdisciplinary activities will become the foundation of a new discipline. So the process goes on and, at any stage, a discipline may seem (or be made to seem) as if it is simply natural, despite the fact that its development involved a significant level of contingency.

This is only a sketch. There have been a myriad processes by which different disciplines and sub-disciplines have been formed but the model is useful for thinking about disciplinary boundaries. The main point it brings out, and the point several of our own respondents made, is the primacy of the research question over whatever disciplinary boundaries happen to exist at any one time. Often, new research questions are imposed from outside academia, for instance, as a way of meeting large societal challenges (as in environmental studies, which demand the pooling of intellectual resources from history, philosophy and many of the social and natural sciences).

At any rate, for those who endorse the priority of research question over existing disciplinary boundaries, it is all the more important to face up to institutional barriers to interdisciplinary research.

Except where otherwise noted, this work is licensed under a Creative Commons Attribution 3.0 Unported License. To view a copy of this license, visit http://creativecommons.org/licenses/by/3.0/

OPEN

7
Funding and Infrastructure

This chapter is concerned with the questions: Is funding for the humanities adequate? Do we have adequate infrastructure for humanities research? Are the institutional parameters of the humanities fit for the challenges of the 21st century? The chapter will not look into general questions of university frameworks, relevant as that would be, but it will focus on the perspectives of humanistic researchers themselves, as evidenced by our interviews, and how they experience financial and infrastructural support for their research and how these are conditions changing. Not surprisingly, we found that there are huge levels of inequality within the world of the humanities and that different regional funding systems, even within the developed world, may have hitherto neglected consequences for humanities research practices.

Core funding for research

By far the majority of interviewees came from publicly funded universities and, while many identified other sources of funding for research, the role of state financing was clear in all continents. We had representatives of a few private universities with large endowments, all of them North American.

All interviewees were asked to give their view of recent changes in the budget situation for the humanities for their university. Because of the financial crisis of the last years it might have been expected that many would report declining funding levels, but this was not the case. Only seven interviewees reported a decline in overall budget (two Europeans, three Africans, and two North Americans). No change was reported by 25 respondents, with some indicating that, while some revenue sources were declining, others had evened out the loss. Positive changes were noted by 13 (four Asians, four Russians, two Latin Americans, and one each from Europe and North America). Half our respondents, 43, however, did not express a view on change. The non-respondents were evenly spread across countries that had experienced positive and negative growth.

These responses should not be taken as an accurate reflection of the funding situation for the humanities. While some of our respondents were in positions of budgetary insight, others responded simply from their own experience. What we can say, however, is that the perception of our interviewees was one of relative stability and maybe even some improvement globally. Our interviewees certainly did not indicate that funding for the humanities had been dramatically cut.

The overall picture of relative stability changes, however, when one looks at individual countries. In some regions, such as the Mediterranean countries, cuts have been severe and are reported by our interviewees, and in some North American universities state funding and some endowments have declined badly, similarly noted by some interviewees. In other countries, most notably in China, Brazil and Russia, budgets for the humanities have gone up quite perceptibly and in some cases even dramatically.

Notions of relative stability depend, of course, on the absolute level of funding. While the interviews did not indicate that humanities in African universities had experienced an adverse trend in recent years, the level of funding was a problem in itself:

> *(Af8)* As in many African universities funding brings many challenges. During the post independence period, UEM was mainly funded for research by Nordic agencies, such as SIDA/SAREC, the Ford Foundation and other agencies, and the government of Mozambique. Since the mid-1980s, and particularly after the 1990s, funding became a huge problem. Government funding covers, with difficulty, teaching activities, salaries and some other institutional support, but very few research programmes. The situation is particularly difficult for young scholars that have to face a lack of books and of research and teaching material, a lack of funds to participate in conferences, and a lacking of funding to publish their work. Publication is a problem at the university. Firstly, because many scholars teach in different (private) universities to earn some money, as the salary at public universities is not sufficient, or serve as consultants, with no time to undertake research; secondly, with a lack of funds to do research we have very few incentives to research and publish.

While South Africa has an advanced university system the legacy of apartheid is still felt in formerly black universities, which struggle with huge number of students and are really teaching universities (Af13).

The evidence from Africa reveals government pressure on universities to raise their income by other means than taxes, such as in this case from an East African country:

> *(Af3)* The government has been the primary funder of public universities, but its funding is gradually declining and universities are expected to raise more from student fees, research income and from other income-generating activities. These might, for example, involve providing particular services or facilities to the local community.

This experience is a far cry from that of Chinese colleagues who reported that funding has been steadily rising for the last five years by about 15% per annum (As16). With increased funding comes problems of transparency as to which subjects and disciplines get the lion's share. Such problems are elucidated by evidence from Russia, which has also seen increased levels of funding. In an attempt to boost the research capability of Russia's best universities, the Federal Ministry for Education and Research devised a vertical hierarchy of institutions of higher education. At the top are federal and research universities, each with a federal development grant (Rub 1 bln/year in 2010–14). This money was to be spent according to a development roadmap (R6). According to our interviewees the humanities have seen little benefit from this investment. The main issues seem to be a lack of transparency for the majority of funding, which is retained at the discretion of central authorities, and an over-emphasis on rewards for publication in peer-reviewed journals and the use of citation indexes. Most humanists publish in Russian and receive little benefit from this system. Another possible funding source is the European Union:

> *(R2)* However, our managers also encourage us to find additional financial support for our research from foreign sources (European especially), probably because they see it as a way for internationalisation of the University.

Funding may be tied very directly to political favour. The Russian Presidential Academy and the Higher School of Economics in Moscow are two of the major political players among Russian universities. They were established during the first years of reform and, according to our interviewees, were seen as a liberal ghetto during the first decade of Putin's government. In recent years they have received political credit to host important and well-funded think tanks for economic reforms. These resources were allocated for a series of new departments and research centres, including for philosophy and sociology. However, such favouritism may prove short-lived and potentially difficult to balance with academic freedom.

The Taiwanese system represents another extreme where funding has been stable for half a century and little incentive is evident for the humanities to be more enterprising:

> *(As14)* Our funding comes from Taiwan's Ministry of Education. However, some of our applied fields, like engineering and business, get a lot of feedback money from their alumni. Besides such donations and support, the colleges of engineering and business will engage in a lot of industry–academy collaborative work. Thus, they can get funding that would never be available to the humanities programme. The extra money that the humanities programmes get tend to be the research grants that the professors receive from the National Science Council or else from cooperative research projects, either locally or internationally funded by various sponsoring organisations. But, I think our humanities colleagues and programmes have to start thinking more deeply about how to increase their financial resources so that they can offer more in their programmes. It's been the same model since day one, I guess, for 50 or 60 years. The principal funding always from the Ministry of Education, that's why we're not so enterprising.

In the United States the funding models are quite diverse, with public universities relying on state grants and tuition fees to varying degrees, while private universities differ according to their historical portfolio of endowments and attractiveness to donors. The financial crisis of recent years has hit some universities badly while others have been insulated against adversity. One interviewee described the situation at a large private university, which was highly dependent on tuition and had a limited endowment.

> *(NA6)* I was chair of the department from 2008–12, right when the great recession hit, and it was quite a hit. My first year as chair was spent dealing with mandatory furloughs for faculty and staff, a 20% targeted cut in soft money and structural funds that primarily funds TAs and lecturers

Another interviewee at a very well-endowed university talked about the implications of imminent changes to the federal budget:

> *(NA5)* Just this morning, we (the other deans, President and Provost) were talking about the potential sequestration issues. If sequestration kicks in, the trickle-down for us will be substantial. If core departments in the sciences lose money, the humanities will take a hit because of the science and engineering emphasis, in perhaps a disproportionate kind of way.... this would mean a loss for everyone.

However, in this case the outlook for the university might still have been relatively stable as funding from foundations and alumni was pretty steady: 'Down in 2008, but basically back where it should be. We don't live on our tuition the way other universities do.' (NA5)

Non-governmental funding in developing countries

A host of private and semi-private international funders play a very important role for some developing countries. In developed countries such foundations may also play an important role for certain areas, but will typically play a much lesser role for the research budget in total.

Outside private funding may be controversial with some governments. Western donations were crucial for the establishment of the European University of St Petersburg, and a few other initiatives in Russia in the 1990s, but this legacy was seen as highly suspect by the Putin government and foreign funding streams have now effectively dried up. Therer was a similar situation in parts of the Middle East before the regime changes of recent years:

> *(ME4)* Under the previous regime it was forbidden to get funding from abroad (except for scholarships). All funding had to come from national public sources.

In most developing countries foreign research donations are welcome supplements to core funding. Public and private donors often collaborate directly or through the African Humanities Program. Staff training is mainly supported by national governments but receives valuable aid from various consortia, including PANGeA (Partnership for African Next Generation of Academics), and several links programmes in languages (Af5). In many countries donors such as the World Bank, EU, UNDP and national aid agencies work directly with local government and agencies.

However, for humanities scholars access to such programmes is not easy and depends on the scholar's abilities to establish international links:

(Af1) Rare, but done. In 2008, I became part of a Volkswagen Foundation research network, which acts as a research hub connecting German (Freiburg), Swiss (Basel) and African (Bayero, Yaoundé and Witwatersrand) universities.

Such breakthroughs are limited to a few scholars:

(ME1) Since 2000, I have received some EU funding that's dedicated to the Mediterranean region. In some cases I work on aspects of funded projects. There are many such projects funded by the EU. Their objective is to create networks in the Mediterranean. EU states need a non-EU partner to apply for such projects. Another source from which I have obtained funding is France's Institut de Reserche pour le Développement, also the American University of Beirut. In such cases I tend to be approached, rather than making the approaches myself. Since most [Arab nationality] don't speak English, they can't access these sorts of funds, so they concentrate on teaching. In this sense, I'm in the minority.

Access to funding may depend on access to colleagues who do have such international contacts:

(Af7) My research is largely supported by funding received from partners as part of collaborative projects. In some cases I do carry out self-supported research because in my field as a historian it is possible to do archival research without large sums of money.

Competitive funding streams in developed countries

Since the 1970s most governments in developed countries have gradually increased a third funding stream of competitive funding administered by research councils or directly through ministries. The funding model was often found in the United States, which introduced the National Science Foundation immediately after World War II to develop the sciences. The National Endowment for the Humanities was funded to a much smaller extent and today plays a relatively small role. In many west European countries, on the other hand, humanities were seen as part of the sciences and shared a considerably larger portion of the total research funding made available through this competitive funding stream. With the development of the European Framework Programme for Research and Innovation, EU funding is now playing an increasing role, also for partner countries outside Europe.

Not surprisingly, European interviewees identified research agencies as crucial funders, although they often change their guidelines:

> *(E12)* Research Council funding is always developing its focus and nature, and we have been challenged to keep up. The most recent developments have encouraged collaboration, longer, larger projects, and the demonstration of impact, which have all moved the emphasis away from the lone scholar model of research that many of us were familiar with up to the turn of the century.

National research agencies in Europe have increasingly focused on excellence programmes of various sorts, which diverts more money to a few elite universities, not least in Germany:

> *(E2)* German universities have not seen drastic funding cuts comparable to what happened, for example, in the UK, although the situation differs among the various German states. The state of Baden-Württemberg is relatively prosperous and hosts several of Germany's most prestigious universities with great traditions in both the sciences and the humanities, including Heidelberg, Freiburg and Tübingen. Moreover, in 2005 the federal government launched the, so-called, competition for excellence that brought several billion Euros to the successful applicants.... Moreover, the state government has invested considerable amounts of money to improve the teacher–student ratio in large departments such as history. Basically, the funding situation of German universities varies according to two factors: the state of public finances in the respective states and the ability to acquire third-party funding.

Another German interviewee confirmed this picture and drew attention to the risk that temporary funding leads to an increasing number of temporary jobs and that young researchers are finding it difficult to establish themselves:

> *(E15)* Over the last decade, funding continues to come mostly from particular states (*Länder*), and this source of funding has remained steady. But third-stream funding (*Drittmittel*) has been

increasing. Third-stream funding supports research projects (as *Sonderforschungsbereiche*), which attract, for the most part, postdoctoral researchers. But there is now a surplus of these, i.e. people who will not find permanent university jobs but will only get jobs on such projects. When I was for the last time involved in such a project, I only took PhD students as collaborators, so as not to create still more researchers who would not get permanent jobs.

The big money allocated through competitive grants is seen by some interviewees as alien to the research environment of the humanities as it forces researchers to team up:

(E5) The overall change is that more funding for research in general is in the competition stream...there is a move towards more strategic research and also there is a move towards more technological research. It means that the humanities will ultimately be seen as an aid to other types of research; those more technically orientated, more research on health topics and so on. Life sciences and, of course, climate change are another two major areas. Also, it's one of the big winners in the battle for strategic money, so the humanities have more of a struggle to have a position that researchers can compete on. It's not that there's less money for humanities research but it's within this overall stream of this competitive stream. There's less of a position for the humanities in general to even enter a competition. In order for this to happen you have to have a window of opportunity; you have to have had something that will be relevant for humanities researchers.

One interviewee made a strong plea for block government funding for research as against competitive and private funding. The interviewee was from an affluent non-EU country that had retained a strong block funding system. The argument put forward was directed against a perceived American funding model but seemed also to go against the European funding model:

(E14) Private funding remains rare and sporadic. I hope it stays so, because private research provides advantages, but it is not a perennial source of funding. Research funded by private institution is usually short-term and its results have to be produced at an unsuitable pace. Therefore it seems very important to me to keep a majority of state funding for our research so that we can be free to decide how to

conduct it and for how long. Besides, this allows our chairs to be more stable and unthreatened, contrary to what is happening in many US universities. Research in the humanities covers different aspects from the kind of research funded by private institutions. It is worth noticing here that private funding favours interdisciplinary and collective research, which is less suitable with what we used to do in the humanities. Moreover, it is important to keep some monodisciplinary and individual research, even though interdisciplinary research is not to be rejected.

A Brazilian interviewee noted the same resistance to collaborative work, but in this case the opposition was identified not in the research community but in a conservative funding system:

> *(LA1)* One change that could be pointed to is the search for private funding or partnerships, specially among natural and applied sciences. The humanities are still controlled by the dominant view that to remain independent and critical one cannot be subject to any funding outside the public ones. And those are controlled by a few networks of people that tend to reproduce the same patterns and knowledge already acquired, and prevent innovation.

Despite such resistance another Brazilian interviewee had found increasing opportunities to develop large-scale projects because of the overall increase in higher education funding and overheads on collaboration with the private sector (LA2).

The Australian funding model similarly relies overwhelmingly on block grants, though the role of research agencies is considerable:

> *(Au1)* In Australia, humanities research is almost all funded by the federal government (although there are also opportunities for collaboration with local bodies, e.g. Newcastle City Council might part fund a project on local history). My university receives some research funding as a block grant, determined by a range of research indicators. There are also grants available from the Australian Research Council (ARC) through the Discovery Projects Scheme. I'm working on one of these at the moment. The block grant is not being reduced that much, though priorities are changing as universities look to fund research that will be seen as more strategic or marketable (depending on conditions). The ARC grants are not in decline, though the chances of being successful in the SSH continue to be about one in five.

The last comment reveals that funding chances in Australia seem considerably better than in Europe, where success rates for both European and national funding for humanities projects are often less than one in ten. Another Australian respondent confirmed that government research funding has been good:

> *(Au3)* It tends to fund much more pragmatic, problem-based projects. So I don't think I've ever directly got funding for one of my monographs on, say, [unclear]. I have had large funding for youth cultures of obesity, that sort of thing. And I've always encouraged my colleagues to think about it in those ways.

Some south east Asian countries have introduced research funding agencies on the European model in recent years. However, funding has come with an increased burden of bureaucracy:

> *(As13)* The problem is not so much lack of funding. But the major obstacles are the endless paperwork the professors are required to do, mostly in the name of accountability. They are mostly written prop-ups of quantities to fulfil government targets or outputs.

Such complaints are often heard in Europe and seem to be inherent in the current funding model.

Despite differences in funding models there seems to be a trend towards larger collaborative project funding in both Europe and North America. One interviewee put it this way:

> *(NA6)* Funding has been very good, partly because I'm in the digital humanities field. I've been pushing my colleagues to apply for more collaborative-scale research grants. The grants for scholars for monographs keep going down. The future of research funding for the humanities in the US lies in collaborative grants, projects, activities. Spinning off individual projects before and after. Having said that, the collaborative grants in the humanities are modest in scale and subject to fees and overheads. If the institution is going to take 50% off of a grant, it often leaves you below the threshold of sustainable activity.... I like to tell junior colleagues that grant writing and organising research projects is new normal. Collaborative project work based on grants doesn't take away from research but it spurs your own research, talks and classes. Your independent work can also get channelled back into the collaborative work. One kind of activity spurs the others and vice versa.

Research institutes

While funders may have increased the pressure on the humanities to develop larger research teams and adhere to certain research metrics, universities themselves have developed humanities centres and institutes that often put emphasis on the individual scholar and provide a sheltered research environment. The model originally emanated from the Institutes of Advanced Studies (IAS) such as developed at the Princeton IAS and later also in Europe and Japan. The IAS model was developed to cater for researchers from all university disciplines but perhaps proved especially attractive to the humanities and social sciences. In the 1970s the first humanities centres were established in the United States and, particularly in the last two decades, the global Consortium of Humanities Centers and Institutes (CHCI) has grown to about 180 member institutions. With proliferation the model has changed and many centres now see themselves taking a leading role in certain interdisciplinary fields with an emphasis on grand challenges and teamwork. However, this statement by a director of a humanities and social sciences institute in Asia does capture much of the ethos of such centres:

> *(As7)* I think the most important thing for an institute such as this is to create a social ambience. Create an atmosphere where you can think a lot.

Space is often at a premium in the humanities. Academics most often have an office or cubicle but there is little or no room for meetings and workshops:

> *(NA11)* Literally, we need spaces to have events and meetings. And there is not enough space. Just to get six people in a room is a headache and an energy suck. Partially so busy, so much going on. When something goes on, there's a constant distraction. People feel scattered. Getting people together and especially sustaining meetings over a term – that is the biggest challenge. Getting the same three to four people together on something for a semester is a pain. I'm not sure if that qualifies as infrastructure, but it is a problem of mechanism or something.

In these conditions it is easy to see why a humanities centre may come as a relief, even if it offers no more than what would count as a break out space in a science lab. The availability of such places of refuge is also precarious at times of financial stress:

> *(NA10)* In the last two years, our funding has been very rather dramatically cut. This was part of a set of cuts that all centers and institutes in the College of Liberal Arts underwent. We're located in the College of Liberal Arts, even though we're supported by the university as a whole. In those cuts, we went from being supported by the college to being supported by endowments. We lost a full-time program administrator, which was a huge loss. My only staff right now are hourly employees, mostly students.

The same centre did have its own resources but they had been donated for specific purposes:

> *(NA10)* The endowments were primarily designed to bring visitors to campus, so that has affected our ability to provide the kinds of programming we were able to do in the past. Our funding is primarily restricted gifts. But I think we are in a point where we can start building up again.

Another director reported that in the UK some institutes have a precarious funding position. For instance, two were closed down soon after being established because of the financial crisis. Of those now existing some are required to generate funding through grant applications for projects. The director was, however, optimistic about the future:

> *(E9)* Approximately 50% of our funding comes from an endowment, 50% on an annual basis from the College of Humanities and Social Sciences. The latter has remained relatively stable (though, because it has not increased with inflation, it has declined slightly in real terms). The income from the endowment suffered along with the fall in the stock market after the financial crisis; it has recovered slightly since. There's also a third stream of funding, though it varies greatly from year to year. This is funding from foundations to support particular themes or visiting scholars, e.g. Leverhulme, Carnegie and Mellon. For instance, we got $150,000 from the Mellon Sawyer Seminar scheme recently, to run a series on 'Bringing the Sense back to the Environment' – six day seminars with a public lecture attached to each, followed by a culminating three-day conference. This funding brings out a general and very important fact about

the humanities. For a relatively small sum (e.g. £40,000) we can set up a really significant project (e.g. involving a leading visiting scholar working [at our Institute] for six months, to the benefit of all [national] universities).

It is clear that, while some centres and institutes have been struggling in recent years, others have benefited from targeted funding, coming from either private or government sources. One American director said:

> *(NA1)* We received a $10 million dollar naming gift two years ago. [We're s]upported both by gifts and the university. Recently we received a $775,000 additional Mellon grant to support a three-year university-wide seminar on the topic of violence.

A Japanese director reported on the government-supported programme 'Global Centre for Excellence' in the Humanities, in Japan, which has funded research centres in the last five years:

> *(As8)* The funding was substantial, although my institution also provided supplementary funding for running the programme for them. Basically, it currently has a tendency to shrink but, on the other hand, it is becoming more selective and for those select institutions and organisations they have a chance to get more funding. This means that the Ministry of Education in Japan is trying to give more focused support for key institutions and trying to make them global Centres of Excellence.

The Japanese programme highlights an ambiguity in the support for humanities centres. While most have been established with a view to providing generic support for the humanities and have therefore facilitated individual researchers to pursue their own research interests, there is clearly a tendency for humanities centres to pool faculty resources and to bid for targeted programmes. A UK director put it this way:

> *(A9)* We are now involved in our first ventures into collaborative EU funding bids; this may be the way of the future.

Infrastructure

Humanities centres and institutes highlight the problem of basic support for research, or what may be termed research infrastructure. Of course, the needs differ immensely across disciplines. Many of our interviewees had very simple demands for such support:

> *(NA11)* Office or quiet space. Library with books and Internet access. Computer. We don't need a lot, but that's not so true for people doing visual and sound studies and new media. They need more sophisticated computers. All of these things are available on this campus.

The notion that the humanities are cheap, as in they do not require a lot of infrastructure, was mentioned by several interviewees. One respondent said:

> *(NA7)* Science requires a team of senior investigators and an army of graduates and postgraduates and you need space and expensive equipment. But in the humanities, it's difficult to recruit grants to remove you from teaching. I am on a number of grant evaluating committees, and we have a deliberate policy of trying to weight our provisions for junior faculty because they really need it. I'm taking a sabbatical year next year, which is three years overdue. I need to finish a book, and what I need is time to sit at home in my pajamas and write. We're about to lose our offices that we have right now, and we're moving to a new site, which just has cubicles. But that doesn't bother me too much.

This sentiment was echoed by a Russian scholar who did not identify any special needs:

> *(R2)* Nothing special, actually; every anthropological research is usually done by a single scholar, we do not work in teams as sociologists usually do, so that in this respect we are closer to historians and philologists.

Another respondent identified infrastructure as research time:

> *(NA10)* I think part of the infrastructure of a university has to be regular time to do research. I think that's being questioned, due to a lot of budget cutting. I think universities that can bring in large grants, so it's the lab sciences. I think the humanities are having a hard time establishing the need to do research. There is a feeling that the research can be done on the side in inexpensive ways. But, of course, it takes time and travel. Our university has dramatically improved its

funding for travel, but for the humanities in general there is certainly not enough support. If you look at funding profiles of humanities scholars as opposed to social sciences scholars, there's just much less out there. And if you compare it to the natural sciences, it's even more dramatic.

Often the library is identified as the core support structure:

> *(E14)* In the humanities, the highest cost comes from subscriptions to magazines, journals and reviews (online or not), which tend to be really expensive because of some editors' monopoly. Some disciplines also require special materials, e.g. linguistics, but generally speaking infrastructure costs in the humanities are low, for we do not need laboratories, machines and so on, like in the sciences. We do not have enough rooms for offices because places were built and attributed according to the approximate number of intern ordinary professors (and collaborators); this did not include visiting professors or research fellows, PhD students, etc. It is difficult to deal with this issue and find sustainable solutions. Besides, funds allocated to indirect expenses for infrastructure, maintenance and administration of research projects, which are called overheads, cannot help us to solve this problem.

It is clear, however, that support needs are developing:

> *(NA7)* I needed research assistants to gather data, I needed statisticians, so then you need a team. That's why my RO1 needed $2 million over five years. I would need equipment and I would need to rent space. And that's typical for scientific research and why it needs so much funding.

Another respondent felt that, while digital equipment needs for humanistic research are increasing, the major investment needs are in the collections and repositories:

> *(ME2)* The humanities tend to work with a rather light infrastructure, if any. A desktop and a laptop, some basic software, a scanner and a digital camera are very often sufficient to perform the major tasks of the craft. The weight of infrastructural investment is rather on the side of service rendering institutions, such as libraries and

archival centres. Digitisation, online accessibility, etc. are increasingly becoming necessities in the field. So I would stay that is really where most of the infrastructural needs are concentrated.

An African respondent was clear about the basic infrastructural needs at his university, and the failure to meet them:

(Af1) Fast broadband Internet access, better cameras for field recording, better editing software (Final Cut would do nicely, although it needs outrageously expensive Mac computers. Sigh.) Is there adequate funding for such infrastructure in your institution? What a lovely question! It is my absolutely pleasure to answer an emphatic NO!

African respondents repeatedly lamented the deficiencies of ICT resources and the library:

(Af1) The only online archives we have access to are JSTOR and parts of EBSCO Host. I would give my keyboard for access to SAGE, ProQuest or Project Muse; perhaps chuck in the screen for Wiley, Cambridge, Routledge (I can use a cheap cloned tablet PC to replace the keyboard and screen!). Once in a blue moon though SAGE gives out free journal access for a month to some select titles they probably want to push along. We call it the downloading period! Log in and get whatever you can. It is easier to chuck it later than gnash your teeth about not having it when the opportunity came!

Another respondent was similarly emphatic about whether infrastructure was adequate:

(Af6) NO! This is more so since the neo-liberal policies of the IMF/World Bank in the 1980s that required governments in Africa to reduce their investment in the education sector.... [The needs are:] reliable Internet connectivity (with enough broadband) to allow the trafficking of vast amounts of data; access to working computers for staff; a book allowance to procure books to supplement library resources (e-journals) available at the university; a proper research office whose role is not merely vetting research proposals but one that can fund research; upscaling of training for researchers; leave time to allow academic staff to conduct research.

Another respondent, a historian, similarly pointed to ICT and library deficiencies:

> *(Af7)* My field does not require much infrastructure for researchers to do their work. However, inadequate office space has been affecting the work of researchers because they have to share space. This has tended to lower the morale of researchers. The major challenge for researchers at the university is inadequate ICT facilities. The library too has not been keeping up to date with secondary sources. While the population of undergraduate students and researchers (postgraduate students included) has grown over the years, the library is not growing at the same pace. Secondary material is therefore a challenge to access.

While digital resources may be easily identified as deficient, some respondents felt that the real need may be caused by a legacy of a lack of investment in print books in the past: 'There is an improvement in digital libraries, but mainly where journals are concerned, rather than monographs. The lack of print books is still a barrier to humanities research in Africa' (Af2). An Indian respondent (As1) felt that infrastructure is 'completely inadequate for books, library materials, old manuscripts, private book collections'.

The dependence on Internet resources as a way of overcoming obstacles of distance and a lack of physical resources is apparent in interviews from other continents as well. A Middle Eastern respondent said:

> *(ME3)* Databases of information are available for my kind of research. The Internet is important, as it's very costly to bring people here from other countries. So if you want to collaborate you have to use Skype or speak by phone. But, compared to the rest of the region, [my country] is weak in terms of this sort of infrastructure. Telephone lines are poor and expensive.

In Russia, digital library resources are accessible in leading institutions while many provincial universities are suffering from a lack of access:

> *(R4)* Apparently, one of the kinds of such infrastructure is access to digital libraries and databases; this type of infrastructure exists in both universities I'm working in. Higher School of Economics is one of the few Russian universities which has subscriptions with basic digital journals (JSTOR, MUSE, Taylor & Francis), and databases (Web

of Knowledge, Scopus). Moscow City Pedagogical University has a subscription with Russian digital library system, Knigafond. Both universities give access to these databases to their members. However, Higher School of Economics is funded better and could afford more. This kind of subscription is very much needed in Russia, as normal paper libraries are very poorly supplied with books and magazines.

An academic located in a provincial university confirmed 'there is a problem to access academic journal database that requires institutional subscription' (R5).

One Russian academic felt that travel support is the most urgent need:

(R6) Most universities in provincial Russia act as isolated islands, with researchers well acquainted only with the work of schools of thought and methodology accepted within the micro-community of their department. Thus, grants and travel aid is of utmost importance to overcome this form of alienation. Grants in humanities are usually meted out by the Russian Foundation for the Humanities, with its ever-dwindling budget. For most young researchers in provincial universities, the main issue is being stranded in their research, with little communication with colleagues in different cities and minimal conference exposure (their own institutions either do not support conference visits at all due to lack of funds or are simply not interested in researchers' professional growth since they see them only as teaching automata). A conference trip can be purposefully made Kafkaesque (e.g. a researcher is ready to pay out of her own pocket, but has to sign the same amount of forms anyway, waiving their right for financial support back to the university). A number of academic researchers have got used to relying on foreign grants and/or own sources to finance research trips and conference visits, arranging their short periods of absence at their universities with their superiors. My institution is no exception to this trend. In more innovative aspects of the humanities, such as cultural studies, Russia is starting to witness the rise of the itinerant researcher, who often changes affiliation and earns money through grants and lecture trips.

Corruption is a real problem when it comes to large infrastructure investments in Russia:

(R8) Infrastructure is the easiest way to 'assimilate resources' [Russian idiomatic expression used to identify semi-corrupt or almost

non-corrupt ways to spend extra funds allocated to governmental institutions]. That's why in terms of infrastructure governmental universities such as ... are in a much better position.

Digital technologies may be seen by many humanistic scholars as simply a question of increasing accessibility to resources, but others identified real changes to their own methods of work:

> *(Af3)* Digitisation is significantly changing research practices. There is now much greater access to resources, it is easier to analyse data using both qualitative and quantitative packages, and referencing has become much more straightforward with access to tools like EndNote. Digital tools have also made consultation easier, and benefited peer review and the reporting process to research communities and individual academics.

With the increasing emphasis on digital resources, there may be an increasing need for training. While most did not identify digital competency as a problem, some identified it as a major issue for academic staff. A respondent from an organisation working to improve research systems and infrastructure in African and other countries identified a need for training as much as for physical infrastructure. He had reviewed a number of universities in Africa, where there had been philanthropic initiatives to create online journal access and found that the resources were much less used than expected.

> This was a cross-disciplinary study, but with sizeable humanities participation. There's a huge question around information/digital literacy. Academic teachers are not inducting their students in how to navigate online journals (or encouraging and expecting them to look at online journals in the first place). There's a lack of familiarity with both sources, physical and online journals and how to navigate them. When you haven't had access to the physical journal, but do have online resources, you treat articles as fragments (by using Google to search for them), rather than as contextualised in journals, i.e. as episodes in a long-running debate. This isn't an African issue, the same would probably be true of a student entering HE in recent years, when everything was online. My overall point is that, where online resources are concerned, there's a difference between their availability and the ability to search, find, navigate them. There are quite a number of African universities creating institutional

repositories, but there don't seem to be many projects about creating online repositories of research materials within or across disciplines, countries (in the humanities) (Af2).

As the respondent states, the concern with the lack of digital competencies is not restricted to one continent, although an African colleague made the same comment:

(Af3) In addition to e-journals, I make use of e-books and electronic teaching and training materials. Researchers do not always have the necessary skills to make use of these resources however. Many do not have the skills to operate resources like digital libraries and electronic packages, and many of these are not easily available.

An American respondent saw a need encompassing the entire ICT field:

(NA3) What we need: 1) human resources; 2) software/other platforms; 3) hardware resources. Humans with the knowledge, training, imagination. We need the programming and platforms. We need the hardware, in all senses, to carry out our work. When you think of a big project like the MLA commons, we have a grant from the Mellon Foundation (the Mellon foundation is ahead of the curve on digital humanities, the NEH as well). I think we have some excellent infrastructure in the form of these two offices in particular. But it's a drop in the bucket compared with what the scientists have access to from the NSF and NIH. Support isn't spread evenly. Grants from the NEH and Mellon are seed money for projects that will eventually be self-supporting. Considering the decreased budgets of schools, it's very hard to sustain these projects that take a great deal of money; to fund things like software engineers and human resources to create and curate these materials. Great deal of interest in preserving in a sustainable way to fund what we're creating. There is funding to make things possible, but not from sustainable resources. Most humanities don't have full access to the pie. Unless they are a revenue generator, the projects are difficult to sustain.

For certain disciplines the change of practice and needs were very evident:

(As2) Film studies ideally need good screening equipment, tools for creating images as well as for dissecting them, etc. My institution,

being public funded and based in an economically disadvantaged place, finds it too difficult to get adequate resources.

Other disciplines, however, have also changed in perceptible ways, which may also call for a restructuring of budgets:

> *(Au1)* Classicists have been well to the fore in the use of digitisation and other kinds of technology. In the US especially, a lot of money has been going into infrastructure to support classical projects. This ought to lead to savings elsewhere (e.g. fewer borrowable copies of books are needed in libraries). As the example of multispectral imaging shows, special equipment for working on material remains of antiquity can be very useful.

Archaeology is another discipline that is experiencing increasing needs for infrastructure:

> *(NA8)* Obviously, for archaeologists you need all kinds of other things: support for in field; particularly if you're working in other countries, you need permits and support from other governments. So in a field like that, there is a substantial need for, so-called, infrastructure.

An African archaeologist identified a lack of basic tools to do the work:

> *(Af5)* Not adequate funding for infrastructure, such as trowels, spirit levels, strings, ropes, plumb bobs, buckets, global positioning system (GPS) sets, ground penetrating radars (GPR), metal detectors, magnetometer, total stations, light microscopes, computers (both laptops and desktops), 4WD vehicles, camping gear, etc.

In conclusion, while the evidence of the interviews indicates that many humanists still identify basic needs such as office space, personal computer equipment and access to the physical and digital resources of a library or other repository as the essential requirements of infrastructure, there is a growing demand voiced by others. The demand stems in part from new technologies, which are being put to use in traditional humanistic disciplines and they stem from the fact that teamwork generates new demands for support structures and communication. The awareness of rising opportunities, thanks to new infrastructural facilities, will probably inspire humanist researchers to raise new questions and stage new types of research, for instance historians carrying out agricultural experimental studies. A positive loop may follow: new technologies, new questions, a quest for another renewal of technologies, and so on. To the question of whether there was adequate infrastructure in place one respondent answered:

> *(NA5)* Of course not. We produce a lot of research, but we could do more. For example, most faculty do not have anyone helping them write grants. Other universities hire grant writers. We don't have much in the way of research assistants, unless a department has a doctoral programme, and only five departments in the school have doctoral programmes. Within the doctoral programmes, faculty might have research assistants, or not. Don't have work study, but we have something better, undergraduate research opportunities. Working in a lab instead. The idea is that they are actually working on research with faculty. Students really love it, internal internship either paid or for credit. In the humanities [it is] a little harder to understand what that would look like (Xeroxing or running errands). We don't have anyone helping with the low-end stuff, and we haven't figured out how to use the mid-level stuff.

Another respondent similarly pointed to a change in work practices that will end the days when the humanities could be called cheap:

> *(NA6)* We are beyond the era in which all you need is your workstation and researchers sit alone by themselves. We are in the era in which we now need to seek, for example, start-up packages for hiring and retention. We need more interesting start-up packages that include not just ordinary technologies for individuals, but those that serve both original research and collaborative research. We need state of the art web conferencing and scanning. We need a whole fleet of project-scale technologies. The funding is inadequate at most campuses.... There are many scholars in this nation and elsewhere, at small liberal arts colleges or community colleges and second or third tier universities who are eager to do research but they just don't have R-1 infrastructure. The infrastructure issue is not at R-1 level, but anything below, the vast majority of institutions in the US and elsewhere.

Conclusion

The voices of the interviewees represent a broad spectrum of personal perceptions and interpretations by humanistic scholars about their own workplace. It is striking that, although the financial concerns of recent years have impacted some badly, the vast majority have not experienced major changes. It is clear that a sea change is taking place in countries like China and some Latin American countries, with rapidly increasing investment in the humanities. Because of the large number of universities and their ambitions to aim for the top, the world of humanities institutions is going to change markedly in coming years.

We identified two major financial models for the humanities: a North American model, which has a focus on individual research supported by major endowments and tuition fees and is often facilitated by sabbatical programmes housed at humanities centres; and a European model, which emphasises competitive funding streams that encourage the formation of large research teams. A general striving for excellence tends to concentrate more money in top institutions both in east Asia, North America and Europe. The digital revolution of the last 20 years has facilitated access on a global scale to key resources, but access is still very uneven across continents, and African humanities in particular suffer from a history of deprived institutions. Problems of corruption and the conservatism of governing structures are said to impact humanities research in some BRIC countries, despite sometimes rapid growth.

Our interviews bring out clearly that globalised access to libraries and databases is the main desideratum by researchers on any continent and that digital platforms – although far from perfect and certainly not available in equal measure – are creating new possibilities of communication, knowledge sharing and collaboration.

If the digital transformation is very much a process that is working its way through humanities institutions, pressures of budget models are reshaping humanities institutions from without. We have identified two main budgetary models, the American and the European, and while mixes of the two certainly exist and other models may be developing, we believe it is generally fair to say that the two models are driving the humanities in opposite directions. On the one hand, there is the world of the tenured American professor, who is essentially free to pursue individual research interests, whose main source of research support must be sought within the institution – except for occasional sabbatical fellowships at a humanities centre or archive. While academic freedom is maximised at the American university, the humanist is restricted by the fortunes of the institution as endowments and tuitions are influenced by the market. The European model, on the other hand, depends on the willingness of the taxpayer to invest in research and, while the state provides a core grant to the institution, the enterprising academic is encouraged to apply for large grants for teams to address grand research challenges.

The two funding models have created two very different academic structures: the American humanities centre which essentially provides research space for visiting scholars and engages in public lecture programmes; and the European research centre, through which a small number of faculty promotes a targeted research agenda with a host of postdoctoral and graduate students. Between the two extremes, blends of both do occur.

So, are academic institutions fit for the 21st century in terms of budgets and infrastructure? If we had had the resources and access to information, it would have been interesting, for example, to study a large number of academic biographies to see if they reveal specific institutional structures that have been conducive to high-quality research. As it is, however, we have had to take the simpler approach of asking researchers for their impressions. Looking back at these interviews, the overall problem is one of inequality. At the end of the day, access to information, collaboration, and indeed computation, is determined by budget rather than academic excellence. The humanities are not a level playing field.

Except where otherwise noted, this work is licensed under a Creative Commons Attribution 3.0 Unported License. To view a copy of this license, visit http://creativecommons.org/licenses/by/3.0/

OPEN

8
Humanities and Public Policy

This chapter deals with the interaction of the humanities with the political system. How do humanities representatives argue the case for the humanities, and what do political systems expect of the humanities? We shall examine various policy documents, such as national reports and international research programmes designed by non-academic bodies. The aim is to identify how humanities' interests are being voiced and promoted and what the regional characteristics of the public role of the humanities are. We concentrate on US and EU cases specifically but will make some observations on other regions for contrast. The information for US, EU, China and India is drawn from our own desk research, while information for other regions is based on country reports for the EU METRIS project.

Political processes involve many actors and motives. We do not pretend to present in-depth analyses but simply identify some of the main advocates for humanities funding, and evaluate the political take up as expressed by budgets (given that funding levels may be a better proxy of goodwill than stated intentions). This chapter pays special attention to humanities policies in Europe as the EU and a few national governments combined provide by far the largest public funds for humanities research globally. As most of these funds are open to non-EU citizens they attract worldwide attention. This chapter raises questions of the *quid pro quo* when the humanities engage with societal concerns. The potential benefits of increased funding may come with questions about the independence of the research.

The United States

Generally, American universities are funded by a mix of student fees, endowments and state funding. In addition, researchers rely on public and private foundations for competitive grants. Public funding – federal and state – is generally much lower than in most other countries in the world, and humanities public policy is therefore also quite different from most other countries. We limit ourselves to a discussion of the role of federal funding as individual states may differ very much in their support of universities. It should be noted that while most states have shrunk their funding of the university sector considerably, states like California, New York and Michigan still make substantial funds available to the sector and indirectly to humanities research.

The main US public foundations for research, the National Science Foundation (NSF) and the National Institute for Health (NIH), by and large do not fund humanities research. It may throw some light on the political expectation of the usefulness of the humanities to consider the vote by Congress in March 2013 to limit funding for political science in the budget of the National Science Foundation (NSF). In the language of Senator Coburn who proposed the amendment, this was to 'prevent wasting federal resources on political science projects, unless the NSF Director certifies projects are vital to national security or the economic interests of the country'.[1] The Senate carried the amendment without opposition. We have found no recent direct policy statement on the role of the humanities in and for society. Considering the enormous soft power of American culture this may be seen as an anomaly but it probably simply reflects the fact that private enterprises in the global market have promoted American culture unchallenged since the Second World War. It is also important to note that in the USA elite universities are well-endowed and private foundations play a large role in supporting humanities research. Most public resources are directed to, so-called, STEM research (science, technology, engineering, and mathematics), whereas very little money is funneled to the humanities.

In light of this, it may be understandable that the US National Endowment for the Humanities (NEH) couches its budget request to Congress in very defensive terms: 'While many still think of humanities research as a dusty, unchanging, and solitary endeavor – the lone scholar ardently sifting through archives and libraries – scholarly research in the 21st century is dynamic. It is grounded in traditional scholarly methods and best practices, but informed by international networks of scholars and enhanced by new methods of accessing vital documents.' The NEH avoids talking about the role of the humanities in society except in very broad terms. Its mission is summed up in this way on its website homepage: 'Because democracy demands wisdom, NEH serves and strengthens our republic by promoting excellence in the humanities and conveying the lessons of history to all Americans.' The NEH Strategic Plan 2013–17 identifies its role as to serve and strengthen 'our nation by supporting high quality projects and programmes in the humanities and by making the humanities available to all Americans.' The NEH budget request argues 'Many NEH-supported projects have direct relevance to current events', and in support of this claim lists books on the Taliban, the Darfur crisis, financial history and global power balance. It further argues that there is a strong public interest in American culture and the Civil War, serviced by NEH-funded books. The books singled out for mention tend to address themes of contemporary topical interest in the American news media.

The NEH's annual budget of around 150 million USD amounts to probably around 0.45% of the federal research budget.[2] The budget of the NEH waxes and wanes as congressional majorities change, and the Republican Party has, at times, attempted to abolish the funding altogether, most clearly in 1998.[3] The NEH budget is divided between eight grant-making offices, only one of which directly funds research with an allocation in 2012 of 14.5 million USD. Most of the rest of NEH funding goes to community college programmes, teacher support, outreach and infrastructural programmes, which may include some research funding.[4] In total, we would estimate that, at best, some 25 million USD funds direct research. It should be mentioned that 80% of awardees report that the NEH award enables them to leverage additional support from their employers or another funder.

The NEH primarily funds 'research by individual scholars (fellowships, summer stipends, documenting endangered languages, and awards for faculty); long-term, complex projects carried out by teams of scholars (scholarly editions and translations and collaborative research); and focused, individual projects that draw upon the collections and expertise of leading humanities institutions and overseas research centers (Fellowship Programs at Independent Research Institutions)'. The NEH does have a budget line for collaborative research but the funds are small. The fellowship programmes would mostly be in support of multiple individual scholars. In 2012 the NEH carried out a full-scale evaluation of the long-term outcome of awards made from 2002 through 2004. Over 96% of the awards resulted in a publication and 70% in a book. Although the NEH flags its support for new work models the funding seems overwhelmingly to be in support of individual scholars writing a book.

While the NEH is reluctant to engage in direct public advocacy of the usefulness of the humanities to society except in the broad terms indicated above, more explicit statements are made in the 2013 report for the American Association for the Advancement of Arts and Science, *The Heart of the Matter*. The report particularly underlines the value of the humanities for American society and security. The humanities (and social sciences) are said to be a 'source of national memory'. They 'remind us where we have been and help us envision where we are going',[5] they guide us to respect 'communalities and differences' between people of the world,[6] and '... they help us understand what it means to be human and connects us with our global community'.[7] All these specific assets should be employed in order to make competent, self-fulfilling and independent citizens of people, reach out to citizens, integrate with other fields of research and respond to the grand challenges. Humanist scholars are encouraged to respond positively, both to challenges common to humankind in general, such as clean air and water, food, health, energy, universal education, human rights and physical safety,[8] and to specific national ones, such as US war missions and the preservation of its leadership in the world.[9] Basically, it is stated, everything 'scholars do to connect with the broader public advances their case for support, and everything they neglect to do weakens that case'.[10] The report emphasises the importance of the humanities to understand 'foreign histories, social constructs, belief systems, languages and cultures' for providing 'experts in national security, equipped with the cultural understanding, knowledge of social dynamics, and language proficiency to lead our foreign service and military through complex global conflicts'.[11]

In conclusion, the American funding system reflects a perception of the humanities as detached from direct importance to ongoing political concerns. The NEH emphasis on the role of wisdom as the main contribution by humanities to society is interesting. Although some humanities advocates identify an applied use of some humanities knowledge in strengthening homeland security, the underlying impression is one of a disconnection between the humanities and society, agreed by both parties.

China

In China there seems to be increasing political interest in the humanities. As noted in previous chapters funding is increasing, there is a strong interest in building networks and inviting scholars from abroad, and leading universities are developing humanities programmes fast. We have not conducted an in-depth study of the Chinese policy behind these developments but, in addition to growing student interest, there is no doubt that there is increased high-level political interest in the field. We are not aware of any open policy documents but impressions from visits by the authors to the country leave a sense that there are both economic and political values in play. The economic value of the humanities seems to be related to a sense that future growth will depend not only on technological progress and the availability of labour but also on well-educated professionals with sophisticated taste and an ability to overcome cultural and linguistic barriers. In this respect Chinese politicians seem to realise that there is a need to invest in human cultural capital as a means to sustain future growth. A second impetus for increased investment in the humanities is Chinese foreign policy, which includes a focus on soft power. The remarkable establishment of more than a hundred Confucius Institutes in major cities and universities across the globe is an indication of the priority put on developing an understanding of China's role in the world by sustaining cultural interaction. Western intellectuals have criticised the Confucius Institutes as vehicles for an antidemocratic regime and some potential host universities have declined an offer to establish an institute. In this respect, the positive development of the humanities in China comes with very real concerns about issues of free speech and thought.

South Africa and Australia

In South Africa and Australia the humanities seem to have a recognised societal importance, which is not however fully developed and in recent years may even have diminished. A public policy report on the humanities in South Africa stands out for stressing the importance of the humanities to social cohesion. The report claimed that societal problems of national concern, such as 'violence, corruption, innovation, the gap between rich and poor, the issue of race' all have 'their solutions...in the Humanities'.[12] It is also stated that the humanities, dealing with 'human communication', tell 'us who we are' and teach us 'to see other ways of seeing', as in the social value of tolerance towards others.[13] Knowledge about interlocutors from different cultures gained in anthropology, sociology and cultural studies, is put into practical use in diplomacy, journalism, teaching and so on,[14] proving the social value of the humanities (in this case very broadly defined to include parts of the social sciences). The South African report also pointed out that the humanities build bridges between past and present, particularly referring to archaeology research.[15] In contrast, the economic value of the humanities, or rather policy makers' stress on economic growth, was not only downplayed but thoroughly criticised for being narrowly utilitarian; instead of building community, this goal has atomised society, bringing with it a series of problems – global warming, global poverty, global epidemics – which can no longer be managed but will only be solved through the community-centred perspectives championed by the humanities.[16] 'Building community', or the promotion of the common good, is seen as the very essence of the mission of the humanities.[17]

The South African report is striking, not only for claiming a societal role for the humanities but also by being critical of the current paucity of society's expectations of the humanities. The report stated that, originally, the humanities were thought of as *'interpreters* (facilitating an understanding of social process and social innovation), *change agents* (facilitating technological change), *generators of policy, critics and producers of knowledge*, and finally as *educators*...', but current use has narrowed their role down to being just 'handmaidens of innovation activities initiated in other science domains'.[18] According to the report, there are no longer any references to the humanities making scientific contributions 'in their own right'.[19] In turn, this has meant a declining support of the humanities in relation to other fields. The report also observed that the post-1994 period of democratic reconstruction, and reorientation of science policy, saw a progressive narrowing of the role of humanities disciplines, a growing instrumentalisation of the humanities in the service of innovation, and a decline in funding and the support base. The report found that this detrimental development for the humanities in the NSI (National System of Innovation) of South Africa may be explained by a lack of serious intellectual engagement with this conceptualisation by academics and researchers, and a lack of humanities' champions in the Department of Science and Technology and the Department of Education to argue their use.[20] We cannot assess these assertions but they do seem to be corroborated by government policy. The National Research Plan of 2009 mentions the humanities only once, as a conditional and auxiliary addendum to research on global human–ecological change.[21]

In Australia questions of aboriginal rights and environmental concerns have given prominence to the humanities. In recent years the Australian Academy of the Humanities (AAH) has submitted five to seven documents annually, advising on issues such as national research priorities, research training, cultural policy, research infrastructure, excellence in research and the future of scholarly publishing.

The AAH is a government-funded independent organisation of some 500 fellows and one of its key roles is to provide 'independent, expert advice to government, industry, the media, cultural organisations and community groups'. The visibility of the humanities does expose it to political counter-attacks, however, and one of the political aims of the new Liberal government, which came to power in 2013, was to abolish federal funding for 'wasteful' and 'ridiculous' humanities research. It publicly highlighted research to be scrapped, such as 'sexuality in Islamic interpretations of reproductive health technologies in Egypt', 'how urban media art can best respond to global climate change' and 'The God of Hegel's Post-Kantian idealism'.[22] The Australian case highlights that political attention may come at a cost.

India, Japan and Latin America

In India and Japan the humanities seem to be low on the political agenda. The India Foundation for the Arts (IFA) provided a report mapping the humanities in 2010.[23] It contrasted the funding position of the social sciences with the humanities and concluded that the humanities in India were not flourishing and were inadequately supported. While the social sciences were better off due to the existence of specialised agencies, corporate interest and project-based funding from the World Bank and other foreign institutions, the humanities relied on government funding by the Indian Council of Historical Research (ICHR) and the Indian Council of Philosophical Research (ICPR). The budget of the ICHR budget was 106 million Rs in 2008–9 and has increased since, while the ICPR reported a declining budget of 63 million Rs in 2009–10. Relative to the size of the academic communities of the country the budgets are very small. According to the IFA report, 'professional philanthropy in the arts and humanities in India is still a nascent area' (p. 27), although clearly growing with the Sir Ratan Tata Trust, which funds some major humanities research centres. The report also stated that funding for literature and languages has 'shrunk considerably' (p. 8). In general, the mapping indicated that the social sciences had taken a privileged place in India, linked to public welfare policies, while the funding for the humanities and their societal role remained limited.

Japan has one of the largest numbers of humanities graduates in the world and new large-scale infrastructures and projects, which specifically address humanities subjects, are underway in geospatial and digital applications. Nevertheless, the humanities do not seem to be called on to address the huge demographic, environmental and economic issues that the country has faced in the last two decades. Science and technology studies are viewed as the best bets for the future.[24]

Relative neglect seems also to be the case in Latin America. In Brazil the National Council of Science and Technology seems to have limited interest in drawing on the social sciences, not to speak of the humanities.[25] The HWR workshop on Latin America did point to questions of social cohesion and religion as areas where the humanities have had a societal impact, not least in Mexico, but overall governments seem little interested in mobilising the humanities for policy advice.

The European Union

In Europe, on the other hand, the language and reality are very different from the American situation, despite the fact that many scholars have close ties across the Atlantic. While the single states of the US have very limited, or non-existent, budgets for the humanities, most of the national states of Europe have significant public humanities budgets. In terms of soft power Europe is not one entity but many national cultures, each with varying takes on the humanities. National research budgets in north west European countries, such as Germany, France, UK, Benelux and the Nordic countries are substantial and far outweigh the importance of the EU contribution to humanities research in these countries, while EU funding is crucial to many southern and eastern countries. The challenges of a communist past in Eastern Europe and the postcolonial realities of countries like the UK, Spain and Portugal also contribute to European diversity and global reach. There are substantial private foundations for the humanities in some countries, such as the Volkswagen Stiftung in Germany, the Leverhulme Foundation in the UK and the Carlsberg Foundation in Denmark. However, relative to the American tradition of private funding, humanities scholars in Europe must look more to the state for funding.

With few exceptions, European countries (EU and non-EU) have research prioritisation plans that identify policy-relevant research topics. Some of these topics explicitly call on the humanities although funding is typically limited relative to science budgets. A review of these national priorities reveal a few top areas as listed in Table 8.1.

Other main areas include topics like behaviour and cognition, democracy, families and lifestyles, while topics like conflict and peace studies, gender, globalisation, migration and international relations are prioritised by only a couple of countries.

Table 8.1 European humanities-relevant national research priorities

Priorities	Number of countries (total 29)
Education, lifelong learning	16
Social cohesion, inequality, poverty	14
Cultural heritage	14
Sustainable development	12
Health	11
Identity, religion, language, multi-culturalism	10

Source: METRIS dashboard, policy priorities. http://www.metrisnet.eu/metris/index.cfm/init/dashboard.

The European Union of 29 countries in 2014 is increasingly a funder and policy maker for the humanities. In principle, research is funded by the nation states, and European funding is only allowed when a case can be made for European added value of joint funding. In accordance with the European Treaty all funding must contribute to European Union aims, primarily economic growth and European integration. The research budget has increased rapidly as knowledge and innovation has been identified as the main competitive factor in the global market. In financial terms the EU budget allocates more money to the humanities than the US, even though comparisons are difficult. The European Parliament votes on the research budget every seven years. Since 2007 the research programme has included support for free, bottom-up research, as proposed by the researchers themselves, and strategic or policy-oriented top-down programmes.

The European Research Council (ERC), which grants the awards for bottom-up free research, acknowledges the humanities as part of the sciences. Significantly, the programme is open to applicants from any country in the world and 17% of its budget goes to the humanities and social sciences, or about 325 million euro per year projected for the seven-year period from 2014 under the new Horizon 2020 programme. Recent practice shows that the money is split equally between the two domains, making some 160 million euro per year available for humanities research. Other 'free' money is made available through the Marie Curie programme for researcher mobility, which funds a substantial number of humanities researchers. Based on past shares, the humanities may expect funding of around 36 million euro per year. The humanities share of the top-down funding stream is much more difficult to estimate. The budget of Social Challenge 6, which will include the bulk

Humanities and Public Policy   169

of targeted humanities research, is unlikely to exceed 50 million euro annually. In addition, some humanities researchers will receive funding as partners of multi-disciplinary teams including the natural sciences and engineering. A rough total estimate of EU funding for bottom-up and top-down humanities research is around 250–80 million euro per year. This would indicate that EU expenditure on humanities research is ten times that of the US federal budget, as calculated above.[26] Still, the humanities share of total EU research funding is only about 2%.

In the EU, the social sciences and humanities are usually treated together as a single SSH field. The inclusion of the humanities is a fairly recent phenomenon as part of a gradual widening of the remit of the EU research budget. It is of interest to study in some detail the development of the humanities policy agenda. In 1994 the European Council decided to launch the Targeted Socio-Economic Research programme to provide evidence-based knowledge for science and technology options, education and social integration.[27] The launch of the Sixth Framework Programme in 2000 inaugurated broader support for social science research. The inclusion of the social sciences encouraged national research councils, primarily in Denmark, the Netherlands and Ireland, to join forces to raise the voice of the humanities. A conference in 2002, 'Humanities – Essential Research for Europe', gathered some sixty representatives of national research councils and academies and agreed a mandate for a European Network of Research Councils for the Humanities (ERCH). The objective of the ERCH was to 'work to strengthen the Humanities in Europe at the political and organisational level' and a declaration identified four action points for the national councils at the European level:

- to stimulate and focus basic research in the humanities, e.g. by doing comparative research
- to develop a European research infrastructure for the humanities
- to increase the role of the humanities in future integrated projects of the European Framework Programme
- to define the role of the humanities in the European Research Area and in particular to identify and build structures to achieve this aim.[28]

The Odense Declaration identified an agenda for the humanities for the next decade. As a direct result, the EU Commission for Research invited the ERCH to apply for matching funds to set up a pilot scheme for humanities funding at the European scale, primarily addressing the first and last of the action points above. In 2005, on receipt of EU funding, the ERCH morphed into HERA (Humanities in the European Research Area), a partnership that now consists of 21 national funding bodies in Europe. To date HERA has launched three thematic calls, mostly funded by the partners but also by a third of the total funding costs paid by the European commission as a part of its ERA-NET initiative to develop the European Research Area as an entity. Two of them were launched simultaneously, one on 'Cultural Dynamics – Inheritance and Identity', the other on 'Humanities as a Source of Creativity and Innovation'.[29] The first was an invitation to humanist scholars across Europe to study 'the way in which cultural exchanges and dynamics cross between social strata, between countries, and between media'. Three topics were outlined, the first about collective 'identities before and after the nation-state', the second on culture 'as self-reflection' and the third cultural 'practices between "high" and "low", local and global, performance and ownership'. The intention of the second call was to generate new knowledge and develop new perspectives on creativity and innovation research. In 2012 a new programme was launched, rather similar to the first one, called 'Cultural Encounters', with a focus on peaceful and conflict-ridden encounters between people from different cultures.[30]

The second action point, infrastructure for the humanities, informed humanities action in ESFRI, the European Strategy Forum on Research Infrastructures. This body was set up by the Commission and the Member States in 2002 to develop a joint strategy for future investments. While ESFRI was not intended to include the humanities, active lobbying secured the inclusion of two important facilities: the Common Language Resources and Technology Infrastructure (CLARIN), with an estimated operational cost of 7.6 million euro per year; and the Digital Research Infrastructure for the Arts and Humanities (DARIAH, 2.4 million euro per year). CLARIN aims to provide easy and sustainable access for scholars in the humanities and social sciences to digital language data (in written, spoken, video or multimodal form) and advanced tools to discover, explore, exploit, annotate, analyse or combine them, independently of where they are located. To this end CLARIN is in the process of building a networked federation of European data repositories, service centres and centres of expertise, with single sign on access for all members of the academic community in all participating countries. DARIAH aims to facilitate long-term access to, and use of, all European arts and humanities digital research data. The DARIAH infrastructure will be a connected network of people, information, tools and methodologies for investigating, exploring and supporting work across the broad spectrum of the digital humanities. Both of these infrastructures are still being built, with a growing number of Member States.

While these developments must be considered a success, the humanities are still struggling for their place in the Framework Programmes. The Seventh Framework Programme 2007–13 (FP7) did call on the humanities for policy advice, but the calls were limited and funding was a fraction of that available for science and technology. Nevertheless FP7 marked a significant recognition of the humanities as part of the knowledge base for policy makers, which has opened up the battle for budgets and action lines in research programmes.

A number of representative bodies and reports have sought to outline how the humanities may turn programmatic intentions of social relevance into reality. In 2007 the Standing Committee for the Humanities at the ESF (European Science Foundation) published a position paper on the nature and importance of the humanities, pointing out the prominent role played by research on 'communicative systems':

> The humanities focus on 'the human element' in the physical, biological, mental, social and cultural aspects of life. They attempt to provide insights into how knowledge arises from the constant interaction between individual and society. When studying culture, the humanities engage not just with its present manifestations, but also with those of the past. All culture comes to us from the past. If traditions, memories and ongoing practices are supplemented and reshaped by individual choices, those in turn are constrained by structural features of the various cognitive and value systems we employ. In this respect we are the product of our past, of the structural properties of our present environment, of our characteristically human capacities such as language, perceptual and communicative systems, and of our bodies.

The document further stressed the significance of the past for contemporary (and future) culture and pointed out the prominent role played by research on 'communicative systems' in physical, biological, mental, social and cultural aspects of life.[31]

Recently, the ESF has been largely replaced by Science Europe as the main association of European funding organisations, and its Committee for the Humanities has developed a focus on the cognitive role of the humanities in society. In its very first statement on societal challenges the Committee singles out 'understanding and influencing behavioural change' as a broad research theme which should be imbedded in all research areas, such as energy consumption, food, health and transport. The Committee also sees a direct economic value of the humanities in understanding and developing innovation ecosystems:

> Technologies are shaped by human involvement and in many cases the human aspects of innovation development and uptake are as challenging as the technological aspects. Design is a crucial aspect in the development of products and services, which is under-researched. This theme would include work on how innovation occurs in different areas of work, why some innovations are successful while others fail, and why some societies are more innovative than others – in short, how do we 'make' innovation?

The Committee further argues that humanities research in innovation will bring out the wider social, political and cultural contexts, 'recognising that the value of innovation should not be measured purely in economic terms'.[32] However, it seems fair to say that, while the 2007 ESF document fitted comfortably with statements by our interviewees of the broad social and cultural value of the humanities, the 2013 Science Europe document is a clear statement of direct economic, social and cultural usefulness. Perhaps it is an indication that with increasing engagement in political processes utilitarian arguments become more important.

Meanwhile, the EU process continued to be informed by internal reports. An expert group on the humanities reported in 2007 on how the humanities might contribute to already defined tasks in FP7 and recommended with some success that the wording in the calls be made 'more humanities friendly'.[33] In 2009 the METRIS report for the Commission highlighted that a lack of data 'is the first impediment to a proper understanding of the evolving role of SSH in society'.[34] An evaluation of SSH research in FP5 and FP6, published in 2010, concluded that EU funding is instrumental in creating a European Research Area both in terms of significantly increasing funding levels and fostering cross-national collaboration and mobility. The report also highlighted the benefits of engaging policy makers with ongoing research. However, policy makers found 'that researchers in social sciences in their countries collaborate more than researchers in the humanities. Research in the humanities was perceived as having a national focus, and collaboration with researchers abroad is, if at all, only carried out with those in neighbouring countries.' Policy makers reported that there is little formal engagement between researchers and policy makers. In general, the need for research stated by most national authorities

> ... seems to be on information and data on current issues which are often high on the agenda of those Ministries dealing with public finances. For example, gauging the state of the economy or understanding the issues affecting employment. Many policy makers interviewed acknowledged that there was potential and good rationale for using SSH research in this context. More specifically, policy makers in the Eastern European Member States explained the need for SSH research to assess the impacts on changes in society and lifestyles of citizens. Specific examples of this included examining the options and choices for the development of a knowledge-based society and the implications of European integration and enlargement for governance and citizens.[35]

In 2011 the Commissioner for Research and Innovation announced that the next Framework Programme, Horizon 2020, to be launched in 2014, would not have a specific grand challenge for the SSH and that instead they would be 'mainstreamed across research challenges of climate change, energy, food, health, security and transport'. Broad segments of the SSH community saw the announcement as a threat that SSH research would only become a fig leaf or an add-on to science- and technology-driven research. For the first time a broad coalition of SSH organisations joined forces in a European Alliance for the Social Sciences and Humanities, EASSH, and drafted an open letter to the Commissioner. More than 25,000 SSH researchers signed the letter, arguing that:

> While for many questions, natural, human and social sciences need to join forces, there are also important societal and economic transformations, which can be described as Social Sciences and Humanities (SSH)-centred challenges: they regard areas as diverse as education, gender, identity, intercultural dialogue, media, security, social innovation, to name but a few. Similarly, only SSH research can address many of the key behavioural changes and cultural developments which provide the backdrop to the EU's current approach to 'Tackling Grand Societal Challenges', such as for example changing mindsets and lifestyles, models for resilient and adaptive institutions, or the evolving position of Europe in a global context.[36]

The Commission did change tack and promised to include a sixth challenge. In May 2012 the Council of Ministers for Research decided to include, as a societal challenge, 'Europe in a changing world: Inclusive, innovative and reflective societies', which 'will support social sciences and humanities research'. In addition, the Ministers confirmed that the humanities and social sciences should be mainstreamed across all the grand challenges of Horizon 2020.[37] At the time this seemed like a significant victory for the SSH action but subsequent developments showed that the European decision-making process is often opaque. The positive wording in Horizon 2020 on the value of the humanities and social sciences may be little more than window- dressing. It is clear that the promise of 'mainstreaming' does not ensure anything but ornamental additions to science projects. When the work programme for the sixth challenge, 'Europe in a changing world: inclusive, innovative and reflective societies', was launched in December 2013 it was clear that the budget would be quite small, in the region of 400 million euro, while other challenges would be allocated several billion euro each. However, the Commissioner was very clear in her call on the humanities:

> Europe is still facing many long-term and complex challenges. It takes profound knowledge and insight to really understand these challenges and how they affect us, and to guide us to solutions. That is why the social sciences and humanities are more essential than ever, and why we, as policy makers, are keen to have their contribution. We need them to understand ourselves, our society and the challenges we face. We need them to guide politicians and policy makers and to inform public opinion. Research and technology provide many answers to the challenges we face, but technological fixes alone aren't enough to solve our major, complex problems. A knowledge society needs to know itself, and the social sciences and humanities are the keys to this.[38]

On a global scale the European Union is a unique expression of a political system calling on the SSH for policy advice while also allocating substantial funds for bottom-up research funding. In the last 10–15 years humanists in Europe have engaged in political processes to argue the societal importance of their research and they have had some success in developing an agenda and a legitimate role for the humanities at negotiating tables. It is notable that EU programmes will now call on the humanities to contribute insights into major societal challenges such as health, climate, food and transport. On the other hand, it is clear that, despite some political goodwill, there is considerable resistance or lack of appreciation at many political and bureaucratic levels. The actual wording of work programmes and calls for funding is a battle ground that is still very often held by technocrats who have little appreciation of humanities research. While the humanities now have several important organisational voices, the European process requires follow-up and lobbying, which is still beyond the capacity of the humanities.

Conclusion: the politics of the humanities

The humanities have a unique position in global politics. On the one hand, many politicians increasingly recognise that at the heart of all the grand challenges of the 21st century are questions of human motivation, behaviour and choice. On the other hand, the academic disciplines that wholeheartedly focus on the human are rarely, if ever, called on to inform the political system. Evidently, in many corners of the world the humanities are exposed to certain societal expectations, even if they are not as great many humanists would wish and, in some places, they are far too low. It is also obvious that the humanities deal with themes of high demand, such as cultural identity and heritage, and that this is also what many humanist scholars think they should be dealing with. To be sure, there is still a mismatch between supply and demand. Yet, it appears to be more a matter of quantity (i.e. scarcity of funding) than of quality (i.e. topics addressed).

The humanities cannot expect this situation to change without action. In the EU the humanities have benefited from a close alliance with the social sciences and from a sustained lobbying process, which has included a large number of actors. On a global scale, the EU's recognition of the humanities is unique, expressed in terms of financial support for basic and targeted research and infrastructure, and the words of support from the political side provides a strong contrast to its neglect in the United States and many other countries. In countries like South Africa and Australia, on the other hand, political attention to the humanities has not been without a cost, and the new embrace of the humanities by the Chinese authorities potentially raises ethical problems and questions of freedom of research that may carry a global lesson.

Critics of the rapprochement of the humanities to grand challenge social, political and cultural issues observe that the humanities may lose their way by becoming too utilitarian or embroiled in political expediency. Indeed, the differences between the European and American humanities seem to us to be widening as a result of this process. The American focus on traditional humanities' virtues, such as individualism and book publication, is clearly at odds with a European culture that is increasingly project-funded, goal-oriented and aimed at peer-reviewed journal publication. Critics may see the European way as a Faustian deal. The critique that has been voiced against current research policy in Europe and elsewhere most often concerns the deliberate commodification and commercialisation of scientific research – though, paradoxically, this policy is not pursued in the spirit of the free market, but goes hand in hand with the audit society, with a strong emphasis on planning and control.[39] One of the harmful outcomes of this policy is a transformation of scientific researchers into experts, better suited for an R&D department in a big company than for academia.[40] In order to serve human interests in the broad sense, professionals 'should not have values regarding the development of society; they should not be political', as stated by one critic of research policy.[41] One way of avoiding value bias in research is to keep a certain distance between researchers and those who expect scientific results to be in line with their ideologies or interests. This means that the research community should not get too involved with stakeholders outside academia; nor should it let them interfere with the scientific choice of themes and methods to be applied. Such at least is the view of some critics of current research policy trends in many countries.[42]

On the other hand, a more positive view would see a culture change as a way to revitalise the humanities. In the autumn of 2013, Helga Nowotny, President of the European Research Council, commented on the contrast between the EU and the US in political attitude to the SSH:

> Under its new EU research programme, *Horizon 2020*, the importance of the social sciences and humanities has been formally recognized...More than €28bn is being allocated to tackle societal challenges, including energy efficiency, climate change, health, ageing, security, privacy issues and digitization.... It is obvious that the social science and humanities have a lot to contribute to each of these agendas, and the EU's integrative approach is laudable...the Horizon 2020 programme reflects a strikingly different approach to developments across the Atlantic. In the United States, the social sciences and humanities are under attack. In Europe we are committed to integrating the natural sciences, engineering, and social sciences and humanities...[43]

Similarly positive is the 'Vilnius declaration', conveyed by a consortium of European humanists and social scientists at an EU conference in Vilnius in September 2013. The declaration stresses the importance, significance and even the indispensability of the humanities for addressing profound current societal challenges and applauds the mainstreaming of the humanities across all six priorities of Horizon 2020:

> European Social Sciences and Humanities are world class, especially considering their diversity. They are indispensable in generating knowledge about the dynamic changes in human values, identities and citizenship that transform our societies. They are engaged in research, design and transfer of practical solutions for a better and sustainable functioning of democracy. Their integration into Horizon 2020 offers a unique opportunity to broaden our understanding of innovation, realigning science with ongoing changes in the ways in which society operates.

Furthermore, the Vilnius declaration supports assessment of impact as one of the basic quality criteria of good science, although it is not made perfectly clear whether such assessment is to be one of the criteria for the allocation of research resources, or if it is a *post festum* measure to find out if research results are disseminated and implemented.[44]

So, looking at policy developments in the EU and comparing them to the US, we might find some cause for optimism, even a model for other regions to follow. But, as we saw above, these same developments have their critics. As the authors of this report, where do we stand? The more positive view – in favour of greater engagement between humanists and policy makers – fits well with some of our findings in Chapter 2, where over half of our interviewees identified 'social value' as the most important extrinsic justification for the humanities, defined as a broad concept ranging from moral values to informing social decision-making and contributing to or contesting social cohesion. Another very frequently stressed value was 'cultural heritage', implying the preservation and critical evaluation of material as well as immaterial leftovers of the past. We also saw in Chapter 3 that much humanities research genuinely engages with the social in terms of the themes selected for study.

But there are at least two problems with which we should close. First, in this chapter we have also seen that some policy makers take a much narrower view of the contribution (if any) that the humanities have to make, particularly in promoting economic growth and innovation. The problem is that, as we saw in cChapter 2, our interviewees rarely identified such values and showed very little appetite for seeing them as a goal for humanities research. So, whenever the more narrow-minded policy makers have the upper hand, there will be a serious rift with the humanists. Second, even when policy makers take the broader view and stress the sorts of social goals discussed above, there is a danger that humanists will end up making a Faustian pact; so, how far should they allow their research to be guided by the goals and interests of policy makers?

Clearly, humanities politics are not just a question of raising the voice in favour of more funding. There are issues of social and political engagement that to many humanists may seem alien to what they signed up for and alien to academic life. However, the question will not go away and the discussion is vital to both the future of the humanities and how society will benefit from the humanities.

Except where otherwise noted, this work is licensed under a Creative Commons Attribution 3.0 Unported License. To view a copy of this license, visit http://creativecommons.org/licenses/by/3.0/

OPEN

9
Conclusion

In this conclusion we start by giving an overview of the preceding chapters and finish by making some recommendations based on our research.

Overview

Each of the preceding chapters ended with a summary of the main points discussed. The purpose of this overview is not to repeat those summaries, but to draw out some important themes from the report as a whole.

The social dimension of the humanities

The relation between the humanities and society has featured in numerous ways over the last chapters. Here we highlight three of them.

In Chapter 2 we discussed some of the ways in which researchers and others articulate the value of the humanities. Looking through our own interview results, we found an interesting pattern. When answering for themselves, many respondents embraced the intrinsic value of research. But when asked to justify funding for research 'to an impatient and potentially hostile audience', well over half of them talked in terms of social value. Sometimes they were referring to social cohesion, but just as often they talked about the need for the humanities to help make decisions for society, typically about issues thrown up by technological innovation in the STEM subjects. As a close relative of social value, respondents also voted in large numbers for the value of cultural heritage.

Given the terms of our question, this might seem just a matter of rhetoric with respondents not saying what they themselves thought, but what critics wanted to hear. But in Chapter 3 we saw that their interest in the social value of the humanities is matched by responses to the question about what sorts of themes have been dominating humanities research, or might do so in the future. Most respondents mentioned themes that could broadly be called social. So their sense of what is actually going on in their fields, including what is around the corner or what might even be a source of breakthroughs, matches well with what many would publicly use to defend funding for their subjects.

So far, this is about the attitudes of individual researchers. But in the Chapter 8 we considered the views of humanities advocates in national humanities associations alongside the responses of policy makers, as evidenced in funding decisions. The results are very mixed across different countries. The focus of the chapter was on the contrast between the US and the EU. What is currently happening in the EU looks like a developing success story for the humanities, especially in comparison to the bleak state of relations between the NEH and the US Congress. Not only is the level of public funding promised much higher than in the US; the EU Commission appears to be seriously interested in tapping into humanities research in order to inform its social policy – precisely one of the roles for the humanities we discussed in Chapter 2. So it is beginning to look as if we have an alignment between the aspirations of the humanists (Chapter 2), the kinds of topic they tend to work on (Chapter 3) and what is expected and promised by policy makers in one region (Chapter 8). But, on closer scrutiny, the EU experience throws up many questions and difficulties. Will the funding be as generous as promised? Will the vision of policy makers be broad enough and how enlightened will they actually be when it comes to grasping the real, long-term potential of the humanities to inform social decision-making? Will they show an interest in the content of the research, or merely in micro-managing it? Are institutions geared to support and develop research in ways that will stimulate curiosity and collaboration? As for the researchers themselves, they face difficult decisions about how to negotiate their compact with the policy makers, so are they trained in ways that will enable them to grasp opportunities? And, more fundamentally, can they maintain the distance and neutrality essential for good research, while keeping close enough to secure the trust and confidence of the policy makers they seek to advise?

Crossing boundaries

Another set of themes that has emerged over the course of this report concerns the existence of various kinds of boundary and the prospects or desirability of crossing them.

Conclusion   181

Translating the humanities

In Chapter 4 we looked at the ways in which humanities researchers attempt to bring the results of their work, or even conduct their work, outside the traditional boundaries of academia. What we termed translation (borrowing the word from medical practice) can exist in many different forms: working with museums to reach the public; going out to high schools; broadcasting on TV and radio; working with policy makers; and so on. No one can deny that there is a great deal of translation going on, and we gave examples of different types based on our own interviews and on national reports and other sources. But we also identified various obstacles to crossing the divide between the academic and the non-academic. One lies in academic culture itself. All too often translational activities are actually frowned upon by fellow researchers. We found evidence of such attitudes in countries as far apart as China and the Netherlands. In other countries the opposite is the case; in Russia and some parts of Latin America, the role of the public intellectual is alive and well. Indeed, some academics even wish the boundaries were sharper.

But, aside from the attitudes of fellow academics, we found a more systemic problem in academic managers and institutional leaders failing to incentivise such work. It often goes unrewarded and so can inhibit career advancement. Even if it is actually respected, institutions may do little to facilitate the process of translation, and the lone researcher has to act as entrepreneur as well as academic researcher to bring his or her work to a wider audience.

We are also aware of the dangers of encouraging translation in inappropriate ways. For example, we are not suggesting that institutional leaders should henceforth require applicants for project funding to build considerations of end use into the very framing of their proposals. Sometimes this may be appropriate, for instance a museum might commission research that will enable it to organise a particular exhibition for the benefit of the public. But it is often discoveries made in the disinterested pursuit of knowledge that result in the most important translation. So the ways of facilitating translation that we wish academic managers to find may typically come once research is well under way. We need to allow for serendipity; let humanists, like researchers in other fields, pursue their research on grounds of intellectual curiosity, without any explicit or conscious regard for what application or social value it may have. Our interest is in what happens when the results of the research turn out to be of immediate public interest or directly relevant to policy making. It needs to be possible for the researcher to cross academic boundaries and reach other constituencies by established and recognised pathways, without having to do it unaided.

Disciplinary boundaries

The issue of interdisciplinary research has featured in two separate parts of the report. In Chapter 3 we looked over our interview responses to see what patterns, if any, existed when respondents talked about methodological trends in current or future research. More than half our respondents pointed towards cross-fertilisation as being the source of current or emerging research trends. This could involve some kind of intercultural comparison (e.g. comparing different philosophical traditions), but what many respondents had in mind was interdisciplinarity, whether among humanities subjects themselves, or between the humanities and the sciences (social or natural).

Then, in the first part of Chapter 5, we focused directly on interdisciplinary research. As well as reporting our respondents' views as to what it means to be interdisciplinary, and the advantages and disadvantages of such research, we also looked to see what they said about the institutional conditions that might inhibit or promote interdisciplinarity. We found anxieties expressed in quite different parts of the world about the tension between two forces: strategic support for interdisciplinary research and monodisciplinary bias in the criteria for hiring and promotion (especially as mediated by publication requirements). Thus, the academic boundaries that already exist are being reinforced by more general institutional conditions.

The digital humanities: technology versus tradition

In Chapter 6 we turned to the ways in which digitisation is transforming, or not, the humanities. After surveying what is happening globally in the field of the digital humanities, we turned to the attitudes of humanities researchers themselves. We pointed to the existence of blogs and other commentaries by staunch critics of the DH, and then looked at our interview sample to see how they viewed the field. While finding very little hostility, we did find a distinct lack of engagement. It seems that the DH are in danger of developing into their own clique and creating their own disciplinary silo, at the expense of alienating more traditional humanists. Our respondents welcomed the greater accessibility and convenience that digitisation brings, but very few identified the intellectual breakthroughs such technology might bring in its wake. In short, their knowledge of the field was sketchy and their enthusiasm for it quite weak. The development of the DH has, for whatever reasons, helped to create a boundary between technologists and traditionalists. Even if this is not a boundary marked by any great hostility, there is a degree of passive resistance, or at least relative ignorance and indifference on the part of most humanists.

Internationalisation

The last kind of boundary we wish to mention here is that of the nation state. It is no surprise that, traditionally, the humanities have often reflected national perspectives and ideologies (especially given their well-established role in cultural heritage). On the other hand, some scholars have always aspired to cross national boundaries. But the trend towards globalisation has brought the whole issue of crossing nationally imposed (or created) intellectual boundaries to the forefront. In the second half of Chapter 6 we looked at our respondents' attitudes to this phenomenon. One might think that internationalisation can only be good for the humanities. As we saw in Chapter 3, some humanists think cross-cultural comparisons a fertile source of research breakthroughs and something that goes hand in hand with internationalisation, including the building of transnational research teams. Internationalisation is also a good means of building support and morale for researchers in countries where funding is poor or governments may be hostile to their work. This was certainly the message we received from respondents in quite different regions, from Russia to sub-Saharan Africa.

On the other hand, not everyone agreed that breaking down the boundaries is an unqualified benefit. Some complained about the growing homogenisation of research, which this might come about by: the imposition of a single research language (English) on publication and dissemination; or the growth of institutional rankings encouraging researchers around the world to chase after the same publication outlets, leaving the editors of international journals free to impose similar research agendas worldwide. Whether these fears are misplaced is a matter of debate. But, as academia inevitably becomes more global, we need to face up to the question of whether homogenisation will lead to something essential to the humanities being lost?

Another point about national (or regional) boundaries can be drawn from Chapter 7 on funding and infrastructure; that internationalisation tends to benefit stronger partners with abundant financial resources and infrastructure. As infrastructure needs to increase there is a risk of growing inequalities in the potential to do excellent research in underfunded research environments.

Finally, although globalisation tends to bring the world of researchers into dialogue, our interviews left us with an impression of clear regional patterns of research language and research culture. At least three main spheres of dialogue are evident: English language and norms dominate North America, Northern Europe, Australia and large parts of South and East Asia and Africa; French, Spanish and Portuguese languages and traditions dominate Southern Europe, Latin America and parts of Africa; big countries like China and Russia retain their own research cultures and native languages. Global humanities research is still very far from being the norm. Research excellence relies on international collaboration and competition that ultimately must build on mutual intelligibility of methods and a lingua franca. The challenge for the future is to ensure that the diversity of human experience is not lost. A point we shall return to.

The nature of the humanities

In Chapter 3 we looked at the way our interviewees viewed the nature of the humanities. Our own specific interest was in the nature of the humanities as truth seeking academic disciplines.

We found very few of our interviewees resistant to the idea that the humanities seek to advance knowledge. In this respect, they did not drive a wedge between the humanities and the sciences. Many, in fact, were happy to use the term findings to describe the outcome of humanities research. We would now like to develop this issue a little further.

The very concept of research in any domain, that of of *searching*, brings with it the hope of *finding* something, of discovery. If there is no prospect or interest in finding anything, it is entirely natural to ask what the point of any research is. And if there is going to be a process of finding, at least a successful one, it ought to be possible to articulate ways in which our knowledge or understanding of a particular area, object or field has been advanced. In short, we ought to be able to say how we are better off in terms of knowledge than we were before we started the research. This, we claim, follows quite naturally from the very concept of research, whatever the academic field.

Now consider disciplines outside the humanities. Whether in the natural or social sciences, in technology or medicine, researchers do not hesitate to talk about the outcome of their work in terms of discoveries, findings and results. Of course, any scientific finding might have to be revised, but accepting the possibility of revision in the future does not mean that one need be reluctant to talk about progress in terms of knowledge or understanding gained.

So, after looking at the very concept of research and then surveying all other academic disciplines, one might reasonably conclude that the same will apply to the humanities. Why should the humanities be different in this regard? If one insists that they are, one would have to explain what it is about the nature of their objective that might lead to a difference. When we study the human, or the human condition, or human culture, decision-making, ideas, texts, and so on why should it be that we are suddenly unable to produce findings and advance knowledge? Is the nature of these topics so much more intractable than, for instance, distant galaxies, mathematical proofs or long-extinct species? As authors of this report we would find this anomaly, if it does exist, quite baffling and it seems our respondents, on the whole, agree.

We would go further, or at least be more explicit. We view the humanities, no less than the other sciences, as truth seeking. Although we only discussed this issue explicitly in Chapter 3, it is strongly related to the two broader issues we have been discussing in this conclusion. First, those who try to split the humanities from the sciences in the ways described are in effect creating yet another kind of boundary to be negotiated. In our view this boundary is fictitious, not to say unhelpful. There are better ways of making distinctions between academic disciplines, which cut across the humanities/sciences division, for instance: some areas of philosophy, with their particular focus on proof, have much in common with mathematics; historians, archaeologists, geologists, astronomers study the past; engineers and students of the arts engage in the creative manipulation of materials for problem-solving. So there are different and quite subtle ways of thinking about the similarities and dissimilarities between academic disciplines that would avoid us making wrong-headed assumptions about our identity as humanists.

Second, the issue about the nature of the humanities connects with the relation between the humanities and society. As we have just argued, the model of research as essentially concerned with advancing knowledge is deeply intuitive, so that the public and policy makers will most likely endorse it and expect researchers to be concerned about making new gains in knowledge and understanding. Yet, if some humanists dispute the model for their own fields, how will they then present themselves to society? What account will they give of themselves to justify their support, and more generally, their value? Admittedly, they will have no problem expressing the value of the humanities in terms of critical thinking, but other values will be deeply problematic, like how are they supposed to inform social decision-making if they don't actually advance knowledge? Now, humanists who genuinely reject the truth seeking model are entitled to do so. But it is hardly a choice to be taken lightly and it needs to be defended rigorously, not assumed as a dogma. And the consequences of taking this view of the social standing of the humanities need to be thought through carefully and consistently.

Like many humanists, we are concerned about the low social esteem in which our subjects are often held (a point discussed at the end of Chapter 3). Part of the reason for this low esteem may lie in the fact that humanities disciplines cannot hold up obvious examples of utility as easily as, say, medicine and engineering. But we also think that the unfounded (or at least uncritical) rejection of the humanities as disciplines that advance knowledge creates a serious problem for public esteem. Thus, we welcome the fact that most of our interviewees were prepared to talk of humanities research in terms of advances in knowledge and understanding.

Recommendations

In closing, we offer some more extended thoughts as to what might be done to address the challenges to the humanities as we see them. We start with some specific recommendations, which follow quite straightforwardly from the preceding chapters. We then turn to some broader considerations about the future of the humanities.

Specific recommendations

The nature of the humanities

Following on from the previous section, we recommend that we reinstate confidence in the humanities as truth finding disciplines, through which we can claim to advance knowledge while being fully aware of the contingent character of our results. Certainly, we need to communicate that much of our work involves talking around a phenomenon, expanding on context and criticising assumptions, as in all fields of research. Still, we do seek and find truths; we do generate answers, as well as questions. We should be prepared to insist that, in this respect, the humanities do not differ from other academic disciplines.

Translation

We have found that there is currently insufficient support for researchers who want to bring their work to a wider audience, or work with stakeholders outside academia. All too often these researchers end up being lone actors, having to play too many roles at once, and their labours are not adequately recognised even when they succeed. We recommend that institutional leaders think more clearly and practically about support systems for effective translation and create real incentives to encourage more academics to engage in it.

The digital humanities

In Chapter 4, we found evidence of a culture gap between traditional humanists and experts in the digital humanities. This gap urgently needs to be bridged. One initiative might be taken by DH experts to start the process of bridge-building. We believe it would be useful to highlight – in terms that will resonate with the traditionalists – several case studies illustrating the *intellectual* power and potential of the DH: how have they thrown up radically new research questions or new ways of thinking about old ones? How are they more than just a means of making research materials more readily accessible? These were exactly the questions we found many of our respondents unable to answer. A second initiative may be for funders and universities to consider how successfully we are training the next generation of humanists to exploit the potential of digital technologies and methods. Are doctoral supervisors only too happy to see well-known methods used by young researchers or are they actively encouraging the use of these new approaches?

Interdisciplinary research

The quest for interdisciplinarity should not be treated as an end in itself, either by researchers or by research funding authorities and policy makers. The most important thing is to ask good questions, sometimes requiring an interdisciplinary effort, sometimes not. However, there is no doubt that interdisciplinarity does have considerable value in numerous contexts and many of our interview respondents reported genuine enthusiasm for it. At the same time it faces significant institutional barriers. Where these exist they should be seriously addressed. In particular, we recommend that promotion criteria are reformed so as to give due weight to interdisciplinary research, in such a way that it no longer appears risky in terms of publication and career advancement.

Humanities and public policy

In Chapter 8 we paid special attention to developments in the EU regarding humanities policy. There is the potential for substantial increases in project funding, as well as a reported willingness on the part of EU leaders to seek advice from the humanities on policy matters. Alongside the opportunities, however, there are challenges: will the humanities succeed in achieving significant funding increases, and how will they keep an appropriate academic distance from those they advise? Will funders understand the importance of investing in research on long-term human challenges? We recommend that these developments be watched closely as they unfold, not just by Europeans, but by others who would like to see the humanities take a much more prominent role in society and social decision-making in their own countries. We think that all parties concerned will benefit from increased scrutiny of these developments to see how well they maintain academic freedom alongside social influence.

Wider considerations and recommendations

The preceding recommendations are all practical in nature. However, we want to highlight some considerations that may be less easy to act on but may help articulate how and why the humanities might matter more in the future. We shall consider them under three headings: the diversity of the human experience; articulating the relevance of the humanities; and integration of knowledge.

The diversity of human experience

The humanities are a unique repository of knowledge and insight into the rich diversity of the human experience, past and present. We draw on this insight for pleasure and wisdom as much as for direct utility. We derive insights from social and cultural diversity and understanding of human responses, motivations and actions in the face of direct and indirect challenges. We draw on the wealth of artistic and intellectual representations to learn how the human race grapples with existence and understands its place in the universe.

A loss of linguistic and cultural competence diminishes our collective intelligence. We cannot know when or how we may want or need to command specialist skills and draw on comparative insights. Therefore, we need to protect and develop humanistic competencies in their full diversity.

UNESCO maintains lists of tangible and intangible human cultural heritage which are used to preserve highlights of the human experience. In a wider sense the humanities safeguard human existence by recording and unlocking traces of the human mind through time.

In this regard, our endeavours are no different from the incessant strife to document and protect the biodiversity of the world. In defence of natural life, it is often argued that the greater the biodiversity the greater nature's resilience to environmental stress will be. It is also frequently maintained that species and habitat diversity combine to provide yet more diversity in the world, and that any loss reduces the human quality of life.

Such arguments in favour of diversity are sometimes ridiculed by arguments that nobody will suffer from the disappearance of the last few specimens of a butterfly. Similarly, nobody will suffer bodily harm from losing our competence to understand an arcane language or losing insight into the religious practice of a long-lost tribe. But we believe that, while a single loss may be deplorable, a succession of losses may turn into an intellectual cancer.

In this sense, the humanities' intrinsic value is that they provide a key to human diversity without which we cannot understand ourselves.

Articulating the relevance of the humanities

At the same time, there is no doubt that humanities research is instrumentally valuable, whether socially, economically, politically or in other ways. We want to sound a note of warning about how we articulate this relevance. It is not the case that each piece of research can be correlated with a specific benefit. The value of our research tends to fall out of humanities research holistically and over the long-term. Even when a particular piece of research does have a particular application, it may not be evident until long afterwards.

So, on the whole, we should not confront each and every researcher with the 'so what?' question, as in 'what is the usefulness of your particular research?' Of course, some researchers will find the question entirely appropriate and not difficult to answer. There are cases of 'low-hanging fruit', where particular results have an obvious application (bioethics, linguistics, musicology, environmental history, etc.). Researchers should be encouraged to make the applications and this is part of our discussion in Chapter 5 on translation. Also, some humanists are very good at drawing out the long-term value of their fields by looking holistically at their discipline and seeing how it translates into current and future social benefit.

As a fictitious example, imagine some research done in medieval Florentine love poetry. Such research may not be of immediate social use, and yet it is precisely the unique insight into human relations in another time and setting that can provide essential insights into human nature. Sometimes the insight may only be at a comparative level, at other times it is possible to generate wider general statements based on research findings.

Many humanists are expert at drawing out such connections, but not everyone is or needs to be, and such work depends on others having pursued their research in an 'ivory tower' kind of way. So, just like all other curiosity-driven scientists, humanists should not typically be expected to answer the 'so what?' question. On the contrary, querying the potential impact of research could actually be damaging to the ability of the humanities to produce socially beneficial research over the long term.

The integration of knowledge

Our final recommendation concerns the integration of knowledge. In our specific recommendations above, we included a section on interdisciplinary research. This recommendation was intended to ensure that those working on interdisciplinary questions are not penalised by current criteria regarding career advancement. This is a recommendation to ensure that such arrangements avoid any kind of monodisciplinary bias by those charged with hiring, promotion or tenure decisions. The recommendation does not attempt to challenge current institutional structures, but it does involve adjusting arrangements within existing structures. In this way it is a proposal for the short- or medium-term.

The issue of integrating knowledge can be discussed in a more radical and far-reaching way. First of all, we need to take stock of the wider problem. The professionalisation of academic research in the natural, technical and social sciences, as well as in the humanities, is based on a division of labour and expertise. This is probably an inevitable result of the ongoing progress of knowledge in all fields of research, of the fact that each of us only has a limited capacity and of the diversity of nature and culture. However, as knowledge is compartmentalised, wisdom may be sacrificed to expediency and our collective intelligence may suffer.

On the other hand, we have seen at several points in this report that there are counteracting developments, such as digital methodologies enabling researchers to draw on and collate data of multiple origin and form. New approaches have given rise to multi- and interdisciplinary fields, such as cognition, medical humanities and environmental humanities. New uses of humanities research are also helping to integrate scholarship and other types of knowledge, as now occurs in the use of historical data for public planning, of narrative models for business, of arts technology for media, and of philosophy for bioethics. Furthermore, long-standing disciplines, such as languages, literature and history of ideas, are becoming ever more important to overcoming cultural borders in a globalising world.

In our view, something radical is needed to address the problems of disintegration and take advantage of these opportunities. What we have in mind is to create integrative platforms as spaces for networking, capacity building and preparation of research on questions at the core of our interest in understanding the human condition. By platforms we intend something larger and more long-term than research projects and centres. Many important crossroads, centres and institutes already exist that address important research questions in innovative ways. They often come with funding instruments such as a web platform, a postgraduate or doctoral school, visiting fellowships and stakeholder interaction. What we imagine is something that would go beyond such initiatives, which are often limited in scope by institutional frameworks and funding horizons.

Integrative platforms may be entirely virtual in the early stage, while physical entities may be useful later. The platforms should bring together experts from all fields of science and scholarship to identify, review and develop current knowledge – for examples in the fields mentioned above – and to identify what we know and what we might know, given a large effort of money, collaboration, methodological improvement and theoretical honing. Such grand research challenges would mean identifying approaches that are not only broad and long-lasting enough to integrate intellectual energies and resources right across the humanities, but also in a way that reaches out to other disciplines. They should aim to lower the barriers between the human, the social and the natural sciences; multiply the learning capacity of many excellent research environments; and enable knowledge transfer and co-production among researchers and other societal actors. Moreover, the transnational structure of such platforms, and the reflective processes of working groups, would develop new best practices for global humanities research.

How would these platforms be developed? Funders would clearly play a major role. Integrative platforms would require substantial investment and long-term dedication over and above current three- to five-year cycles of funding. They would also require a commitment to furthering global humanities without regard to national priorities. Intellectual commitment must be the guiding light. Whatever research challenges are chosen, they must come from a commitment to fulfilling the promise of the humanities in helping us understand the human condition: how do we perceive the world, what motivates us, and what may cause us to change direction?

Our concern here is not to second-guess what the research challenges, integrating themes and methodologies might be. This would require a sustained conversation among interested parties from different fields and regions. That intellectual conversation needs to happen first. Funders might want to organise workshops and conferences, perhaps supported by some of the numerous humanities centres around the world.

We make this proposal because there is a crying need for experiment over and above the traditional university and its disciplinary divides. There is a need for institutional and funding developments that promote the integration of knowledge. However, the establishment of integrative platforms is not intended to replace current structures, but to supplement them. In the end the platforms would depend on research done in traditional university departments and the benefit would run in all directions.

Envoi

At the beginning of this report we said we would not be raising a battle cry for the humanities. All too often, commentators talk about the 'Crisis of the Humanities'. Indeed, as soon as one hears the word humanities, one suspects the word crisis is just around the corner, but the humanities are not in a crisis. Although funding is an issue, we did not find general evidence of disproportionate decline. Epistemologically, the humanities are divided, but not in the strong sense that is often implied; that of a loss of confidence in humanistic knowledge resulting from the postmodernist trend of the 1980s, which has largely been overcome. The world, of course, is beset with crises: lack of trust in financial institutions; inaction in the face of planetary environmental threats; and inequality of opportunities and resources across the world. These are all very human problems, and the humanities have a vital part to play in their solution. But, rather than talk about a crisis in the humanities, we have sought to pinpoint specific and longer-term challenges, such as the need to integrate research more systematically than we do at present. Only if these challenges are met can we realise the full potential of the humanities to help us understand ourselves and make a better world.

Except where otherwise noted, this work is licensed under a Creative Commons Attribution 3.0 Unported License. To view a copy of this license, visit http://creativecommons.org/licenses/by/3.0/

Appendix: The Interview Questionnaire

VERSION 1

HWR interview questions

Interviewee:
Date:
Interviewer:
Introduction:

This is a questionnaire for the Humanities Worldwide Report. We'd like to elicit your views on the current state of the humanities and of the challenges facing them in the future.

We shall collate the results of these interviews anonymously and use them alongside data collected from reports and other surveys.

Questions for interviewees

1. To start off, please say in a few sentences a little bit about yourself and your role in your university/organisation.

2. Funding

    Please give a brief description of the funding sources that support your institution. Is your funding situation undergoing any significant changes?

3. Major research themes

    What themes have been dominating your own field?
    What themes do you expect to dominate your field?
    Where do you see the potential breakthroughs in your field?

4. Interdisciplinary research

    Is your own research monodisciplinary or interdisciplinary? What are the benefits or disadvantages of each type of research?

5. The digital humanities

Is the development of digitisation changing the nature of research practice in your field?

Do researchers in your field have the necessary skills to make the most out of the digital resources available to them?

6. Research infrastructure

   What kinds of research infrastructure are needed in your field?

   Is there adequate funding for such infrastructure in your institution?

7. Publications and career development

   How do publications affect the way research is done, in particular through the assessment criteria they provide for hiring and promotion? What effects do the demands of getting published have on the work of younger researchers?

8. Ranking systems (e.g. university rankings, citation indices, national assessment systems)

   What effects do ranking systems have on research, on the behaviour of researchers and on the management of research in your area? (Give examples to illustrate your answers.) What views do you hold on efforts to measure the wider social impact of research?

9. Internationalisation

   What effects is internationalisation (e.g. in recruitment patterns, institutional collaboration, networks) having on research and research activity?

   Do researchers in your field have sufficient language skills for their work?

10. Government policies

    How do government policies currently affect humanities research?

11. The nature of the humanities

    What are the major similarities and dissimilarities between the humanities and the sciences in the ways they conduct and present research? Could you give some examples (up to three) of important findings gained in the humanities? Aside from your own views, how do you think the humanities are perceived in this respect? And what impact does the perception of the humanities in comparison to the sciences have on funding?

12. Translating the humanities

    How are you or members of your organisation working with or exchanging knowledge with stakeholders outside academia? (If possible, please give some concrete examples, e.g. in media-related activities, museums, policy making or social innovation.) What support systems are in place for translational research?

13. Justifications for humanities research

    'Why fund research in the humanities?' If you had to give a succinct answer to this question, what would it be? How would you articulate the value of the humanities research to an impatient and potentially hostile audience?

VERSION 2

HWR interview questions

Interviewee:
Date:
Introduction:

This is a questionnaire for the Humanities Worldwide Report. We'd like to elicit your views on the current state of the humanities and of the challenges facing them in the future.

We shall collate the results of these interviews anonymously and use them alongside data collected from reports and other surveys.

Questions for interviewees

1. To start off, please say in a few sentences a little bit about yourself and your role in your university/organisation.

2. Funding

    Please give a brief description of the funding sources that support your institution. Is your funding situation undergoing any significant changes?

3. Major research themes

What themes have been dominating your own field?

What themes do you expect to dominate your field?

Where do you see the potential breakthroughs in your field?

4. Interdisciplinary research

   Is your own research monodisciplinary or interdisciplinary? What are the benefits or disadvantages of each type of research?

5. The digital humanities

   Is the development of digitisation changing the nature of research practice in your field?

   Do researchers in your field have the necessary skills to make the most out of the digital resources available to them?

6. Research infrastructure

   What kinds of research infrastructure are needed in your field?

   Is there adequate funding for such infrastructure in your institution?

7. Publications and career development

   How do publications affect the way research is done, in particular through the assessment criteria they provide for hiring and promotion? What effects do the demands of getting published have on the work of younger researchers?

8. Ranking systems (e.g. university rankings, citation indices, national assessment systems)

   What effects do ranking systems have on research, on the behaviour of researchers and on the management of research in your area? (Give examples to illustrate your answers.) What views do you hold on efforts to measure the wider social impact of research?

9. Internationalisation

   What effects is internationalisation (e.g. in recruitment patterns, institutional collaboration, networks) having on research and research activity?

Do researchers in your field have sufficient language skills for their work?

10. Government policies

    How do government policies currently affect humanities research?

11. The nature of the humanities

    What, in broad terms, are the major similarities and dissimilarities between the humanities and the sciences in the ways they conduct and present research?

    Please give up to three examples of things that, due to humanities research, we know today that we did not know before, either in your own field or in the humanities in general.

    Do you think it is appropriate to describe the results of humanities research as findings?

    What impact does the public perception of the humanities in this respect have on funding?

12. Translating the humanities

    How are you or members of your organisation working with or exchanging knowledge with stakeholders outside academia? (If possible, please give some concrete examples, e.g. in media-related activities, museums, policy making or social innovation.) What support systems are in place for translational research?

13. Justifications for humanities research

    Here are some ways of expressing the value of humanities research:
    i. Intrinsic value
    ii. Informing social policy
    iii. Understanding cultural heritage
    iv. Promoting economic value
    v. Contributing to other academic disciplines (e.g. in the natural or social sciences)
    vi. Promoting personal and spiritual development
    vii. Feeding through to undergraduate education
    viii. Promoting critical thinking and innovation

Which of these in your own view is (or are) the most important? Which of these is considered most important in your country/region?

'Why fund the research in the humanities?' If you had to give a succinct answer to this question, what would it be? How would you articulate the value of humanities research to an impatient and potentially hostile audience?

Notes

2 The Value of the Humanities

1. Fish (2008).
2. Quoted by Menand (2010) p. 49.
3. Menand (2010) pp. 57ff. also offers a critique of non-instrumentalism.
4. Nussbaum (2010) 'Afterword'.
5. Popular interest in literature and history needs little documenting; but, for the remarkable growth in popular archaeology, see Parker Pearson (2011). In the UK, Melvyn Bragg's work on TV and radio, especially *In our time* (BBC Radio 4) has established a widespread interest in philosophy, the history of ideas and of language. The German publisher C. H. Beck (http://www.chbeck.de/) provides another good example.
6. For this point, see Collini (2012) pp. 96-7.
7. Nussbaum (2010) makes the case for the social value of specific disciplines across Chapters 3-5 as a whole.
8. *Consensus Study on the State of the Humanities in South Africa* (2011) p. 29.
9. See McMahon et al. (2011).
10. Participants included congressional staff from the House and Senate. The meeting was intended to show 'how research projects funded by the National Endowment for the humanities helped foster a better understanding of foreign cultures – particularly in Afghanistan, Pakistan, Iraq, and Iran – and how that knowledge has assisted U.S. military, aid, and diplomatic efforts in those countries'. The meeting discussed research into Iranian civilisation, Chinese historical figures, the history of uranium production in Africa, Arab demographic trends, and newspapers across Latin America – in general, research that has 'deepened America's understanding of other countries with which it regularly engages'.
11. According to the METRIS reports, cultural heritage is also among the leading thematic priorities in most former Eastern bloc countries. For instance, the authors of the report on Poland state: 'the research schemes of the National Programme for the Development of Humanities have a particular focus on research projects in the domain of national heritage' (p. 20). But this is part of a pattern common to several other countries. For specific references see Bulgaria p. 9, Croatia p. 20, Czech Republic pp. 22-3, Latvia p. 12, Lithuania pp. 2-3, Romania pp. 2-3, Serbia p. 2, Slovakia p. 19 and Slovenia p. 13. Contrast the METRIS report on the UK, where heritage hardly figures at all. (Page numbers refer to the relevant METRIS reports for each country.)
12. For an account of the controversy, see Evans (2013). For a possible US parallel in the state of Texas, McKinley (2010).
13. See the example above, *Addressing National Security & Other Global Challenges Through Cultural Understanding*.
14. A point implicit in some of the METRIS reports referred to above.

15. See *Leading the World: the Economic Impact of UK Arts and Humanities Research* (2009) pp. 12–24.
16. This will be discussed in some detail in Chapter 8.
17. See Matthews (2012).
18. *Consensus Study*, pp. 31–2.
19. See Fish (2008) and Nussbaum (2010), esp. Chapters 1–2.
20. See Parker Pearson (2011).
21. See e.g. Gurr (1981), Eisner (2003) and Spierenburg (2008).
22. See Overy (2011).
23. For two disparate examples, see *Playing to Our Strengths*, Irish Research Council, p. 3, and *Consensus Study*, South Africa, p. 44.
24. For a US/Australian example, see Golsby-Smith (2011).
25. E.g. Isaacson (2011) discussing Steve Jobs. (Jobs' view on the humanities is discussed below.)
26. *Leading the World* (2009) pp. 22. See also Press (2011), who details cases where research in art and design has led to business innovation.
27. On the distinction between economic and social innovation in the context of the humanities see the *South African Consensus Study* (2011) p. 40.
28. Nussbaum (2010) Chapter 4.
29. Cf. Karl Popper's claim that progress in science operates through conjectures and refutations.
30. Kronman (2007), critiqued by Fish (2008).
31. See McDonald (2011). He argues that literary scholars should espouse this role. If they do not, literary disciplines start to lose their identity and merge into subjects such as history, cultural studies or philosophy.

3 The Nature of the Humanities

1. Most respondents who referred to some form of cross-fertilisation only referred to one of the categories above. But some of the Asian respondents who stressed interdisciplinary research trends also mentioned comparative approaches, and vice versa. So, in the ten Asian interviews where cross-fertilisation featured, there were actually seven references to interdisciplinary and eight to comparative research.
2. To an extent this trend overlaps with a tendency towards the socially relevant themes discussed above, because some forms of interdisciplinary, collaborative and intercultural research are societal in focus. But the two notions do not necessarily converge.
3. We call this reaction *mildly negative* because, unlike the previous quote (NA10), it seems to allow for the possibility, in principle, of making findings in the humanities. This was quite a common reaction within this category. Indeed, it is useful to wordsearch 'findings' throughout an interview to see if they use the word elsewhere, even if they appear negative in this particular question.
4. These results include both batches of interviews.
5. For want of a better one we use the term to describe those who think the humanities do not aim to make discoveries resulting in truth.

4 The Digital Humanities

1. Spence, P. 'How Do You Define DH? | Day of DH 2012.' Accessed July 26, 2013. http://dayofdh2013.matrix.msu.edu/members/.
2. Spence, P. 'How Do You Define DH? | Day of DH 2012.' Accessed July 26, 2013. http://dayofdh2012.artsrn.ualberta.ca/dh/. See also: Heppler, Jason. 'What Is Digital Humanities?' Accessed July 26, 2013. http://whatisdigitalhumanities.com/.
3. 'Our Mission | ADHO.' Accessed July 26, 2013. http://adho.org/.
4. 'The Association for Computers and the Humanities | Membership.' Accessed July 26, 2013. http://ach.org/membership/.
5. Others include *Digital Studies/Le champ numérique*, an open-access peer-reviewed electronic journal from CSDH/SCHN *DH Commons*, an open-access peer-reviewed electronic journal forthcoming from centerNet, *Computers in the Humanities Working Papers*, an online preprint publication, *Text Technology*, a free electronic journal published by McMaster University.
6. 'THATCamp | The Humanities and Technology Camp.' Accessed July 26, 2013. http://thatcamp.org/.
7. See for example: 'The Medici Archive Project | The Medici Archive Project.' Accessed July 26, 2013. http://www.medici.org/.
8. Galina, Isabel. 'Is There Anybody Out There?' http://humanidadesdigitales.net/blog/2013/07/19/is-there-anybody-out-there-building-a-global-digital-humanities-community/ (Accessed July 26, 2013).
9. 'centerNet | An International Network of Digital Humanities Centers.' Accessed July 26, 2013. http://digitalhumanities.org/centernet/. Home | EADH - The European Association for Digital Humanities.' Accessed July 26, 2013. http://www.allc.org/.
10. For example, the 'Digging into Data Challenge' is an initiative funded jointly by organisations in Canada, the Netherlands, the United Kingdom, and the United States. 'Digging Into Data > Home.' Accessed July 26, 2013. http://www.diggingintodata.org/.
11. Galina, Isabel. 'Is There Anybody Out There? Building a Global Digital Humanities Community | Humanidades Digitales.'
12. *ibid.*
13. 'About | Centre for Educational Technology.' Accessed July 26, 2013. http://www.cet.uct.ac.za/aboutCET.
14. 'About the Programme.' Accessed July 26, 2013. http://www.ulwazi.org/index.php?option=com_content&view=article&id=1&Itemid=4.
15. 'centerNet | An International Network of Digital Humanities Centers.' Accessed July 26, 2013. http://digitalhumanities.org/centernet/.
16. 'People - Digital Humanities Hub - ANU - Digital Humanities Hub - ANU.' Accessed July 26, 2013. http://dhh.anu.edu.au/people.
17. '[FOCUS] Digital Humanities Research in China.' *DH101*. Accessed July 26, 2013. http://dh101.ch/2012/10/16/focus-digital-humanities-research-in-china/.
18. *ibid.*
19. 'centerNet | An International Network of Digital Humanities Centers.' Accessed July 26, 2013. http://digitalhumanities.org/centernet/.

20. UCL puts it at 25 in 2011. 'All Sizes | Infographic: Quantifying Digital Humanities | Flickr - Photo Sharing!' Accessed July 26, 2013. http://www.flickr.com/photos/ucldh/6730021199/sizes/o/in/photostream/.
21. 'Home | EADH - The European Association for Digital Humanities.' Accessed July 26, 2013. http://www.allc.org/.
22. 'People : CIRCA.' Accessed July 26, 2013. http://circa.ualberta.ca/?page_id=9.
23. 'McGill Digital Humanities.' Accessed July 26, 2013. http://digihum.mcgill.ca/.
24. UCL puts it at 44 in 2011. 'All Sizes | Infographic: Quantifying Digital Humanities | Flickr - Photo Sharing!' Accessed July 26, 2013. http://www.flickr.com/photos/ucldh/6730021199/sizes/o/in/photostream/.
25. See, for example: 'View All Projects | DHCommons.' Accessed July 26, 2013. http://dhcommons.org/projects.
26. 'Old Weather - Our Weather's Past, the Climate's Future.' Accessed July 26, 2013. http://www.oldweather.org/.
27. 'POxy Oxyrhynchus Online.' Accessed July 26, 2013. http://www.papyrology.ox.ac.uk/POxy/.
28. 'TEI: Text Encoding Initiative.' Accessed July 26, 2013. http://www.tei-c.org/index.xml.
29. Lee Woolgar, Country Report, Social Sciences and Humanities in Japan, 2011 Report, Metris, European Commission, DG-Research, p. 19.
30. Gold, Matthew K. 'Debates in the Digital Humanities.' Accessed July 26, 2013. http://dhdebates.gc.cuny.edu/debates.
31. Sinclair, S., Ruecker, S., Gabriele, S., Patey, M., Gooding, M., Vitas, C. & Bajer, B. (2011). Meditating on a Mandala' Accessed July 26, 2013. http://mcp.educ.ubc.ca/book/export/html/3.
32. 'Metadata and Text Markup » Tooling Up for Digital Humanities.' Accessed July 26, 2013. http://toolingup.stanford.edu/?page_id=141. See also: 'Text Analysis » Tooling Up for Digital Humanities.' Accessed July 26, 2013. http://toolingup.stanford.edu/?page_id=981.
33. 'TAPoR.' Accessed July 26, 2013. http://portal.tapor.ca/portal/portal.
34. 'Textal.' Accessed July 26, 2013. http://www.textal.org/.
35. 'Voyant Tools: Reveal Your Texts.' Accessed July 26, 2013. http://voyant-tools.org/.
36. 'WordSeer Project Page.' Accessed July 26, 2013. http://wordseer.berkeley.edu/.
37. 'Overview | Geographic Information Systems.' Accessed July 26, 2013. http://www.esri.com/what-is-gis/overview.
38. A large number of projects can be found at 'Zotero | Groups > humanitiesGIS > Library > Literary Spaces.' Accessed July 26, 2013. https://www.zotero.org/groups/humanitiesgis/items/collectionKey/ED4MRWHI. See also: 'Research | Spatial Humanities.' Accessed July 26, 2013. http://spatial.scholarslab.org/collections/?colnum=8EB7UQHC.
39. 'Mapping St Petersburg | Experiments in Literary Cartography.' http://www.mappingpetersburg.org/site/ ; 'Mapping the Lakes: Home Page.'. http://www.lancs.ac.uk/mappingthelakes/index.htm; Hui, Barbara. 'LITMAP: Mapping Literature.' http://barbarahui.net/litmap/; Charles Travis, Digital Literary Atlas of Ireland. http://www.tcd.ie/trinitylongroomhub/digital-atlas/. Accessed July 26, 2013.

40. 'China Historical GIS.' Accessed July 26, 2013. http://www.fas.harvard.edu/~chgis/.
41. ibid. http://www.fas.harvard.edu/~chgis/data/chgis/downloads/v5/about/.
42. 'Pleiades Project | Ancient World Mapping Center.' Accessed July 26, 2013. http://awmc.unc.edu/wordpress/blog/category/pleiades-project/; 'NGA: GNS Home.' Accessed July 26, 2013. http://earth-info.nga.mil/gns/html/.
43. Lee Woolgar, Country Report, Social Sciences and Humanities in Japan, 2011 Report, Metris, European Commission, DG-Research, p. 19.
44. Information from Digging Into Data Challenge website: http://www.digging-intodata.org/ (Accessed October 20, 2013).
45. For examples see the list of project presentations at Duke University http://www.cs.duke.edu/~emonson/FridayForum/spring_2013.html. Trevor Harris' work see: http://pages.geo.wvu.edu/~tmh/?page_id=169.
46. P. Svensson, The Landscape of Digital Humanities, http://digitalhumanities.org/dhq/vol/4/1/000080/000080.html (Accessed October 17, 2013).
47. P. Bradley, http://chronicle.com/blogs/profhacker/where-are-the-philosophers-thoughts-from-thatcamp-pedagogy/37408 (Accessed October 17, 2013).
48. http://dgmyers.blogspot.com/2013/04/digital-humanities.html (Accessed October 17, 2013).
49. R. Grusin, http://www.c21uwm.com/2013/01/09/dark-side-of-the-digital-humanities-part-2/ (Accessed October 17, 2013).

5 Translating the Humanities

1. Duke Translational Medicine Institute http://www.dukemedicine.org/Initiatives/ClinicalAndTranslationalScience.
2. Vision statement of the PennState Clinical and Translational Science Institute http://ctsi.psu.edu/?page_id=27.
3. Wainwright et al. (2006).
4. John Galloway, Translation: Beating Scientific Swords into Medical Ploughshares. http://www.nimr.mrc.ac.uk/mill-hill-essays/year/2010/.
5. Martin et al. (2008) p. 39.
6. On the other hand, it is worth mentioning European initiatives that support translation between humanities and business. The Flexit programme of the Riksbankens jubileumfond 'aims to build bridges between humanities and social science research and companies and organisations outside the academic world'. (http://www.rj.se/en/Funding-opportunities/2014/Flexit-Call-2014/) Similar programmes are funded in the Netherlands by the NWO Humanities and in Denmark by InnovationsFonden.
7. *Reinvigorating the Humanities,* AAU (2004).
8. *The Nairobi Report* (2009) p. 1.
9. The Economic Role and Influence of the Social Sciences and Humanities: A Conjecture (http://www.sshrc-crsh.gc.ca/about-au_sujet/publications/impacts_e.pdf), p.31.
10. DJØFbladet 2013:2 http://www.djoef.dk/blade/defacto/udgivelser/2013/nummer-2/~/media/Documents/Djoef/D/DeFacto/2013/2/Produktiviteteffekter%20af%20uddannelse%20i%20den%20private%20sektor.ashx.

11. http://www.torch.ox.ac.uk/node/336.
12. See American Academy of Arts and Sciences, *Humanities Indicators*, (Part III. The Humanities Workforce: Section B. Career Paths of Humanities College Graduates). http://HumanitiesIndicators.org.
13. http://www.almedalsveckan.info/6895.
14. See for example http://humanities.ku.dk/research/industrial_phd_programme/ (Accessed January 1, 2014).
15. http://www.dublintellectual.ie (Accessed January 1, 2014).

6 The Culture of Humanities Research

1. This issue is discussed in more detail by Mamdani (2012).
2. In contrast, it is worth quoting another part of E14's interview referred to above: 'in some countries, e.g. Sweden and Netherland, my...colleagues do write only in English. Their research is therefore totally disconnected from the population of their country.'
3. Unless one counts the following comment from R7 as negative: 'the EUSP is a highly untypical institution for Russia in the sense that it requires international publications (in WS indexed periodicals) as a condition for promotion to professorial positions. That creates some pressure towards choosing topics which may be of more interest for an international audience (e.g. comparative, or dealing with global processes), to the detriment of those which have more relevance for intellectual and political debates inside the country.'
4. However, one of them (As6) did make an interesting comment that conflicts with the general tendency to think homogeneity is on the rise: 'in one sense of internationalisation this is happening a lot (especially over the last 10–15 years). New funding is coming in internationally – government funding collaborates with private (international) funders; the Internet has created new international networks. But this is not to be confused with intellectual internationalisation, which is quite old. In fact, this kind of internationalisation is declining, as research becomes more regional (because of the postcolonial emphasis).'
5. See *Arts and Humanities Research Mapping, India* (2010) pp. 9–10.
6. Latin America was the one region where all respondents were interdisciplinary.
7. There is a closely related issue. In discussions of interdisciplinarity one can easily take a sceptical position, arguing that there is something artificial about disciplinary boundaries. Only two of our respondents raised this issue, but we shall return to it in the conclusion. For further discussion, see Menand (2010) Chapter 3, on the link between academic professionalism and anxieties over interdisciplinarity.
8. In this connection, it is interesting that six respondents claimed that their own fields are, by nature, interdisciplinary and that monodisciplinarity is not really feasible. These fields were anthropology, education, film studies, sociology, environmental history and social history. The respondents making this point were from Algeria, Australia, India, Jordan, Mozambique, Russia and the US.
9. The METRIS reports contain useful discussions of interdisciplinarity. In each report, the topic comes in Section 4.5.2. The relevant section of the Germany report is particularly interesting (pp. 66–9). On interdisciplinarity in India

see *Arts and Humanities Research Mapping, India* (2010) esp. p. 24, though the topic recurs at frequent points in the report. A useful guide for the US can be found in Sa´ (2008). See also Holm et al. (2013).
10. See E15: 'An organisational problem is that if you publish in interdisciplinary edited collections, people in your own discipline may not read it. In fact such collections may attract rather few readers.'

8 Humanities and Public Policy

1. http://www.gpo.gov/fdsys/pkg/CREC-2013-03-20/pdf/CREC-2013-03-20-pt1-PgS1975.pdf, p. S1976 and 1978. For a European perspective on the US debate see Helga Nowotny, 'Shifting horizons for Europe's social sciences and humanities', in http://www.theguardian.com/science/political-science/2013/sep/23/europe-social-sciences-humanities.
2. 4humanities.org/wp-content/uploads/2013/07/humanitiesmatter300.pdf.
3. C. Koch, 'The Contest for American Culture: A Leadership Case Study on The NEA and NEH Funding Crisis' http://www.upenn.edu/pnc/ptkoch.html.
4. NEH, Appropriations Request for Fiscal Year 2014 http://www.neh.gov/files/neh_request_fy2014.pdf (Accessed October 27, 2013).
5. http://www.humanitiescommission.org/_pdf/hss_report.pdf, p. 9.
6. Ibid., p. 57.
7. http://www.humanitiescommission.org/_pdf/hss_reort.pdf, p. 9.
8. Ibid., p. 44.
9. Ibid., p. 39.
10. Ibid., p. 40.
11. Ibid., pp., 17, 39.
12. *Consensus Study on the State of the Humanities in South Africa* (2011) p. 25. Curiously enough it is also claimed that all these problems have their 'roots' in the humanities. We cannot tell what was intended by this.
13. Ibid, pp. 26–7.
14. Ibid., p. 27.
15. Ibid., p. 26.
16. Ibid., p. 31.
17. Ibid., p. 28.
18. Ibid., p. 44.
19. Ibid., p. 45.
20. Ibid., p. 47.
21. http://www.info.gov.za/view/DownloadFileAction?id=104227, p. 5.
22. 'Ending more of Labor's waste', https://www.liberal.org.au/latest-news/2013/09/05/ending-more-labor's-wast (Accessed October 30, 2013).
23. *Arts and Humanities Research Mapping, India* (2010).
24. *METRIS Country report. Social Sciences and Humanities in Japan.* http://www.metrisnet.eu/metris//fileUpload/countryReports/Japan_2012.pdf.
25. *METRIS Country report. Social Sciences and Humanities in Brazil.* http://www.metrisnet.eu/metris//fileUpload/countryReports/Brazil_2012.pdf.
26. We compare the calculated NEH research expenditure of 2011 of 25 million USD with the estimated annual 220 million euro for the humanities in ERC by inflating to 2013 prices and conversion rate.
27. Kastrinos (2010).

28. *Humanities – Essential Research for Europe* (Danish Research Council for the Humanities, 2003). http://fivu.dk/en/publications/2003/files-2003/humanities-essential-research-for-europe.pdf (Accessed October 28, 2013).
29. http://www.heranet.info/hera-joint-research-programme-1.
30. http://www.heranet.info/system/files/HERAJRPdocuments/hera_a4_26sept.pdf.
31. http://www.esf.org/fileadmin/Public_documents/Publications/SCH%20Position%20paper_01.pdf, p. 12.
32. Science Europe Position Statement, Embedding Social Sciences and Humanities in the Horizon 2020 Societal Challenges. January 2013 http://www.scienceeurope.org/uploads/Public%20documents%20and%20speeches/SE_SSH_Pos_Statement_Jan.2013.pdf (Accessed October 24, 2013).
33. Positioning Humanities Research in the 7th Framework Programme http://ec.europa.eu/research/social-sciences/pdf/egh-report_en.pdf (Accessed October 29, 2013).
34. METRIS Monitoring Emerging Trends in Socio-Economic Sciences and Humanities in Europe (Brussels, 2009, EUR 23741, ISBN 978-92-79-11136-5, DOI 10.2777/57083) http://ec.europa.eu/research/social-sciences/pdf/metris-report_en.pdf (Accessed October 29, 2013).
35. Evaluation of the impact of the Framework Programme on the formation of the ERA in Social Sciences and the Humanities (SSH) ftp://ftp.cordis.europa.eu/pub/fp7/ssh/docs/evaluation-fp-ssh_en.pdf (Accessed October 29, 2013), pp. 62, 74.
36. http://www.eash.eu/openletter2011/.
37. http://www.era.gv.at/attach/ST10663.EN12.pdf (Accessed January 15, 2014).
38. Máire Geoghegan-Quinn in a speech 'Horizons for Social Sciences and Humanities', Vilnius, September 2013 http://europa.eu/rapid/press-release_SPEECH-13-740_en.htm (Accessed January 11, 2014).
39. See e.g. Radder (2010).
40. Hyvönen (2013) p. 98.
41. Hasselberg (2013) p. 139.
42. Nybom (2013) esp. p. 26ff. Except in the EU itself, this trend is visible in many research policy documents, e.g. from the Netherlands, France, UK, Sweden, Norway, and Denmark. See http://www.nwo.nl/en/our-ambitions;_http://www.agence-nationale-recherche.fr/Intl; http://www.ahrc.ac.uk/News-and-Events/News/Documents/AHRC-Strategy-2013-18.pdf; http://www.forskningsradet.no/en/Main_strategy_of_the_Research_Council/1185261825635.
43. Nowotny, op.cit.
44. http://horizons.mruni.eu/ (Accessed December 30, 2013).

References

Academy of Science, South Africa (2011). *Consensus Study on the State of the Humanities in South Africa: Status, Prospects and Strategies.*
American Association of Universities (2004). *Reinvigorating the Humanities: Enhancing Research and Education on Campus and Beyond.*
American Association of Universities (2011). *Addressing National Security and Other Global Challenges through Cultural Understanding.*
Arts and Humanities Research Council (2009). *Leading the World: The Economic Impact of UK Arts and Humanities Research.*
Bate, J. ed. (2011) *The Public Value of the Humanities.* London: Bloomsbury Academic.
British Academy & Association of Commonwealth Universities (2009). *The Nairobi Report: Frameworks for Africa-UK Research Collaboration in the Social Sciences and Humanities.*
Collini, S. (2012) *What are Universities for?* London: Penguin Books.
Eisner, M. (2003) 'Long-term historical trends in violent crime', *Crime and Justice*, 30, 83–142.
European Commission, DG-Research (2009). *METRIS (Monitoring European Trends in Social Sciences and Humanities).*
Evans, R. J. (2013) 'Michael Gove's history wars', *The Guardian*, Saturday 13 July.
Fish, S. (2008) 'Will the Humanities save us?', *The Opiniator, New York Times*, January 6.
Golsby-Smith, T. (2011) 'Want Innovative Thinking? Hire from the Humanities', *Harvard Business Review* blog, March 31.
Gurr, T. R. (1981) 'Historical trends in violent crime: critical review of the evidence', in Morris & Tonry, eds. (1981) 295–353.
Hasselberg, Y. (2013) 'In defense of discretion', in Rider, Hasselberg & Waluszewski, eds. (2013) 137–44.
Holm, P. et al. (2013) 'Collaboration between the natural, social and human sciences in global change studies', *Environmental Science and Policy*, 28, 25–35.
Hyvönen, M. (2013) 'The foundations of knowledge according to the knowledge foundation', in Rider, Hasselberg & Waluszewski, eds. (2013) 97–110.
India Foundation for the Arts (2010). *Arts and Humanities Research Mapping.*
Irish Research Council (2010). *Playing to Our Strengths: The Role of the Arts, Humanities and Social Sciences and Implications for Public Policy.*
Kastrinos, N. (2010) 'Policies for co-ordination in the European Research Area: a view from the social sciences and humanities', *Science and Public Policy* 37:4, 297–310.
Kronman, A. T. (2007) *Education's End: Why Our Colleges and Universities Have Given up on the Meaning of Life.* Yale: Yale University Press.
McDonald, R. (2011) 'The value of art and the art of evaluation', in Bate, ed. (2011) 283–94.
McKinley Jr., J. (2010) 'Texas conservatives win curriculum change', *New York Times*, March 12.

McMahon, A., Barras, W., Clark, L., Knooihuizen, R., Patten, A., & Sullivan, J. (2011) 'Language matters 1: linguistics', in Bate, ed. (2011) 247–58.

Mamdani, M. (2012) 'Advancing the research agenda at Makerere University', *Makerere Institute of Social Research Working Paper* No. 9.

Martin, P., Brown, N. & Kraft, A. (2008) 'From bedside to bench? Communities of promise, translational research and the making of blood stem cells', *Science as Culture* 17:1, 29–41.

Matthews, D. (2012) 'Defending British universities', *Inside Higher Ed*, November 8.

Menand, L. (2010) *The Marketplace of Ideas: Reform and Resistance in the America University*. New York: Norton & Co.

Morris, N. & Tonry, M. eds. (1981) *Crime and Justice*, vol. 3. Chicago: University of Chicago Press.

Nussbaum, M. C. (2010) *Not for Profit: Why Democracy Needs the Humanities*. Princeton: Princeton University Press.

Nybom, T. (2013) 'Power, knowledge, morals: society in the age of hybrid research', in Rider, Hasselberg & Waluszewski, eds. (2013) 21–38.

Overy, K. (2011) 'The value of music research to life in the UK', in Bate, ed. (2011) 184–96.

Parker Pearson, M. (2011) 'The value of archaeological research', in Bate, ed. (2011) 30–43.

Press, M. (2011) ' "All this useless beauty": the hidden value of research in art and design', in Bate, ed. (2011) 156–70.

Radder, H. ed. (2010) *The Commodification of Academic Research: Science and the Modern University*. Pittsburgh: University of Pittsburgh Press.

Rider, S., Hasselberg, Y. & Waluszewski, A. eds. (2013) *Transformations in Research, Higher Education and the Academic Market*. Dordrecht: Springer.

Sa', C. M. (2008) ' "Interdisciplinary strategies" in U.S. research universities', *Higher Education* 55, 537–52.

Spierenburg, P. (2008) *A History of Murder: Personal Violence in Europe from the Middle Ages to the Present*. Cambridge, UK: Polity Press.

Wainwright, S. P., Williams, C., Michael, M., Farsides, B. & Cribb, A. (2006) 'From bench to bedside? Biomedical scientists' expectations of stem cell science as a future therapy for diabetes', *Social Science & Medicine* 63:8, 2052–64.

Index

3D immersive visualisation, 72

AAH (Australian Academy of the Humanities), 165–6
AAU (Association of American Universities), 20, 104, 105
academia.edu, 96
ADHO (Alliance of Digital Humanities Organizations), 65
aesthetic appreciation, humanities, 13, 35–6
Africa, 4, 6, 34, 38, 61, 81, 96, 104
   community engagement, 93, 94
   evidence from national reports, 105–6
   funding, 136–8, 140–1, 151
   political role of humanities, 99, 100–1
   socially relevant themes, 45
   translational research, 92
AHRC (Arts and Humanities Research Council), 26, 30, 128
American Association for the Advancement of Arts and Science, 163
Arab countries, political role of humanities, 99–100
archaeology, 27, 95, 156
Asia, socially relevant themes, 45
Australia, 4, 6, 66
   digital humanities, 66
   engagement with public institutions, 102–3
   public policy, 164–6
   research funding, 144–5
   socially relevant themes, 45–6
   translational research, 91
Australia Research Council (ARC), 144

big data, digital humanities, 71–2
bioethics, 13, 20, 45, 46, 47, 102, 126, 189, 190
Bradley, P., 73

British Academy, 70, 105
Buddhism, 34, 35, 43, 67
businesses, translational research, 101–2, 203n6

Canada, 4, 6, 66
   digital humanities, 67
   evidence from national reports, 106–8
Canadian Social Sciences and Humanities Research Council, 107
career development
   attitudes to publication, 112–13
   interdisciplinary research, 131–3
   interview questions, 194, 196
Carlsberg Foundation, 167
CDBU (Council for the Defence of British Universities), 26
centerNET, 66, 67, 201n9
CHCI (Consortium of Humanities Centers and Institutes), 146
China, 6, 20, 22, 25, 34, 47, 60
   digital humanities, 67
   engagement with media, 97
   funding, 138
   public policy, 163–4
Chinese Academy of Social Sciences, 67
CHNM (Center for History and New Media), 67
CLARIN (Common Language Resources and Technology Infrastructure), 170
collaboration
   digital humanities, 81–2
   funding, 145
   research, 49–50
Columbia University Digital Humanities Center (DHC), 67
communication, 8, 18, 30, 36, 40
   collaboration, 82, 83
   cultural heritage, 25

communication – *continued*
 funding, 153, 156, 158
 interdisciplinary research, 122–3
 language, 46
 public policy, 164
 social media, 71–2
 translational research, 84–5, 99, 103, 109
community engagement, translational research, 93–6
Confucianism, 23, 34, 35, 76
Confucius, 22
Confucius Institutes, 22, 164
corruption, infrastructure, 153–4
critical discursive mapping, 70–1
critical thinking, humanities, 13, 32–4
cross-fertilisation, humanities research, 48–51, 200n1
crowdsourcing, digital humanities, 71–2
cultural heritage, 199n11
 essentialism, 23–4
 humanities, 12, 22–5
 nationalism, 23–4
 preserving memory and identity, 22–3
Cultural Revolution, 22
culture of humanities research
 attitudes to publication, 112–13
 digital humanities, 76–8
 institutional tensions, 128–33
 internationalisation, 113–22
 setting the scene, 111–12

DARIAH (Digital Research Infrastructure for the Arts and Humanities), 170
DARTH (Digital Arts and Humanities), 67
decision-making, social, 19–21
developing countries
 competitive funding streams in, 141–5
 non-governmental funding in, 140–1
Dharma Drug Buddhist College Library and Information Center, 67
DHII (International Institute for Digital Humanities), 67

Digging Into Data Challenge, 71
digital humanities (DH), 7, 64–7, 82–3
 3D immersive visualisation environments, 72
 beneficial effects, 81–8
 big data, 71–2
 collaboration, 81–2
 crowdsourcing, 71–2
 culture clash, 76–8
 dark side of, 73–4
 democratic potential, 82
 difference between fields, 75–6
 digital collections and archives, 68–9
 engagement, 74–5
 failure to apply to disciplines, 73
 interview questions, 193–4, 196
 interview responses, 74–82
 mapping technologies, 70–1
 networking, 71–2
 reading and analysing electronic texts, 69
 recommendations, 187
 research trends, 68–72
 resistance to, 72–4
 reward structures in academia, 72–3
 scepticism about, 78–81
 social media, 71–2
 technology vs. tradition, 182–3
Digital Humanities Quarterly, 65
digital platforms, 70–1
digital resources, 152–3, 154–5
digital revolution, financial models, 158–9
diversity, human experience, 188–9

Early Americas Digital Archive, 68
EASSH (European Alliance for the Social Sciences and Humanities), 173
East Asia, 13, 34, 35, 66, 76, 97–8, 119, 184
economic value, humanities, 12–13, 25–7, 41
education, translational research, 90–3
Eliot, Charles William, 16
employment of graduates, humanities and liberal arts, 26

Index 211

ERCH (European Network of Research Councils for the Humanities), 141, 169, 170
ESF (European Science Foundation), 171, 172
ESFRI (European Strategy Forum on Research Infrastructures), 170
essentialism, 23–4
Estonia, political role of humanities, 101
EU (European Union), 9, 31
  funding, 138
  public policy, 167–75
EU Commission, 20, 169, 180
EU METRIS project, 4, 160, 172, 199n11, 204n9, 206n34
Europe
  community engagement, 95–6
  digital humanities, 67
  financial models, 143–4, 158–9
  Flexit programme, 203n6
  political role of humanities, 101
  socially relevant themes, 46
  translational research, 91–2
European Framework Programme for Research and Innovation, 142
European Research Area, 170, 172
European Research Council (ERC), 168
European Science Foundation, 131
European Social Sciences and Humanities, 177
European University of St. Petersburg, 140

Federal Ministry for Education and Research, Russia, 138
film studies, 155–6
Fish, Stanley, 16, 27
Florida, Richard, 30
Ford Foundation, 137
Framework Programmes, 171
French Revolution, 49
Fudan University Research Center on History and Geography, 67
funding, 9, 204n3
  competitive streams of, in developing countries, 141–5
  core, for research, 136–40
  financial models, 158–9

infrastructure, 148–57
interview questions, 193, 195
non-governmental, in developing countries, 140–1
research institutes, 146–8

George Mason University, 67
geospatial mapping, 70–1
Germany, research funding, 142–3
GIS (geographic information systems), 70
Global Centre for Excellence, 148
globalisation, 8–9, 12, 25, 45–7, 121, 167, 183–4
global politics, humanities, 175–8
Globe Shakespeare project, 60
Grusin, Richard, 74

Harvard University Digital Arts and Humanities (DARTH), 67
HERA (Humanities in the European Research Area), 128, 170
Hermenuti.ca, 69
Higher School of Economics, Moscow, 138
Horizon 2020 Programme, 20, 168, 173, 174, 176–7
Hypercities, 70

IAS (Institutes of Advanced Studies), 146
ICHR (Indian Council of Historical Research), 166
ICPR (Indian Council of Philosophical Research), 166
ICT resources, 151, 152, 155
IFA (India Foundation for the Arts), 166
IMF (International Monetary Fund), 151
India, public policy, 166
infrastructure, 9, 148–57
  academic journal database, 153
  archaeology, 156
  classical projects, 156
  corruption in Russia, 153–4
  digital resources, 152–3, 154–5
  film studies, 155–6
  interview questions, 194, 196

infrastructure – *continued*
  library, 150, 151
  university, 151
  work practices, 157
innovation
  translational research, 101–2
  value of humanities, 13, 30–2
Institut de Reserche pour le Développement, France, 141
Integrated Database of Classical Japanese Texts in the pre-Meiji Period, 68
interdisciplinarity, 111, 204n7, 204n7–9
interdisciplinary research, 49
  advantages, 125–6
  borrowing methods, 123
  career advancement, 131–3
  communication with other disciplines, 122–3
  description of, 122–5
  disadvantages, 126–8
  disciplinary boundaries, 182
  institutional tensions, 128–33
  interview questions, 193, 196
  mastering other disciplines, 123–4
  multidisciplinary edited books, 133
  post-disciplinarity, 124–5
  recommendations, 187
  value of, 125–8
International Institute for Digital Humanities (DHII), 67
internationalisation, 51, 111, 113–22, 204n3
  boundary crossing, 183–4
  international networks, 114–16
  international ranking systems, 118–20
  interview questions, 194, 196–7
  methodological nationalism, 122
  in publishing, 116–18
  redressing the balance, 120–1
interview questionnaire
  version 1, 193–5
  version 2, 195–8
intrinsic value
  analysis, 16–17
  humanities, 12, 16–18
  hybrid approach, 18
  and justification, 17

Japan, 4, 6, 20, 70, 76, 114
  digital humanities, 66–7
  engagement with media, 97
  Global Centre for Excellence, 148
  public policy, 166–7
  research institutes, 114, 146, 148
JICA (Japanese International Cooperation Agency), 114
JISC (Joint Information Systems Committee), 71
Jobs, Steve, 30, 31
justification
  intrinsic value and, 17
  strategies for, 38–40

Knigafond, 153
knowledge
  advancing humanities, 57–8
  integration of, 190–2
Kronman, Anthony, 34

Latin America, 3, 6, 13, 19, 38, 66, 119
  political role of humanities, 98
  public policy, 166–7
  research funding, 137, 144, 158
  socially relevant themes, 46–7
  translational research, 89, 91
Leverhulme Foundation, 147, 167
library, infrastructure, 150–3
linguistics, 3, 6, 20, 22, 27, 51, 60, 65, 76, 99, 103, 123, 150, 164, 189
Literary and Linguistic Computing (LLC), 65
literature, 3, 6, 12, 15, 17, 18–20, 22–3, 28, 75–6, 126, 166

mapping technologies, geospatial and critical discursive, 70–1
Marie Curie programme, 168
Massachusetts Institute of Technology HyperStudio, 67
media, engagement with, 97–8
medicine, translational, 8, 86–8
Mellon Foundation, 128, 147, 148, 155
MENA region, 6, 38
  political role of humanities, 98
  socially relevant themes, 47
methodological nationalism, 122

Index 213

Mexico, 6, 66, 167
Modern Language Association, 73
Mongolia, 6, 99
MOOCs (massive open online courses), 74, 112
Moscow City Pedagogical University, 153
multidisciplinarity, 123–5, 127, 133
Museum of Memory, 98
music, 28, 29, 35–6, 67, 95, 96
musicology, 3, 13, 28, 189
Myers, D. G., 73

Nanjing Normal University, 67
Nanyang Technological University Research Centre for Digital Humanities, 67
National Autonomous University of Mexico, 66
National Council of Science and Technology, 167
National Humanities Alliance, 20
National Institute of Japanese Literature, 69
nationalism, 23–4, 45, 121, 122
national reports, evidence from, 103–8
National Science Council, 139
nature of humanities
  breakthroughs, 58–60
  cross-fertilisation, 48–51
  interview questions, 194–5, 197
  knowledge, 57–8
  overview, 43–4, 184–6
  perception of humanities, 61–2
  reactions to term 'findings', 54–7
  recommendations, 186
  socially relevant themes, 44–8
  thematic orientations, 43–51
NEH (National Endowment for the Humanities), 9, 71, 141, 155, 161–3, 180, 199n10
NESTA (National Endowment for Science, Technology and the Arts), 30
networking, digital humanities, 71–72
neuroscience, 29
New Zealand Electronic Text Centre, 66

NIH (National Institute of Health), 87, 161
North America
  community engagement, 95
  financial models, 145, 158
  political role of humanities, 101
  socially relevant themes, 47–8
Norwegian Research Council, 114
Nowotny, Helga, 176
NSF (National Science Foundation), 71, 141, 161
NSI (National System of Innovation), 165
Nussbaum, Martha, 27, 199n4, 199n7
NWO (Netherlands Organisation for Scientific Research), 128, 230n6

Odense Declaration, 169
Old Weather, 68
Oxyrhynchus Papyrus Project, 68

PANGeA (Partnership for African Next Generation of Academics), 140
perception, humanities, 61–2
personal development, 13, 34–5
philosophy, 3, 6, 13, 19–21, 22–3, 28–30, 46, 49, 60, 76, 126
politics, humanities, 98–101, 175–78
post-disciplinarity, 124–5
professional schools, humanities and, 28–30
publication
  attitudes to, 112–13
  funding, 137
  international, 204n3
  interview questions, 194, 196
  multidisciplinary edited books, 133
public institutions, engagement with, 102–3
public policy
  Australia, 164–6
  China, 163–4
  EU (European Union), 167–75
  India, 166
  interview questions, 194, 197
  Japan, 166–7
  Latin America, 166, 167
  recommendations, 187–8

public policy – *continued*
  South Africa, 164–6
  United States, 160–3
publishing, internationalisation in, 116–18
publish or perish, 112

ranking systems
  international, 118–20
interview questions, 194, 196
research institutes, funding, 146–8
research trends
  3D immersive visualisation environments, 72
  big data, social media, crowdsourcing and networking, 71–2
  digital collections and archives, 68–9
  digital humanities, 68–72
  mapping technologies, 70–1
  reading and analysing electronic texts, 69
Rhodes University Book and Text Studies, 66
Ritsumeikan University Digital Humanities Center for Japanese Arts and Cultures, 67
Russia, 22
  corruption, 153–4
  digital library resources, 152–3
  engagement with public institutions, 103
  funding, 138
  international publication, 204n3
  political role of humanities, 100
  socially relevant themes, 46
  translational research, 92
Russian Foundation for the Humanities, 153
Russian Presidential Academy, 138

scientific cross-fertilisation, 48–51, 200n1
social cohesion, 18–19
socially relevant themes, 44–8
social media, 71–2, 96
social norms, 21
social value
challenging social norms, 21
  humanities, 12, 18–22
  institution building, 21–2
  social cohesion, 18–19
  social decision-making, 19–21
sociology, 3, 27, 28, 44, 96, 139, 164, 204n8
South Africa, 6, 9, 19, 27, 66, 92, 116
  funding, 138
  public policy, 164–6, 175
spiritual development, humanities, 13, 34–5
SSH (Social Sciences and Humanities), 26, 99, 105–6, 107–8, 144, 169, 172–4, 176
SSHRC (Social Sciences and Humanities Research Council), 71
STEM (science, technology, engineering and mathematics), 32, 37, 39, 49, 60, 107, 122, 161, 179
Svensson, Patrik, 73

Taiwan, 6, 101
  digital humanities, 67
  engagement with media, 97
  funding, 139
Tanzania, 6, 50, 115, 118
Targeted Socio-Economic Research programme, 169
tenure, career advancement, 132
Textal, 69
Text Analysis Portal for Research (TAPoR project), 69
Text Encoding Initiative (TEI), 68
THATCamps, 65
themes, humanities research, 43–51
translation, 8
translational medicine, 8, 86–8
translational research
  academic integrity, 109
  community engagement, 93–6
  educating role, 90–3
  engagement with businesses, 101–2
  engagement with media, 97–8
  evidence from interviews, 88–103
  evidence from national reports, 103–8
  innovation system, 101–2

translational research – *continued*
  interview questions, 195, 197
  political role, 98–101
  practicalities, 109
  practices, 84–6, 181–2
  quantitative evidence, 88–90
  recommendations, 186–7
  risks and opportunities, 109–10
  social media, 96
Truth Commission, 98
Tufts University's *Perseus* project, 68
Tunisia, 6, 99
Turkey, 4, 6, 24, 98, 99

undergraduate teaching, 90–3
UNESCO, 3, 101, 188
United States, 6, 71, 119, 146
  digital humanities, 65, 67
  evidence from national reports, 104–5
  funding models, 139–40
  public policy, 160–3, 175, 176
University College London Centre for Digital Humanities, 67
University of Cape Town Center for Educational Technology, 66
University of Maryland Institute for Technology in the Humanities (MITH), 67
University of Tokyo Center for Evolving Humanities, 67
University of Virginia, 6, 70

value of humanities
  aesthetic appreciation, 13, 35–6
  contribution to other disciplines, 13, 27–30
  critical thinking, 13, 32–4
  cultural heritage, 12, 22–5, 41
  economic value, 12–13, 25–7, 41
  innovation, 13, 30–2
  intrinsic value, 12, 16–18, 41
  personal and spiritual development, 13, 34–5
  social value, 12, 18–22, 41
Vilnius declaration, 176–7
visual arts, 28
Volkswagen Foundation, 128, 141, 167
Voyant, 69

Women Writers Project, 68
Wordseer, 69
World Bank, 140, 151, 166
World Social Science Report, 3
Wuhan University History College, 67

Zambia, 6, 94, 100

The manufacturer's authorised representative in the EU is Springer
Nature Customer Service Centre GmbH, Europaplatz 3, 69115 Heidelberg,
Germany. If you have any concerns regarding our products, please
contact ProductSafety@springernature.com

Printed and bound by CPI Group (UK) Ltd, Croydon, CR0 4YY

23/03/2026

02076663-0017